The Legend of
ALLTEL

Photo by Eric Myer

The Legend of ALLTEL

David A. Patten and Jeffrey L. Rodengen

Edited by Melody Maysonet
Design and layout by Rachelle Donley and Sandy Cruz

Write Stuff Enterprises, Inc.
1001 South Andrews Avenue, Second Floor
Fort Lauderdale, FL 33316
1-800-900-Book (1-800-900-2665)
(954) 462-6657
www.writestuffbooks.com

Publisher's Cataloging in Publication

David A. Patten
    The legend of ALLTEL / David A. Patten,
Jeffrey L. Rodengen. – 1st ed.
    p. cm.
    Includes bibliographical references and index.
    ISBN 0-945903-64-2

    1. ALLTEL Corporation – History
2. Telecommunications – United States – History
3. Telephone companies – United States – History
I. Patten, David A. II. Title.

HE7797.A455R63 2001   384.0673
                             QBI00-286

Library of Congress
Catalog Card Number 99-075889

ISBN 0-945903-64-2

Completely produced in the
United States of America
10 9 8 7 6 5 4 3 2 1

Also by Jeff Rodengen

The Legend of Chris-Craft

IRON FIST: The Lives
of Carl Kiekhaefer

Evinrude-Johnson and
The Legend of OMC

Serving the Silent Service:
The Legend of Electric Boat

The Legend of
Dr Pepper/Seven-Up

The Legend of Honeywell

The Legend of
Briggs & Stratton

The Legend of Ingersoll-Rand

The Legend of Stanley:
150 Years of The Stanley Works

The MicroAge Way

The Legend of Halliburton

The Legend of
York International

The Legend of
Nucor Corporation

The Legend of Goodyear:
The First 100 Years

The Legend of AMP

The Legend of Cessna

The Legend of VF Corporation

The Spirit of AMD

New Horizons:
The Story of Ashland Inc.

The Legend of Rowan

The History of
American Standard

The Legend of Mercury Marine

The Legend of Federal-Mogul

Against the Odds:
Inter-Tel—The First 30 Years

The Legend of Pfizer

State of the Heart:
The Practical Guide to
Your Heart and Heart Surgery
with Larry W. Stephenson, M.D.

The Legend of
Worthington Industries

The Legend of
Trinity Industries, Inc.

The Legend of IBP, Inc.

The Legend of
Cornelius Vanderbilt Whitney

The Legend of Amdahl

The Legend of Litton Industries

The Legend of Bertram

The Legend of Gulfstream

TABLE OF CONTENTS

FOREWORD

BY
JACKSON T. STEPHENS
CHAIRMAN OF STEPHENS GROUP, INC.

ONE MORNING IN DECEMber 1958, the receptionist at my office in Little Rock told me that a young man was in the lobby asking to meet with me. The young man didn't have an appointment, but he insisted that we needed to talk.

That was Joe Ford. He was home from college for Christmas vacation, and when he woke up that morning he decided he needed advice in a hurry. When he told his mother he was going to see me, she said he'd better call first. He told her he didn't have time to call, put on his suit, and went downtown.

I didn't know any of this at the time, but I told the receptionist to send him up. Joe sat down in my office and explained what was on his mind. He said that he didn't have any money, that he didn't know anybody who had any money, and that he didn't know how people went about getting money. Now he was about to graduate from college. What did he need to do, he asked me, to become successful in life?

If I had an answer for that question then, I don't remember it now. I suppose I must have given

Joe a pep talk of some kind. If I did, I hope it was a useful one. At any rate, when our conversation was over, I told Joe to be sure to come back and see me as soon as he was ready to go to work.

I didn't see Joe again until 1962. (This time he made an appointment.) He told me then that he had graduated from college and that he had spent some time in the army. He had also sold advertisements for the Yellow Pages. Now he was working for a little company called Allied Telephone. Joe said he thought Allied had a chance of becoming a big, important company but that it needed to attract some new capital in order to grow. I asked him how much he thought he needed. He told me, and I said the money was his.

That was the beginning of the most profitable investment I have ever made. I don't just mean profitable in a financial sense, although it has certainly been that. My relationship with Allied Telephone—which became ALLTEL in 1983, when it merged with Mid-Continent—has enriched my life in many ways. Joe and Jo Ellen Ford became

CHAPTER ONE

THE TELEPHONE AND THE RISE OF INDEPENDENTS

Let it be known that I, Alexander Graham Bell, of Salem, Massachusetts, have invented certain new and useful Improvements in Telegraphy, of which the following is a specification....

—Patent No. 174,465, United States Patent Office, March 7, 1876

IN 1876, AMERICANS COMMU-nicated over long distances by writing their thoughts in letters and sending them via the post office. If they needed a message to arrive faster, they used message boys or Samuel Morse's invention, the telegraph, which at that time was dominated by Western Union. Most people viewed these methods as sufficient, even convenient, so when Alexander Graham Bell announced that he could transmit voice over wire using electricity, many viewed his invention as nothing more than a "scientific toy." Those who weren't saying that it was impossible were dismissing it as insignificant.

The naysayers couldn't have been more wrong. The telephone has done far more than merely bring convenience to our day-to-day living; the invention has saved lives through links to emergency services and vastly accelerated the rate of scientific and technological change in industry. For better or worse, the telephone even made possible the modern city, for only after the telephone's commercial popularity did we begin building those multiple-floor office buildings known as skyscrapers.

Long before Alexander Graham Bell invented the telephone, people had been finding ways to better communicate over short distances. Trains, steamships, offices, and households used speak-ing tubes to be heard over noise, barriers, and distance, and children played with string phones to magnify their voices. But it wasn't until electricity was applied to the concept that the telephone as we know it was made possible.

The Scientific Toy

Born in 1847 in Edinburgh, Scotland, Alexander Graham Bell moved to Salem, Massachusetts, before beginning his career as an inventor. His father and grandfather were speech experts and his mother and wife were deaf, so Bell had an uncommon appreciation for hearing and a unique insight into sound—a background that no doubt contributed to his invention of the telephone.

Bell had been puzzling over how to transmit speech over wire for several years before that momentous day of March 18, 1876, when his assistant, a technician named Thomas Watson, heard Bell's voice coming over the machine from

A model of Bell's first telephone, through which speech sounds were first transmitted electrically. Thomas Watson, who was a technician, made the original device overnight from June 2 to June 3, 1875. *(Model photographed by Wally Tubbs, courtesy Frank H. Woods Telephone Pioneer Museum.)*

rooms away: "Mr. Watson, come here. I want you!"[1] Eleven days earlier, on March 7, 1876, his twenty-ninth birthday, Bell had received the patent for his "Improvements in Telegraphy." It is now considered the most valuable patent ever issued, though at the time, few people recognized just how important that patent would be to Bell and to those who formed the Bell System, which later became known as AT&T.

When Bell filed for the patent, he was able to transmit sound but not clear speech. An inventor named Elisha Gray had been thinking about a similar invention and nearly beat Bell to the patent office, arriving mere hours after Bell with a caveat—a declaration of his intention to invent the apparatus. Bell's filing with the patent office was an application, which meant he had already perfected the invention, though even he did not yet have a working telephone.[2] There is some evidence that Bell used some of the ideas Gray

had written about to turn his "Improvements in Telegraphy" into what he at first called an "electrical speech machine."[3]

News of the telephone spread, thanks in large part to the publicity generated by Bell's father-in-law, Gardiner G. Hubbard, and Bell's lectures to demonstrate the device. Still, response to the strange contraption was skeptical at best. "The effect is weird and supernatural," said the *New York Times.* And the *Providence Press* cautioned, "It is hard to resist the notion that the powers of darkness are somehow in league with it." It wasn't until the telephone had been displayed at the Philadelphia Centennial for months that it finally attracted enough attention to gain popularity.[4]

In 1877, the first permanent outdoor telephone wire was strung up. It was three miles long. The following year, Bell set up the first telephone exchange in New Haven, Connecticut. The exchange let calls be switched among different subscribers rather than each requiring a direct line. By 1879, there were enough telephone subscribers on each exchange that they needed to be identified by telephone numbers rather than their names.

Growing the Business

The improvements in the telephone system meant increased business, and Bell's little company—which consisted of Bell as inventor, Watson as the builder of the phones, Hubbard as publicist, and a man named Thomas Sanders, who invested the money to get the business started—was having a hard time keeping up. Hubbard was leasing a thousand telephones a month when he decided to hire Theodore Vail as general manager.[5] Under Vail, the Bell System flourished. Thomas Edison had developed a transmitter that was superior to Bell's and was working with the giant Western Union, which had a monopoly on the telegraph business, to market it. Vail helped prevent Western Union from taking the business by sending copies of Bell's patent to every agent, but it wasn't until Francis Blake developed a transmitter as good as Edison's that Bell's company was able to compete with Western Union.

It was Vail's dream to create a national telephone system, and indeed his efforts went a long

Bell gave lectures to demonstrate his telephone, as this engraving depicts, but his invention didn't immediately catch on. *(Image courtesy New York Public Library.)*

way toward connecting people, despite vast geographic distances. Vail struck out on his own to erect the first long-distance line between Boston and New York City in 1884. The connection used metallic circuits and a double line and raised the telephone business to a new level, for it proved that a national system was within reach. The Bell System had previously been skeptical of Vail's plan, but once it realized that the line was a success, the company bought it for its own use.[6]

Improvements to the telephone system continued, keeping pace with the technology of the time. Switchboards got a revolutionary boost in 1888 when Hammond V. Hayes developed the common-battery system. Previously, each unit on an exchange had its own battery, but Hayes developed a central battery that could supply all telephones on an exchange with power. In 1891, a mortician named Almon Brown Stowger invented the first automatic dialing system because he thought someone was stealing his business by rerouting his calls. With automatic dialing, an exchange operator was no longer needed to route local calls. A major breakthrough came in 1906 when Dr. Lee De Forest applied a vacuum tube, which could amplify radio waves, to telephony.

Farmer Lines

By this time, a new generation was finding appreciation for the telephone, and demand was growing. In 1885, the Bell System had decided it needed a holding company for the dozens of Bell companies scattered around the country, and American Telephone & Telegraph, or AT&T, was formed. The telephone business had so much potential that would-be inventors and entrepreneurs were challenging Bell's patents, but in 1888 the U.S. Supreme Court issued a ruling that gave the Bell group a monopoly on manufacturing telephone equipment and, consequently, on providing telephone service. The monopoly lasted until 1894, when Bell's original patents expired.

The telephone systems of the larger cities like New York and Chicago had been allowed to grow and flourish with little if any competition. But things were different in rural areas, where, after Bell's key patents expired, independent telephone companies began to spring up, often to provide

By the turn of the century, the largest cities in America had developed adequate phone systems. Harriet G. Daly, shown here in 1908, was the operator for the U.S. capitol's switchboard. *(Photo courtesy National Archives.)*

service to the rural areas that the Bell system had neglected for the more profitable urban areas. These men and women, many of them farmers, were helped along by a published manual explaining how to develop their own telephone systems.[7]

The independents rose rapidly. In 1893, Bell provided about 266,000 phones in the United States. Ten years later the independent companies had nearly caught up to Bell, serving more than a million people.[8]

As far back as the 1880s and 1890s, a few states had begun regulating telephone service, and there was growing concern in the early 1900s over a Bell System monopoly. AT&T had acquired 495,000 independents in three years. Though its growth was stunted somewhat after being charged with violating antitrust laws in 1912, the passage of the Willis-Graham Act nine years later allowed mergers of telephone companies without antitrust fears, and AT&T once again went on a gobbling spree.

Though the number of independent telephone companies continued to increase, reaching a high in 1927, many of these rural systems were deteriorating. These were tiny organizations, run by families who, as often as not, knew very little about how to run a business. At the same time, telephone subscribers often were unable to pay their bills. To make matters worse, maintenance and repair of the systems were often lax, due to the small number of qualified people and the even smaller amount of capital. Rural residents had to suffer poor telephone service, and other than moving to the cities, there wasn't much they could do about it. Because the tiny exchanges faced so many hardships, many of them were forced to sell to larger, more stable companies, which often meant they were bought by the Bell System.

Help from the Government

The Great Depression didn't help matters, but it did bring President Roosevelt's New Deal, which created myriad alphabet agencies, including the FCC, or Federal Communications Commission. The FCC was created in 1934 to regulate the telephone industry, and the foundation of its telecommunications policy called for "making available, so far as possible, to all the people of the United States a rapid, efficient, nationwide and worldwide wire and radio communication service with adequate facilities at reasonable charges."[9]

The telephone went through a number of transformations in its early years. Pictured from left: Alexander Graham Bell's "gallows" telephone, so named because it resembled a hangman's gallows, circa 1875; Bell's second wall-mounted transmitter, circa 1877; Bell's "coffin" telephone, complete with Bell Butter Stamp transmitter and receiver, circa 1878; the American Cushman three-box walnut wall telephone with black-type transmitter and long-pole receiver, circa 1889; the American Electric "pencil shaft" upright desk set, also known as the candlestick phone, circa 1897; the American Electric "silver dollar" pay telephone with slots on the writing shelf to accept coins, circa 1903; the Kellogg "fiddleback" common battery wall telephone with pay station coin collector, circa 1905; the Stowger upright desk telephone, also called the "secret service system" because no operator was needed to place a call, circa 1905; the Stowger single-box dial wall telephone, circa 1905; the automatic electrical dial upright desk stand, circa 1920s; and the single-box Western Electric wall telephone, circa 1920s. *(All telephones are reproductions of original models, photographed by Wally Tubbs, courtesy Frank H. Woods Telephone Pioneer Museum.)*

Experiments conducted during World War II contributed to the telecommunications boom, filling the postwar years with new conveniences. In 1946, the first commercial mobile telephone service linked a vehicle to telephone networks via radio. Also that year, coaxial cables began carrying transmission, which greatly improved service since electrical interference would no longer interrupt calls. In 1947, microwave radio transmission was used for long distance.

As men and women returned from their overseas duties, demand for more and better telephone service shot up. Exchanges had a hard time keeping up. The small rural systems continued to deteriorate and dwindle in number, but the independent telephone industry got a big boost when, in 1949, Congress authorized the Rural Electrification Administration (REA) to make loans to telephone companies at just 2 percent interest. Many independents that had managed to survive were extremely short on capital. They couldn't get the latest technology that city dwellers enjoyed, and they often couldn't repair equipment if, for example, a storm brought down a wire. Without the low-interest REA loans, many rural customers might not have had telephone

service, as it allowed the independents to provide better, more affordable service to more people. It also allowed them to acquire other independents that were willing to sell.

Still, Ma Bell was determined to have as much of the pie as it could consume, actively discouraging independents from infringing on its monopoly. Despite AT&T's efforts and despite the myriad hardships faced by the men and women who sought to bring telephone service to rural areas, some of the independents were able to grow and prosper. Two such organizations, Allied Telephone & Electric in Arkansas and Mid-Continent Telephone Corporation in Ohio, were able to survive and thrive by bringing an uncommon entrepreneurial spirit, a dedication to serving people, a vast amount of integrity, and all the business savvy they could muster to the often cutthroat telecommunications arena. It was these two companies that would come together in 1983 to form ALLTEL, which by 2000 had evolved into a communications company valued at $7 billion that served more than ten million customers in twenty-four states.

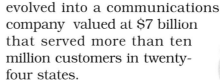

Announcing the Opening of
ALLIED
TELEPHONE &
ELECTRIC CO.

Hillcrest Station
Former Location of
Post Office

2819 KAVANAUGH
PHONE 3-6868

Charles B. Miller

H. R. Wilbourn, Jr.

We proudly offer the Pulaski Heights community a first class service and the following quality lines of merchandise:

GENERAL ELECTRIC
**Refrigerators • Stoves • Heaters • Irons
Fluorescent Lights • G-E Bulbs • Complete Kitchens**

General Line of **TOOLS** • Pittsburgh **PAINTS** • Full Line of **PYREX**
SPORTING GOODS • XMAS TOYS • HARDWARE

 Stromberg-Carlson **RADIOS** Fada **RADIOS**

AND MANY OTHER LINES OF HOUSEHOLD EQUIPMENT

OPEN MONDAY
FOR FRIENDLY NEIGHBORHOOD SERVICE

An advertisement in the *Arkansas Gazette* on December 1, 1945, announces the opening of Allied Telephone & Electric Company in Little Rock's Pulaski Heights community.

CHAPTER TWO

THE ARKANSAS PIECE

1947–1950

The timing was perfect. But we had nothing to do with that except for having a lot of desire to succeed.

—Hugh R. Wilbourn, on how he and Charlie Miller built
Allied Telephone & Electric Company[1]

MEN WHO WOULD CONSIDER it an acceptable business proposition to operate a strand of telephone wire for twelve miles along an Arkansas dirt road to serve only seven poor homes would be no one's candidates to father a global communications company. That brothers-in-law Hugh R. Wilbourn Jr. and Charles B. Miller, saddled with $40,000 of debt at the lingering edge of the Great Depression, could even make a go of one little rural telephone company with archaic equipment was itself a notable accomplishment. That they might build a company that would one day be on the vanguard of breathtaking communications technology would have seemed an absurd premise.

A half century later, Wilbourn, at eighty-five, would attribute it all to eternally smiling fortune, good family, and hard work. "I have been blessed," he said. "Everything I ever touched turned out well."[2]

The good luck that seemed to follow all the risks that Wilbourn, Miller, and their successors took may have been simply their shared determination and capacity for relentless labor. But the same lucky star or the same stubborn will had guided the progenitor of the Wilbourn family as he settled in North America.

The Founders' Roots

A Welshman named John Wellborn (the name eventually evolved into Wilbourn) was one of a handful of hardy survivors of five hundred emigrants bound for the Jamestown colony in 1609. But storms scattered the ships of the ill-fated expedition, and Wellborn bailed for three days and four nights before his boat sank in the rocks off Bermuda's shore. Wellborn and a small band clambered ashore and survived on the island for ten months before journeying in makeshift boats to the starving Jamestown colony, itself decimated by disease.[3]

The Wellborns scattered south and west until settling close to Oxford, Mississippi. In 1900, Wilbourn's father, also named Hugh, migrated from Mississippi to England, Arkansas, a few miles southeast of Little Rock. There he met and married Willye Mae Bonner, the daughter of an

The Kellogg single-box telephone, a magneto-operated variety commonly in use in the rural exchanges bought by Allied Telephone from the 1920s into the 1950s, when they were replaced by dial phones. *(Photo courtesy Frank H. Woods Telephone Pioneer Museum, Lincoln, Nebraska.)*

Arkansas farmer. The elder Hugh Wilbourn was the station master of Rock Island Railroad and later became the freight claims agent for Missouri and Arkansas, a job that seemed to entail, at least in Wilbourn's case, endless hours and days. Wilbourn was dedicated to his work, his family, and the Pulaski Heights Baptist Church near his home on Cedar Street. The son would follow his example as nearly as he could, down to serving, like his father, as a deacon in the same Heights church.

Hugh Randolph Wilbourn Jr. was born in Little Rock on September 13, 1915, the second of three children. A younger brother, William Bonner, died at the age of seven. His older sister, Marion, fell in love with an aspiring journalist, Charles Beverly Miller, at a church camp in the remote Ozark mountain town of Siloam Springs in northwest Arkansas.

Charles Miller was born July 23, 1908, the son of a hardware store owner in Gravette, Arkansas, near the Missouri and Oklahoma borders. His parents were separated early, and he was reared by grandparents. Miller's grandfather, a circuit-riding preacher with a penchant for music that he imbued in the whole family, was a prominent citizen of the town and often took the extended family with him to sing at churches and religious festivals.

A gifted writer, Miller wanted to be a journalist and for a couple of years attended the University of Missouri at Columbia, the nation's oldest journalism school. Even long after he abandoned the notion of a writing career, he usually had a camera slung around his neck wherever he went. But during his college sojourn he also took courses in engineering, which may have proven more useful in later years than his journalism training. After falling in love with Marion Wilbourn and moving to Little Rock, Miller tried his hand at odd jobs during the early stages of the Depression. He became fast friends with Edward J. Hopkins, boyfriend of Marion's best friend. Hopkins, who would go on to a distinguished career in the U.S. Air Force, became principal of Ruraldale School, a small school about thirty-five miles south of Little Rock, and he hired Miller to teach the second grade. Miller was a wonderful teacher, Hopkins recalled, but it was obvious that he didn't expect to make it a career.[4] He taught only briefly before he and his

future brother-in-law, Wilbourn, were lucky enough to be hired at Southwestern Bell.

Wilbourn, who thought he might be an engineer, had journeyed after high school to Ouachita Baptist College, a small liberal arts school at Arkadelphia, south of Little Rock. Certainly a business career did not seem to be on either young man's mind at the threshold of the Depression. After a year of college, Wilbourn dropped out as well, for this was the hardest time of the century in the hardest place in the country to live and prosper. A business career was hardly thinkable. Mere employment was difficult enough.

But even then Wilbourn showed the entrepreneurial impulses that would mark his telephone career. At loose ends after quitting school, he noticed a vacant root beer stand on the city's Main Street off the downtown business district and learned from the owner that he could rent it for $25 a month. He went home, fetched a skillet and a few more cooking utensils, and telephoned the Coca-Cola and Nehi bottling companies and the Mayflower Ice Cream Company. Very soon, Wilbourn had soft drink boxes, an ice cream cabinet, and an inventory of snacks. From the Reed Music Company he rented a piano and a piano box, and he hired a piano player to entertain. He called it the White House, and the parking lot filled up.

In the meantime, Wilbourn recalled, "My mother was tearing her hair out because her son was down there late at night in that neighborhood, which was not a very good one." So when a young man who had made money in a South American scheme asked him to sell, he did. The two men drove around to all of Wilbourn's creditors, the man paid the outstanding bills, and Wilbourn handed him the keys to the White House. "I took my skillet and went home," Wilbourn said.[5]

The Bottom Rung

Steady, paying work was hard to find anywhere in 1934, so it was double good fortune when Miller and Wilbourn both landed jobs that were stable and that gave them entry into the field in which they would establish their names. The Depression hit the telephone industry as hard as any, as thousands of people in the state halted service, counting telephones a luxury. Nevertheless, two men from the Pulaski Heights Church—an accountant and an engineer at Southwestern Bell Telephone Company—encouraged the young men to apply for work at Bell. Miller and Wilbourn both were hired as construction workers, Wilbourn as a splicer's helper and testman and Miller as an outside construction worker, called a "combination man."

Miller was dispatched to the town of Nashville in southwest Arkansas. There was no featherbedding on the telephone team, and Miller did everything there was to do, from setting poles and stringing lines to installing and repairing telephones and switches. In the fall he married Marion Wilbourn, Hugh's sister, and brought her to Nashville.

Meanwhile, Wilbourn was on a construction crew operating out of Little Rock, which entailed trimming trees away from lines, digging trenches, setting poles, and installing phones. In 1936, he married his Little Rock sweetheart, Edith Morris, whom he met while organizing a coed church softball team.

His break at Bell came one day when he was waist deep in a muddy trench on the main street in the delta town of Marion, across the Mississippi River from Memphis. Three Bell officials stood to the side as the crew was laying a cable to the town's hotel. As Wilbourn was throwing dirt out of the trench, one of them shouted for him to join them. Wondering what he could have done, Wilbourn climbed out of the ditch. "So there I am standing with these powerful men who ran Bell Telephone in that part of the country," Wilbourn remembered. "One of them was from St. Louis, and he said, 'How would you like to change jobs? We're going to send you over to Fort Smith and put you in the office.' Man alive, to come out of the ditch and go into

the office was a turning point in my life! From then on, I went on up through Bell and had all the advantages you could possibly get."[6]

Thus Wilbourn moved to Fort Smith, Arkansas, an old frontier town on the Oklahoma border and by then the state's second largest city. Bell sent him to school to learn the intricacies of switching—how to build, install, and maintain switchboards—and the managerial operations

Below: Charles B. Miller and his wife, Marion Wilbourn Miller, soon after their marriage in 1934. Her brother Hugh and Miller had worked at Southwestern Bell and would later form one of the businesses that became ALLTEL.

Bottom: Hugh R. Wilbourn Jr. and his wife, Edith Morris Wilbourn, soon after their marriage in 1936.

of the telephone office. In his new position, Wilbourn observed the complicated procedure for responding to orders for new service and repairs and for keeping records of the service. Someone took the order downstairs, and it was routed upstairs, where the address was tracked on massive maps that gave house numbers and terminal numbers. Then the information was transferred to another set of books.

"One day I thought, 'You know, there's a better way to do this,'" Wilbourn recalled. When the district plant manager passed through, Wilbourn stopped him and explained how it could be simplified with a Cardex system, which automated the system on cards without all the maps. "Where'd you get that idea?" the manager asked. "Right here," Wilbourn replied, tapping his forehead. Very soon Wilbourn found himself developing a Cardex system for Fort Smith. The task meant logging home and business addresses, terminal numbers, and pole numbers, and it gave Wilbourn an intricate grasp of the network from exchange switchboards to the receiver.[7]

The brothers-in-law spent ten years with Bell. Cumulatively, they gathered all the expertise in operating a telephone company that could be had and gained considerable moonlighting experience as well. Small rural telephone companies in their areas, usually husband-and-wife operations, had little expertise, and a breakdown could mean days or weeks of disruption. Independently, both Miller and Wilbourn lent their know-how to nearby towns on weekends and evenings to repair and install equipment. And as their reputations spread among the independents, the demand for their services grew.

The Alliance

At last Wilbourn and Miller decided to pool their knowledge and skills and see if their sideline business would support a career. In July 1943, they both quit Southwestern Bell and opened a telephone business in Little Rock called Communications Repair Service. The headquarters was a rented post office box. They bought an old half-ton pickup truck at a bankruptcy sale for $25 and purchased a few tools for $35, then sent notices to more than one hundred independent telephone companies in Arkansas, telling of their availability to perform all sorts of technical services.

Weeks passed and nothing happened, but finally one request came in. Ouita Felker, owner and operator with her husband, Mark, of the Felker Telephone and Oil Company at Mulberry, wanted the partners to come up to the little Ozark mountain town above the Mulberry River southeast of Fort Smith to set poles and string cables. Setting telephone poles, backbreaking toil under the best of circumstances, was not exactly what the men had in mind when they quit Bell, but they loaded their tools, piled in their truck, and drove the 125 miles to Mulberry. Over time, they wound up rebuilding the little exchange, sometimes borrowing Southwestern Bell crewmen on weekends.

Wilbourn remembered the Felkers fondly. Mark, who was "strong as a horse," helped them set poles, and Ouita told other telephone people what Wilbourn and Miller had done for them. Seven years later, the Felkers' little company would be one of the first that Wilbourn and Miller would buy.[8]

Setting telephone poles, which required nothing more than muscle, sweat, and endurance, turned out to be a frequent order for Communications Repair Service, though it often went along with more cerebral labor. The work was emotionally draining as well as physically demanding because the two men were often away from home for days and weeks at a time.

"Charlie and I worked long, long hours," Wilbourn recalled. "But hours didn't mean a thing in the world. We started digging holes to set poles at daylight, when it was cool in the morning. And maybe we'd be only a little ways down in that [mountain] rock when it'd get so hot, we'd quit, put something over the hole, and go about other business, and then early the next morning we'd come back to that rock hole."[9]

Within a couple of years, Wilbourn and Miller were contracting with more than one hundred rural companies. In 1945, they rented a storefront on Kavanaugh Boulevard in the shopping district of Hillcrest, a fashionable neighborhood that was then on Little Rock's western side, and changed the name of their business to Allied Telephone & Electric Company. By conscious choice, the name, or at least the initials, bore a close resemblance to

AT&T, the holding company of the Bell companies and the manufacturer of communications equipment. Allied Telephone sold General Electric appliances and other equipment up front, and Wilbourn and Miller continued to run their repair and installation business for the independent companies in back. The Hillcrest store gave them a higher profile and a convenient and stylish headquarters for their consulting and contracting, and it enabled them to buy their equipment wholesale.

Business was booming, and by the mid-1940s the company had two crews and had branched into Oklahoma. The partners were no longer engaged in the backbreaking work of setting poles but were engineering, designing, and rebuilding systems. Miller and Wilbourn worked hard to satisfy their customers as residents of smaller

Miller and Wilbourn opened a store in Little Rock's Hillcrest neighborhood in 1945, selling hardware and electrical appliances while running their telephone engineering and repair service from the back.

towns began demanding more modern services, such as dial equipment, that were already available in the cities.

Buying Grant County

The men's good fortune in business, as Wilbourn would later say, owed as much to a few extraordinary relationships with important businessmen as to their own hard work and shrewd risks. Wilbourn's close friendship with R. A. "Brick" Lile, a powerful Little Rock businessman who left his print on the city's skyline, would yield the company vital real estate for its headquarters on the banks of the Arkansas River. Lile secured the land from Winthrop Rockefeller, the state's first Republican governor (1967–1971) since the Reconstruction period and a personal friend.[10]

But no relationship proved as momentous as that with W. R. "Witt" Stephens and, subsequently, his brother, Jackson T. Stephens, other members of the Stephens family, and the Stephens' financial holdings. By the end of World War II, Witt Stephens was fast accumulating

A GOOD CONNECTION TO HAVE

THE MAN FROM WHOM WILBOURN and Miller bought their first telephone company—W. R. "Witt" Stephens—was a genius in his own right, and their connection to him and his family would prove to be extremely beneficial.

Stephens was born and reared in the little farming community of Prattsville outside the county seat of Sheridan, thirty miles south of Little Rock. After selling belt buckles and Bibles in the early Depression years, Witt made his first real money by massaging the government and working with bankrupt local governments and the federal Reconstruction Finance Corporation. This involved refinancing local debts after he had bought many of the discounted securities and then trading on the good will he had earned to capture a big share of the municipal bond business in the years ahead.[1]

Though frequently the object of political storms, Witt was admired personally even by critics, some of whom later would regularly partake of the country vegetables, pork chops, and cornbread at his legendary table in the Stephens Building. His rich, gravelly voice, achingly slow

W. R. "Witt" Stephens, who built a great personal fortune and financial empire, bought the telephone company in his hometown in 1942 so that he could provide a telephone for his mother. He sold the troubled company to Wilbourn and Miller, and it became the foundation of Allied Telephone and ALLTEL.

cadence, and practiced rustic ways charmed competitors and regulators alike.

one of the greatest personal fortunes and financial empires of mid-America.

Stephens had purchased the Grant County Telephone Company in 1942 for $25,000, mainly so that he could run a line out to the farm at Prattsville and talk to his mother on the telephone. He called on Wilbourn and Miller to install the line and phone and continued to call on them for repairs. Over time, the constant complaints by customers grew to be a headache for him, and in 1946, he asked Wilbourn and Miller to operate and maintain the system for him with the understanding that they could keep the earnings.

It turned out to be a headache for Wilbourn and Miller too, so they went to his office on Second Street in Little Rock one morning in 1947 to col-

lect their payments and to tell Stephens they wanted out of the arrangement. Damage caused by a recent ice storm compounded the fact that they were not making any money, and they would have to spend more money to modernize the outdated plant. Stephens followed the men out to the street. As they were walking away, Wilbourn turned around and asked Stephens if he would be willing to sell. "Boys, come on back," Stephens growled. As Wilbourn recalled, "By the time we left that front door on Second Street and got back to his office, he had all the figures out, the percent, the interest, everything—how we would pay him, the whole bit. He just laid it out there. 'Now, we'll do this, this, this, this, and you're going to do this, this, this, and this. Can you boys handle that?' Charlie and I looked at each other and said, 'Well,

When he offered to buy the Fort Smith Gas Company (now Arkansas Oklahoma Gas Company), the object of an antitrust divestiture, for $1.2 million in 1945, Stephens had to appear before the federal Securities and Exchange Commission in Washington for approval of the sale. Securities and loans would cover most of the price, but he had to raise $150,000 in equity capital. A skeptical government lawyer repeatedly asked the evasive Stephens how he could raise that kind of cash. Finally, Stephens fished in his coat pocket and plopped a fat wad of bills on the table. "Judge," he drawled, "I brung it with me." The SEC approved the sale.[2]

No small part of Stephens' business success was owing to his uncanny political influence. He had become, by the late 1940s, the kingmaker of Arkansas politics, raising the essential money and almost singlehandedly determining who would be elected governor or United States senator. His sway reached the state legislature, the state regulatory commissions, and the state's delegation in Congress. When the Arkansas Supreme Court rendered an unfavorable decision on the pricing structure of natural gas on a Monday morning in 1957, Witt drafted a bill, had it introduced in the legislature, passed in committees by both the senate and house of representatives, and signed into law by Governor Orval E. Faubus by Friday afternoon. That single act insured, in virtual perpetuity, the high profitability of his gas company.

Outside the gas company, Witt and his brother, Jack, owned vast energy resources (western bituminous coal as well as natural gas) and extensive banking, transportation, and manufacturing interests across Arkansas and in other states.

By the 1970s, the little investment company he founded in Little Rock during the Depression, Stephens Inc., had become the largest investment banking firm off Wall Street. He had turned over active management of the investment company to his younger brother, Jack, a U.S. Naval Academy classmate of Jimmy Carter, while he busied himself with building a natural gas empire. Witt had acquired from Cities Service Company the controlling interest in Arkansas Louisiana Gas Company—an anemic gas distribution company that served most of Arkansas and part of northern Louisiana in the early 1950s— and, applying his genius once again, built it from one of the least profitable to one of the most profitable utilities in the country.[3]

sure, Mr. Stephens. That's all we do.' And he said, 'Okay, it's yours.'"[11]

Stephens sold them the stock in the company for $40,000 on credit with no down payment. The men didn't have the assets to get a loan, so Stephens carried the note until some years later when Miller and Wilbourn borrowed from Boatman's National Bank in St. Louis and paid the balance. Stephens would later say he never dealt with more honorable men.

One stipulation of the sale was that Wilbourn and Miller would continue to supply Stephens' mother at Prattsville with free telephone service. The regular base charge in those days was about $3 a month. Mrs. Stephens got her phone service free for several years until Allied converted Prattsville to dial service.

Even by rural Arkansas standards, the Grant County Telephone Company was obsolete and decrepit. The exchange had three operators who worked in shifts and 275 telephones of the ancient magneto variety. The magneto was a series of horseshoe-shaped magnets pierced by a shaft and a coil. When you cranked the telephone's lever, the coil produced alternating currents that would alert the operator by causing a little bar to fall on the switchboard. Many of the rural exchanges had not replaced the antiquated system with a common battery, which would supply a charge for the whole exchange and allow people to reach the operator by simply picking up the telephone. Outside town, lines stretched for miles, sometimes on fence posts and trees and under the fragile limbs of yellow pines, and they served few customers. A line north from Sheridan stretched for twelve miles but served only seven homes along the route.

For most country dwellers a telephone was a needless luxury, well down on their list of priorities. Maintenance was a perpetual function, especially in winter, when ice, snow, or a strong breeze could topple a tree or a big limb across a line, knocking out service along its length. People knew enough about the technology available to those in nearby Little Rock to be unhappy about their own cursed phones, and the new owners knew they had to rebuild the whole system and install reliable and modern equipment.

Thus Wilbourn rented and then built a house at Sheridan to upgrade the Grant system. The Sheridan City Council approved a small rate increase for the new company on the condition that the new owners replace the old magneto phones with a common battery and that service be satisfactory. On July 10, 1948, Allied cut the Sheridan exchange over to a common battery.

Extending the Network

In the meantime, Allied's consulting work with independent telephone companies across the state was flourishing. The Sheridan arrangement allowed Wilbourn to perform or supervise the work in South Arkansas while building the Sheridan system, and Miller ran things from Little Rock and supervised work north of the capital.

Their work for the independents and the friendships developed with the mom-and-pop owners would pay off over the next two decades. When independents found themselves without a successor or unable to finance or manage technological change, they sold to the men they had learned to trust.

Hugh D. Straughn, who owned the Southwest Arkansas Telephone Company, summoned the two men regularly to repair lines in his exchanges at Glenwood, Amity, and Norman (towns along the beautiful Caddo River) and Mount Ida in the Ouachita Mountains. Bad weather usually spelled trouble somewhere along the lines, and Straughn was accustomed to wrapping cables with tape and paraffin cloth to stop leaks into the line. After Wilbourn and Miller drove down on weekends with moonlighting Bell crewmen to upgrade the lines, Straughn told them they ought to buy into the telephone business. In May 1950, nearly three years after acquiring the phone company in Grant County, Wilbourn and

An extended family portrait, circa 1949, at the Hillcrest home of the elder Hugh Wilbourn and his wife, Willye Mae (standing rear center). At top left are Charles Miller, a founder and first president of Allied Telephone, and in front of him, his wife, Marion Wilbourn Miller. At top right are Hugh Wilbourn Jr., a founder and later president and chairman of Allied Telephone and a director of ALLTEL, and his wife, Edith Morris Wilbourn, in front of him. The children, clockwise from bottom left, are Hugh Randolph "Randy" Wilbourn III, who would become senior vice president for corporate communications for ALLTEL; the Millers' son Max Miller, who would die the next year; the Millers' son Charles Wilbourn Miller, later executive vice president of ALLTEL; the Wilbourns' daughter Jo Ellen, whose future husband, Joe T. Ford, would become chairman and CEO of ALLTEL; Mary Nell Wilbourn, later Mary Nell Shaw, who died in 1989; and Beverly Wilbourn, later Beverly Pascoe, the youngest of the Wilbourns' daughters.

Hugh Wilbourn Jr. (right) and Carl McGarrity, his plant superintendent, in front of the company's Sheridan exchange in 1950.

Miller bought Straughn's company, which served seven hundred stations, and nearly tripled the phones they maintained. Three of the four exchanges still had magneto phones, which had to be converted to common batteries, so the partners later formed Allied Telephone Company to operate the widening system.

If prosperity did not exactly flood the countryside after the war, at least jobs were prevalent, living standards improved, and the practiced austerity of people in the small towns and rural routes relaxed. They wanted telephones, but not just any telephone. Frequent and long disruptions and crowded party lines were becoming jokes. Pressed by their neighbors and customers for better equipment and service, the family owners of many independents contracted with Charles Miller and Hugh Wilbourn to engineer and build new systems, and if the owners couldn't afford the improvements, they often approached the partners about buying their small companies out.

Money, however, especially in a capital-starved state and for tightly regulated little utilities, was hard to come by at a workable rate for anyone. Few banks were willing to lend money to hard-pressed telephone companies whose obsolete assets and stagnant earnings did not make them attractive risks. For many owners of the rural companies, conservative by their very nature, debt went against their constitutions even if money were easily available. They couldn't win rate increases in advance from the state regulatory commission to pay for the improvements but had to wait until the modernization was complete, and then there was a chance the commission might not condone rates that the company deemed adequate. Equipment and supplies, including cables, had been hard to buy during World War II because natural resources were requisitioned for the war effort, and they were still scarce after the war, particularly for small independent telephone companies.

"It was a good time for us," Wilbourn recalled years later. "The war was over, and everybody seemed to want telephone service. We built an organization that would furnish it."[12]

In most of the small towns served by independents, people were two decades behind their relatives in the larger cities served by Bell, which had begun to install rudimentary dial telephones in Little Rock in 1922. Meeting the growing demands for telephones and for reliable and modern service in a reviving postwar economy was nearly impossible for many of the rural independents, and they began to look for saviors.

Before digital switching, this original toll board at the Fulton, Ohio, office in 1940 represented state-of-the-art telephone technology.

CHAPTER THREE

THE OHIO PIECE

1909–1959

When I tell you that people are the single most valuable asset in any company, I'm not just spouting a cliché. I know it to be true.

—Weldon W. Case[1]

ONE DAY IN THE WINTER OF 1909–10, Weldon C. Wood was translating Morse code in the Western Union office in Cleveland, Ohio, when a lively message from the little town of Hudson south of the city came across his key. James W. Ellsworth, a wealthy philanthropist, was telling rich friends in New York about a fine little brouhaha he had created in Hudson after he had tendered an extraordinary offer to make the town lovelier and more livable. As Wood translated the message, he recognized a golden opportunity. Later it would lead to a sprawling telecommunications empire.

The Underground Debate

The son of a shopkeeper on the village green, Ellsworth grew up in Hudson, but in 1869, two years before the great Chicago fire, he moved to Chicago, where he built a fortune banking, mining, and jobbing coal for midwestern railroads. While he kept a home in Chicago, a brownstone in Manhattan, a villa in Italy, and a castle in Switzerland, Ellsworth summered in a magnificent Queen Anne–style mansion that he called Evamere, which he had erected on the outskirts of his little hometown.[2] When he sojourned in the town, he strolled about in formal clothes and a top hat. He was also prone to grand gestures, such as the purchase of a statue and Daniel Boone's log cabin after

their exhibition at the Chicago World Fair, for which he was a prime mover.[3]

What Ellsworth was proposing to do, he related to his New York friends, had been a point of controversy in Hudson for some time. In 1907, he told the village elders that he would build a water treatment plant and install a new water and sewer system for the town, eliminating the need for backyard wells. He also would build a new electric system, including a generating plant and attractive street lights for the whole town of fifteen hundred. The lines would all be underground.

But Ellsworth attached a few conditions, and it was these conditions that sent the community into a frenzy. The city would have to plant elm trees on both sides of the streets, all the bars in town except one would have to be closed, the city would have to bear the cost of paving the streets, and the two telephone companies in town would have to dig up their poles and plant their lines underground. All of this would have to continue for fifty years, or else ownership of the water and electric operations would revert to Ellsworth or his heirs.

In 1910, Weldon C. Wood was the first to put telephone cables underground. His Hudson Underground Telephone Company would form the foundation for Western Reserve, run by his son-in-law, Harry Case, and would later evolve into Mid-Continent Telephone, run by Harry's son, Weldon W. Case.

Two-thirds of the villagers voted that December to do as Ellsworth proposed. The losers, formulating a new verb, said the town had been "Ellsworthed." They said the part-time resident was trying to be a dictator.[4]

But while most voters embraced the public portion of the bargain, neither they nor the village council could control the two telephone companies, Central Union Telephone Company and Akron People's Telephone Company, which refused to put their lines underground, at least under conditions that the townspeople considered acceptable. Most of the village was served by People's, which later became Ohio Bell, and the rest by Central Union, although only about a hundred people actually had telephones. The companies each had poles and crossarms running up and down the same streets, and the crisscrossing wires were an eyesore. The telephone companies said the expense of buying and burying cables, about $11,500 for each company, was unprecedented anywhere and would be outrageous and the maintenance backbreaking—if indeed it could even be done. Eventually, the companies said they would put the wires underground, but they would raise the rates on town customers and expect the city or Ellsworth to pay for the conduits and materials.

Feelings became inflamed as the improvements were stalled by the phone companies' intransigence, and the controversy raged for three years. By 1909 Ellsworth was calling for townspeople to halt their telephone service and disconnect the wires from their homes and businesses, thereby putting the companies out of business. A few gave up their

telephones but wanted them back after the boycott produced no results. Finally, in August 1909, Ellsworth told the village council, "As many as possible of the citizens should be made to see this and publically denounce every one of those who are standing in the way.... Then, at the end of thirty days, if the poles are not removed, chop them down!"[5]

Western Reserve

From his telegraph desk in Cleveland, Wood followed the debate as he tapped out Ellsworth's cables to New York. Finding Ellsworth in Hudson early in 1910, Wood took a carriage to see the industrialist. Wood said he knew something about the technology and that if Ellsworth and the town would help him figure out a way to buy the companies, he would install an underground telephone system. Ellsworth said he had a deal.

Whether it was from the threat to cut down their poles or weariness from the controversy, the companies agreed to sell. With Wood's savings and $25,000 in bonds that he sold to Hudson businessmen, he bought and merged the companies, calling the new entity the Hudson Underground Telephone Company.

As promised, the village council adopted an ordinance prohibiting telephone or electric poles within the city limits for fifty years. A half century later, when the city council took up an ordinance to allow the power company to install overhead wires, Wood's grandson, Weldon W. Case, who was by then running the old telephone company, told the council that if it granted the waiver to the power company, he would

Above: The Case family farmhouse, where Weldon Wood's son-in-law, Harry Case, was raised and where Harry raised his son Weldon Case, who would later become president of Mid-Continent and chairman and CEO of ALLTEL

Top left: A telephone construction crew for the Jamestown Telephone Corporation, circa 1922

Left: Cora Koontz operates the one-person switchboard at the Newark, Ohio, exchange, circa 1938.

be most happy to resurrect all his cables and hoist them onto poles. Repairs and installation would be a lot cheaper, he said. The council denied the power company's petition and eventually renewed the underground ordinance.[6]

All the underground cabling was completed by the end of 1910, although not without considerable grumbling as customers complained about losing service for a week or longer at a time. But Hudson had the first underground telephone system in the United States. People came from miles around to see the trenching, the construction of oak conduits, and the laying of telephone and electrical cables side by side.

Wood, who was by then forty-four, bought a four-hundred-acre farm west of town and moved there to run his company and rear his family. Over the next seventeen years he acquired several small

telephone exchanges in the area and consolidated them into Western Reserve Telephone Company.

A Family Business

As they would with the little telephone company in Arkansas, marriages would prove to be propitious events for the Ohio business. Wood's daughter, Alice, married the boy on the next farm, Harry N. Case. In 1925, young Case quit the family farm and went to work for the telephone company, which had a single office on the second floor of the bank next door to the town's clock tower. Upon his father-in-law's death in 1936, Harry Case became general manager and president of the company.

The mechanics of the telephone business were not daunting to master. The standard equipment was the candlestick telephone, which the user grabbed firmly with both hands. A party-line phone—twelve families sometimes shared the same line—cost customers $2 a month. When the cradle-model phone came along, a customer had to pay another quarter a month.

Demand was slow. Western Reserve kept an inventory of only five or six phones on hand. One of Harry's four sons, Weldon W. Case, who would later take over and lead the company onto the national stage, recalled many years later that marketing was a foreign notion in the Depression

Harry Case (pictured above right) had four sons—Nelson, Theodore, Weldon, and Baxter—all of whom joined Western Reserve, the family's telephone business.

years. "I'm afraid our attitude toward all those prospects out there was, if you don't ask for a telephone, you probably can't afford it."[7]

Weldon Case was born February 22, 1921. He and his brothers, Nelson, Theodore, and Baxter, all were introduced to the telephone business as youngsters, working summers, weekends, and after school. By 1934, at only thirteen, the eldest son, Weldon, was working on construction crews putting up poles, and he later worked inside on installation and switching. Brother Nelson, a little younger, followed soon after. They worked alongside men who were likely to be jobless and were putting in a few days on the line to work off delinquent phone bills.

Harry Case was known as something of a scrounger. People did not get rich in the independent telephone business, and Case kept the com-

pany afloat and making a little profit by keeping expenses low and helping people maintain their telephone service when they couldn't muster the cash to pay their bills. Weldon Case would recall going on bill-collecting forays with his father on weekends. They would return with a basket of eggs from "the egg lady," as his father referred to her, a chicken or two, a sack of potatoes fresh from the soil, or a jug or two of maple syrup. Maple syrup was a regular and valued payment. In 1936,

a jug of pure maple syrup was considered satisfactory payment for $1.50 of telephone calls.[8] One of Western Reserve's old customers, the Timmons farm, continued to ship buckets of premium maple syrup to Weldon Case at his retirement home in Boca Raton, Florida— though no longer in consideration for telephone service but for friendship—until Case's death in October 1999. Another delinquent customer paid his past bills by turning over a steamroller to the telephone company. It stayed around the premises for years, and Case never did find a use for it. Later, near the end of World War II, when sales were sluggish and marketing costs were high, a northern Ohio manufacturer of go-carts paid off a delinquent telephone invoice by delivering a dozen go-carts to the telephone company. Case stamped the bill paid.[9]

Harry Case had little money, for the company earned little, capital was scarce or too expensive, and, at any rate, he considered debt to be anathema. Bank borrowing was a last resort, something prudent men avoided. To get equipment—wire, poles, insulators, and tools—to enlarge the system or upgrade it, Case used his wits. He made friends easily and widely, including engineers at Ohio Bell Telephone Company. If Ohio Bell abandoned a pole line somewhere in southern Ohio, one of the engineers would mention it to Harry Case. Case would then round up a pole trailer and a couple of crewmen, maybe his eldest son, climb into a

Model A Ford, and head to the area. Farmers along the abandoned line might tell him, "Those guys from the telephone company told us that if we'd take these poles down, we could have them." "Oh no," Case would say, "we're from Western Reserve Telephone Company, and we need to take these poles." He would stack the poles on the trailer and haul them back to Hudson as if he had a contract for them.[10]

It was through just such resourcefulness that Harry Case kept the little telephone company both debt free and growing. But the first task was always to make customers happy. If someone ordered a phone and the company's sparse inventory happened to be depleted, Case would remove the phone in his house, install it at the customer's house, and do without until he could get new phones.

The frugality, the resourcefulness, the ease of friendship, the attention to customers—all were traits he passed along to his sons in the business. But the days would come, after World War II, when demand for these novel communication devices would not be slack and a dynamic business would need bolder and more creative management. It would take capital, lots of it, to meet the demands and inventive management to prosper in the most regulated environment in American business.

Upgrading the System

As a young man, Harry's son Weldon attended Western Reserve Academy, the Case Institute of Technology in Cleveland, and Ohio Wesleyan University in Delaware, Ohio, where he met and married Beatrice Kuhn. He finished college just as the United States was entering World War II. The war proved a career-learning experience as well. He received a battlefield commission, fighting with the U.S. Army 39th Signal Corps Heavy Construction Battalion in England, France, Belgium, Holland, and Germany.

While Weldon was overseas, the owner of the West Richfield Telephone Company, located sixteen miles west of Hudson, sold her company to the Case family because she was unable to find anyone to help her run it. She had had to do all the installation and troubleshooting herself,

including climbing the poles and repairing damaged lines in the brutal winters. West Richfield, in the Cleveland suburbs, significantly expanded Case's company.

When Weldon returned from the war early in 1946, he became the general manager of Western Reserve Telephone Company, now considerably larger than when he left and growing rapidly. It took some time after the end of the war for raw materials and equipment to become plentiful, and meantime the demand for telephones—not merely for telephones but modern ones—often outstripped what independent telephone companies could meet. People were not satisfied with the old hand-cranked magneto phones, long service

Switchboard operator Beulah Baker stands in front of her magneto switchboard, circa 1912. Her salary was $12 a week.

interruptions, noisy and meddlesome party lines, and interminable waits for operators to connect their calls. Ex-GIs were especially impatient, and people in small towns, moreover, were familiar with the quick dial service that people in the cities enjoyed.

Weldon Case was just as impatient. He began immediately to convert all the exchanges to common batteries, eliminating the need to ring up an operator. A customer could simply pick up the receiver and an operator would chime "Number, please." In 1948, he began converting the exchanges to dial service, beginning with the town of Aurora.

Setting up dial exchanges was a big production. Western Reserve built a standard square brick building to house the switching system in each town. But as soon as work started on the Aurora exchange, the bricklayers went on strike. The next day, Weldon Case picked up his cousin, Bill Wood, and drove to Aurora. "Bill, have you ever laid brick?" Case asked. "No, have you?" Wood replied. "No," Case said, "but I'm about to learn." Case mixed the mortar, and they began laying

Inset: Weldon Case (on left), who learned bricklaying on the job during a strike by bricklayers when the company built its first dial exchange, lays a few ceremonial bricks during construction of a Western Reserve exchange.

Bottom: Western Reserve Telephone Company's headquarters on Main Street in Hudson. The building, formerly a dealership for the Maxwell automobile and later a glove plant, was bought soon after World War II. It housed the telephone switching equipment on the first floor, and Harry Case and his wife lived on the second floor.

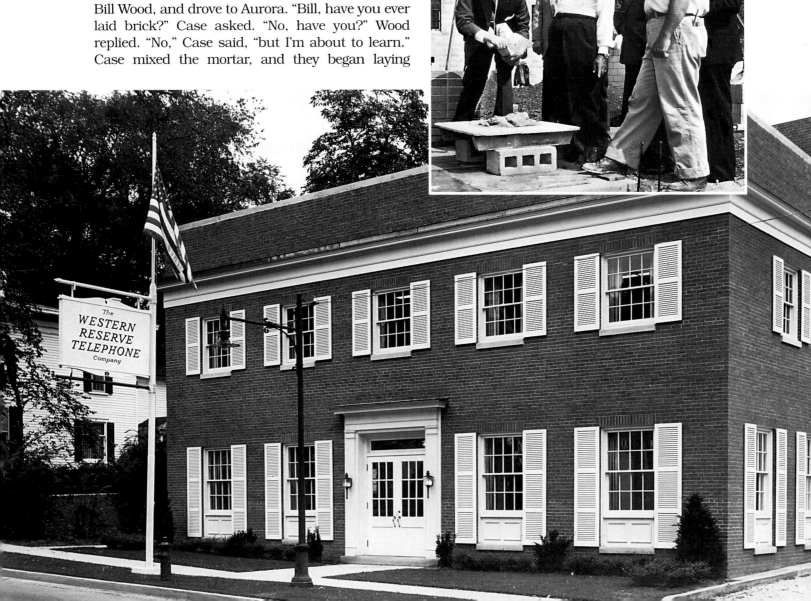

Operators at the common battery switchboard in Hudson, Ohio, before the exchange converted fully to dial in 1954

brick. They had finished the entire east wall of the exchange before the bricklayers returned to work.[11]

All eleven towns in the Western Reserve system —Hinckley, West Richfield, Peninsula, Hudson, Aurora, Bainbridge, Russell, Newbury, Hiram, Twinsburg, and Northfield—had been converted to dial by 1956, well ahead of most independent telephone companies.

Meanwhile, another technology had arrived that would enable people to bypass operators altogether on long-distance calls, and Case and his brother Nelson, then the controller, were eager to put the new technology to work. On October 8, 1954, Hudson became the first town in Ohio and one of the first in the country to dial long-distance direct, beating Ohio Bell by a month.

Finding Solutions

Ohio Bell was the standard, and despite meager resources, Case tried to emulate or beat Bell at everything. Western Reserve's trucks were a hodgepodge of castoffs, but Case had them all painted Ohio Bell's green, with the Western Reserve logo, of course. As the company grew in the 1950s and 1960s, the need for a fleet of trucks grew, but the company couldn't afford new ones. Case learned that Pennsylvania Bell auctioned off its

vehicles, still in generally good condition, after five years. Pennsylvania used sand and cinders on its highways after snow so that trucks that traveled those highways exclusively did not rust like trucks on the Ohio roadways, which were treated with salt in the winter. Case went to Pennsylvania twice a year, bid on Bell's old construction and installation trucks, and brought them back in a convoy to Hudson, where they were repaired and given a fresh coat of green paint.[12]

But the frugality and resourcefulness of Harry Case had its price too. The sons inherited a company that had no capital base upon which to earn a healthy return under the standard regulatory rules. Under the rate-making process in Ohio and nearly every other state then, telephone and other utility rates were predicated upon capital investment. A company invested in capital plant, and then it could seek higher rates that would reflect a suitable return on the investment. A company that had written off everything it had as expenses and, in effect, had no investment, theoretically was not entitled to rates greater than what it took to operate the business. Thus Western Reserve had virtually no book value.

Weldon Case went to the Ohio Utilities Commission in about 1954 to plead the company's case. He told the commission that while his company had no book value upon which to base higher rates, if the commission would grant a rate increase, he would rebuild the telephone system into one the commission would be proud of. The commission waived the rate-making formula and awarded the company a rate increase.[13]

After his father died in 1949, Weldon became president of Western Reserve in 1955, and his mother continued for years to come to the office to write all the checks. All four brothers were working for the company by then, and they concluded that while the business was flourishing, it was too small to support four families. When Ohio Bell approached the brothers about buying the company, they knew the time had come to decide the company's future.

After considering the offer to sell, the brothers decided to branch out instead. Western Reserve bought a 15 percent interest in the Elyria Telephone Company in a city of about fifty thousand west of Cleveland—a huge exchange by their standards. Elyria was a profitable company with modern equipment, but it was managed poorly, and service was abysmal. In 1956, Weldon Case became general manager and vice president at Elyria and a year later its president, commuting the thirty-six miles from Hudson daily. Baxter Case took a similar position with the acquired Chardon Telephone Company east of Cleveland, a much smaller company but one with similar management problems.

Instilling Values

It was in Elyria that Weldon Case demonstrated a management philosophy that would inspire the organization for decades to come—the philosophy that workers come first. A company that values, rewards, and encourages its employees, he thought, is one that will be successful. "Amid the hoopla over technological progress, the most complex and productive telecommunications device available on the market today is still the human element," he said years later. "A tiny, miraculous microchip contains information put there by human minds and hands."[14]

Before Case took over Elyria, the state Public Utilities Commission had held hearings on the substandard telephone service, and townspeople

YOU DON'T HAVE TO BE BAD TO BE GOOD

*E*VEN AFTER HE HAD RETIRED AS *ALLTEL's chairman and CEO, Weldon W. Case's reputation for integrity in business continued to be a model for others to follow. Included here are excerpts from a speech Case delivered to Ashland University's 113th graduating class in Ashland, Ohio, on May 11, 1991.*

Another tenet we live by in our organization is to seek and respect the ideas and opinions of everyone. Henry Ford once said, "If there is one secret of success, it lies in the ability to get the other person's angle as well as your own." That person may be wrong, but he doesn't think so. There is a reason he thinks and acts as he does. Ferret out that reason. Try honestly to put yourself in his place.

* * *

The three most important tools you should bring to work with you every day are a smile, a friendly manner, and a kind word. Don't make the mistake of thinking the business world is too sophisticated and cutthroat for common courtesies.... Any fool can criticize, condemn and complain. But a great man, said English essayist Thomas Carlyle, shows his greatness by the way he treats little men.

In his bestseller *How to Win Friends and Influence People*, Dale Carnegie tells the story of a famous American test pilot. Bob Hoover was returning to his home in Los Angeles after performing with a World War II vintage plane at an air show in San Diego. At three hundred feet in the air, both engines suddenly stopped. By deft maneuvering he managed to land. Nobody was hurt, but the airplane was badly damaged. Alighting from the craft, Hoover immediately inspected the plane's fuel. Just as he suspected, the old propeller plane had been filled with jet fuel instead of gasoline.

He returned to the airport and asked to see the mechanic who had serviced the plane. The man was sick with agony over his mistake. Tears streamed down his face as Hoover approached. He had just caused the loss of a turned out in droves to tell their horror stories. Case sensed the problem. It was not a lack of equipment or staffing but unappreciated and unmotivated employees.

"On the day I took the company over," Case recalled years later, "the average answering time when you dialed the operator to get long distance was 19.7 minutes. We brought that average answering time down to just under ten seconds—on the second day." Editorials in the newspaper saluted him, and he was an instant hero. People wanted to know how he did it. "I'll tell you how it happened," Case said. "I started with the telephone operators. On my first day, I had the chief operator take me around to meet them personally, every single one of them. Up to this point,

they frankly didn't give a damn about their jobs. But they were important to me—and I let them know it. On the second day, the equipment was no different. Nothing was different, except for a dramatic turnaround in the attitudes of the people. From that day the company went on to be extremely successful."[15]

Case kept an open door to employees, organized and participated in company functions, took roles in skits, and generally instilled a family atmosphere. He was slow to rebuke, preferring instead to show by example. On weekends, when other employees were off, Case and son Tom often would collect the complaints at Hudson and make the rounds themselves to repair phones so that customers wouldn't have to do without service

---

very expensive aircraft and could have caused the loss of three lives as well. Can you imagine Hoover's anger? Can you almost hear the tongue-lashing that was about to be delivered for that careless act? But Hoover didn't scold the mechanic. He didn't even criticize him. Instead, he put his arm around the man's shoulders and said, "To show you I'm sure you'll never do this again I want you to service my F-1 tomorrow."

* * *

The most important lesson I hope to impress upon you today is this: If you learn nothing else, learn how to treat people. In the corporate world, in your community, and everywhere you go, treat the next person the way you would like to be treated. Degrees, MBAs, and technical skills are all important in preparing for a life in business. But even more important is your ability to direct and inspire and influence people.

* * *

Corporate wrongdoing is the exception rather than the rule. Most companies have spotless records. But the few incidents of corruption are corroding the public's respect ... for American business. Opinion polls show that most people think U.S. companies are run by schemers and crooks. The truth is, the vast

majority of business executives are committed to upholding the law.

Do you have to be bad to be good at business? Just the opposite, according to James O'Toole, author of several books on management.... [According to O'Toole,] "You can succeed by taking the low road. But you can also succeed by taking the high road. I believe that most people, if given a choice, will take the high road. The only reason they don't is because they're afraid they will fail if they do. They have come to believe that American capitalism requires treating employees badly and cutting corners on the product. But they're wrong. There is a different kind of philosophy—a moral one—by which you can succeed. In the short run you may make more money by cutting corners, but in the long run you won't have created an institution that you can be proud of."

* * *

I hope you will enter your chosen careers and make wonderful successes of yourselves. And when you meet up with Robert Frost's "Two Roads Diverged in a Wood," take the high road. It will make all the difference.

You don't have to be bad to be good in business—or in any other facet of life. I sincerely give you my word.

Both pages: Though the beautiful city of Hudson served as home base for Western Reserve, the telephone company had exchanges in many surrounding cities.

Inset: Harry Case (left) and his wife, Alice, pose with their four sons shortly before the elder Case's death in 1949. The sons are (from left) Theodore, Weldon, Baxter, and Nelson.

until the next week. When calls came during dinner parties, the president of the company would excuse himself, fetch tools, and head into the night to fix someone's phone.[16]

Tom remembered one typical incident that demonstrated his father's way of correcting deficiencies. Case frequently made unannounced visits to all the exchanges in the system. Arriving at a Western Reserve office in August, he saw an eight-foot-square patch of grass in front of the building that was turning brown from lack of water. Case walked around the building looking for a water hose. The commercial manager spotted him and asked if Case needed help. "No, I'm just looking for a hose," Case said. Why did he need a hose? "I'm just going to water that grass down a little." Employees jumped to do it for him. "No, no, that's all right. I'm going to do it myself," he said. Case, who hated yard work, stood in the sweltering heat whistling and watering the little spot for the better part of two hours while his son watched from the shade. "For many, many years after that," Tom remembered, "whenever he went by that Western Reserve headquarters, that patch of grass was perfectly fertilized, watered, and manicured because they knew that if it wasn't, he would go out there again and water it himself."[17]

Weldon Case never expected people to do more than he would do. It was a management code that seemed tailored for small business, a good recipe for running the mom-and-pop outfits that typified most independent telephone companies in the 1950s. But grafting such a code onto a holding company with dozens of subsidiaries and thousands of employees would prove to be a bit more challenging.

When Allied's toll center in Harrison, Arkansas, was demolished after a natural gas explosion in 1979, the community pulled together to quickly restore telephone service. Here, an engineer installs a circuit in the newly rebuilt center in 1980.

CHAPTER FOUR

THE EXPANSION OF ALLIED

1947–1979

My life really changed when I found out these little telephone companies could be bought. It was a whole different story to us. They wanted out, most of them, but no one wanted them.

—Hugh R. Wilbourn[1]

WHEREAS WORLD WAR II brought an interlude in the growth of the telephone industry, the war's end unleashed a demand that the industry, especially rural independent companies, found impossible to meet. The war effort had requisitioned the knowledge and energy that went into development of new technology as well as the copper, lead, and other resources that were needed for cable, insulators, and switching equipment. The quality of telephone service most Americans enjoyed actually declined during the war even though the war mobilization and production left most Americans better able to afford the service. There were long delays in getting telephones installed, and while the number of calls per phone increased due to the separation of families in wartime, the average time that customers had to wait to get an operator and their parties increased.

After the war, twelve million men and women were absorbed back into the economy, most of them into the small towns, suburbs, and countrysides served by independent phone companies, and they brought with them a pent-up appetite for consumer goods and services. Defying predictions of a recession as the country demobilized, the economy soared.[2] In Sheridan and Kirby, Arkansas, as well as in thousands of other small towns, people were demanding things they formerly considered a luxury. They wanted telephones and modern, efficient service.

Small independent companies, hampered by a lack of capital and equipment, couldn't cope with the demand. Even companies of the Bell system lagged in meeting the requests for service. From the war's end through 1948, 11 million phones were added to the nation's telephone network. Although 3 million phones were installed in 1948, by that year's end 1.25 million work orders for new phones were left unfilled.

Telephone companies raised huge sums of capital to carry on the work. During 1948 alone, Western Electric, the manufacturing subsidiary of AT&T, shipped to the Bell companies more than 60 billion cubic feet of exchange cable and enough local central-office dial equipment to serve 4 million telephones.[3] The Long Lines Department of AT&T added more than ten thousand new toll circuits, and the Bell companies rapidly converted customers from the old manual phones to dial.

A Coup for Allied

For struggling companies like Allied in Arkansas and Western Reserve in Ohio, meeting the surging

---

Just like AT&T's famous bell, Allied's logo of the 1960s and 1970s became a familiar icon to many residents of Arkansas.

Hugh Wilbourn's reputation as an honest and innovative businessman helped him secure innumerable deals throughout his long career. Though he was known for never passing up an opportunity, he was always careful to analyze potential acquisitions before acting.

demand for more and better service in their small-town exchanges was far more difficult. By the end of 1949, 40.5 million telephones were in service in the United States, but only 7.2 million of them were in small towns and rural areas served by the thousands of independent telephone companies.[4] The rest were in the Bell systems. For rural companies, progress was slower because capital was scarce, at least at prices a tightly regulated company could afford. But even

more problematic was the continuing scarcity of supplies and equipment long after the demands of the war effort had subsided. The Bell companies had first call on supplies, and independents cadged and scrounged for what they could get.

At Allied, Hugh Wilbourn and Charlie Miller had the good fortune to notice an ad in the *Arkansas Gazette* seeking bids on surplus communications equipment at the Jacksonville Ordnance Plant. The Army operated a big training base on the outskirts of North Little Rock, Arkansas, and ordnance depots in the nearby communities of Jacksonville and Maumelle. It decommissioned the ordnance plants and put the training base in mothballs a few years after the war and began selling off the big stockpiles of defense material.

Wilbourn and Miller decided to bid on the miles of cable, mainly copper, and other communications equipment. Miles of service territory and the little Jacksonville exchange were part of the bargain, and the bidders had to commit to operating the exchange. Allied was the successful bidder, but complications arose. Allied was not unionized; in fact, it had only a few employees, and questions were raised about the little company's capacity to handle the material and operate the exchange. Moreover, Wilbourn and Miller had to scurry to accumulate operating capital. Months dragged on, and the defense bureaucracy seemed immovable.

Finally, the partners went to see U.S. Senator John L. McClellan, the state's senior senator and a rising member of the Senate Appropriations Committee and the Senate Permanent Investigations Committee. It was the first of many instances in which Allied would find Arkansas' congressional delegation, powerful beyond the state's minuscule status, useful. McClellan frankly asked if they could swing the deal and make good use of the material, and Wilbourn assured him they could. Satisfied, McClellan picked up his telephone and dialed someone in the upper reaches of the Pentagon. When he hung up, McClellan told Wilbourn that the deal would be quickly consummated, and, true to his word, it was.[5]

The acquisition was a bonanza for Allied, allowing the company to rebuild and expand the handful of exchanges Wilbourn and Miller had bought in Grant County and southwest Arkansas. Even while operating their own companies, the partners remained in the telephone engineering and consulting business—at least for a while—and the big store of surplus cable and equipment allowed them to service other small companies as well.

Wilbourn would call the buy a breakthrough for the company, both because Allied could modernize its own obsolete equipment and because the acquisition cemented Allied's standing as a pacesetter and savior for the independent companies, most of which already had depended on the two men for years when they needed troubleshooting and repairs. The time would soon come when all small-town operators would be under pressure to sell their systems, and they would think first of Charlie Miller and Hugh Wilbourn.

A Phone in Every Home

Capital was a more daunting problem for independents. Big banks were reluctant to lend to rural utilities because their books didn't inspire confidence. In a capital-starved state like Arkansas, where the state constitution imposed the harshest interest-rate limits in the nation, all the banks were small, and the small-town banks followed unusually conservative lending practices. Despite the heightened demand for service and the willingness of customers to pay, telephone companies could not reap earnings until they invested in the equipment, and they couldn't raise the money to make the investments. Even if banks were willing to lend to rural telephone companies, the interest cost was too high for companies that were limited by state regulators in what they could earn, and the rate increases required to amortize the loans would be too steep for rural customers.

Wilbourn visited with the state's congressional delegation about the problem. In his office, U.S. Representative Wilbur D. Mills, who later would rise to the chairmanship of the Ways and Means Committee and wield legendary power over national tax policy, listened as Wilbourn explained the

dilemma he and other telephone independents faced. Mills summoned several other congressmen to his office, and they discussed ways the federal government could help get modern telephone service to the countryside.

In October 1949, Congress amended the Rural Electrification Act (REA) to extend its loans to telephone companies as well as electric cooperatives. Unlike the electric cooperatives, which were opposed by the major investor-owned utilities, the independent telephone companies enjoyed the favor of the manufacturers—Kellogg Corporation and Stromberg-Carlson Corporation—and AT&T, which saw the expansion of rural service as a chance to enhance their long-distance revenues.[6] The legislation authorized the Rural Electrification Administration to lend to utilities that could provide phone service to rural areas. Rural telephone companies, cooperatives, and mutual corporations could borrow up to 50 percent of their total capitalization and repay it at 2 percent interest over thirty-five years. But the REA had to pass upon the physical condition of the property that would secure the loan, the work had to meet REA specifications, and the REA imposed restrictions on dividends to the borrowing company's investors. Many companies, including Western Reserve in Ohio, would opt out of the deal and find commercial financing, but for Allied, the REA was a lifeline.

"Without it," Wilbourn said, "we could never have served a lot of people." Allied would borrow millions of dollars and string hundreds of miles of cable across the Arkansas landscape in the 1950s and 1960s. And the affordable financing of REA and encouragement from state regulators allowed the company to acquire dozens of exchanges and expand into five other states. Allied could now bring

---

Charlie Miller was known to be a more conservative businessman than his partner, Wilbourn, and was often seen as a balancing force to Wilbourn's more zealous approach.

modern dial service and the other fruits of burgeoning communications technology to tens of thousands of people who previously had no telephones or else were served by contraptions that had been obsolete in American cities since the beginning of the Great Depression.

Networking with Mom and Pop

Small-town telephone exchanges had been a vital institution in rural America. They were typically family businesses. The husband did the outside work, perhaps in addition to another job, and the wife operated the switchboard, which ordinarily was in the living room. Sometimes the couple installed the switchboard by the bed so she could make an emergency connection in the midwatches of the night without having to arise in the dark and stumble through the house to the board. Hugh Wilbourn said it was not uncommon to be summoned to a town to make repairs and sit on the edge of the bed to tinker with the board while the wife slept.

People rang up the operator whenever they needed to place a call. If the operator was at the switchboard, she could make the connection right away, but if she was otherwise occupied, it might take a while. The caller might have to hold the line for twenty minutes for the operator. If a person shared a line with eight or twelve other parties, the wait might be hours. Many exchanges, moreover, shut down each evening and on weekends, or at least on Sunday, so that the operator could enjoy some private life. The operator was the nerve center of the community. She chased down the police, a doctor, or volunteer firefighters for distressed customers. She kept up with the weather and the doings about town. She knew everyone's ailments and distempers. It was an exhausting burden but one that some operators were loath to give up when technology made them anachronisms.

Joe T. Ford, who would become the CEO of ALLTEL, recalled the operator of the exchange at tiny Amity—with about sixty-five phones—in southwest Arkansas. She was disabled and spent most of her adult life in her upstairs bedroom tending to the switchboard. Allied bought the exchange and built her a house and office on the main street for $20,000 in 1959 so that she could go out of the house in a wheelchair. Ford noticed from the books that she never had delinquent collections. For three consecutive months, everyone paid on time, which would be unexpected in an affluent community and downright mysterious in a depressed one like Amity. Ford suspected that she knew all the customers and their problems and couldn't let them be delinquent or cut off their service. Questioned about the 100 percent collection rate, she acknowledged that she sometimes paid bills for people. "They'll pay me back sometime," she said. Most of them did.

Demand for new phone service and unhappiness with the old crank phones, the long delays, the frequent breakdowns in equipment, and the interruptions when trees and ice-laden limbs fell across lines put the mom-and-pop companies under duress. Everyone knew that better phone service was available elsewhere, and people were impatient. By the late 1940s, the old equipment, which was made by Kellogg or Stromberg-Carlson, was barely holding together. The lines were worse. The poles and crossarms, often erected in the 1920s and 1930s, had deteriorated. In some places, lines were even strung on fence posts or attached to trees. Modernization was long overdue. But both the new technology and the prospect of borrowing sizable amounts of capital to finance it, even at the REA's 2 percent, were daunting to most owners. Debt was improvident, if not sinful, a thing to be avoided except for a home or a family car. Short-term installment purchases for a new refrigerator or freezer were things people talked about openly only with some chagrin.

Complaints about telephone service flowed into town councils and to the state Public Service Commission in Little Rock, which sometimes conducted public hearings where customers told horror stories about delays and brushes with tragedy because their phones didn't work or they couldn't reach the operator.

By the early 1950s, owners of the more than one hundred independent companies in Arkansas were looking for relief. "As the business grew, it got technically more complicated," explained Emon Mahony, a lawyer who was introduced to Allied through legal work he completed for the company while at Friday, Eldridge & Clark and later an ALLTEL board member. "There were demands for capital, and the owners said, 'Hey, I'm sixty years old, and the kids don't want to carry on the business. I need the capital.'" But as Mahony pointed out, they were willing to "hang up the business" only if they knew someone would take care of their customers.[7]

They frequently sought out Miller and Wilbourn, who had performed construction work for all of them. Wilbourn had been in their homes, often with his wife, Edith, and they had socialized in the Arkansas Telephone Association and the United States Independent Telephone Association. "My wife was a wonderful partner," Wilbourn said. "She had met all these people. I mean she knew every one of them. She had a wonderful mind for people. I was trying to buy companies and grow. We'd go to a meeting, and I'd put her in front and say, 'Now, baby, who is that?' And she'd tell me it's so-and-so from such-and-such town. When we would go to a little company, she would get with the lady who operated the switchboard, and they would go back in the kitchen and talk about cooking and sewing. Then we'd all get together, and we'd make them an offer. We'd do it on a yellow piece of paper. 'We agree to sell' and 'We agree to buy.'"[8]

In 1950, Allied bought the Felker Telephone and Oil Company in Mulberry from old friends Ouita and Mark Felker, whose mountainside telephone system Miller and Wilbourn had rebuilt when they started out in the independent telephone consulting business during the war. The next year, Allied acquired the Quitman Telephone Company, which served the hamlets of Quitman, Vilonia, Pangburn, Rosebud, Morganton, and Greenbrier northeast of Little Rock. In 1955, the partners bought the exchange at Murfreesboro, a county-seat town in the Ouachita Mountains and the site of the only diamond mine in North America. The following year they purchased Public Service Corporation, which served Tuckerman and Swifton, farm towns in northeast Arkansas.

Managing the Business

By 1957, Allied was a company scattered across a rural state with poor roads and still served fewer than six thousand customers. Miller and Wilbourn and small crews were trying to tend to widely separated exchanges, each serving no more than a couple hundred customers. Because they had more than they could do managing, upgrading, and repairing their own company's lines, they were forced to stop consulting, engineering, and constructing for other independents. They had acquired so many companies that in 1954, they formed Allied Telephone Company as a holding company for the burgeoning operating companies with Miller as president and Wilbourn as secretary-treasurer.

The partners informally divided the state in half between them, and Allied moved its headquarters from the old Hillcrest neighborhood to the Little Rock airport. Miller, in charge of the southern half of the state, earned his pilot's license and bought a little single-engine Cessna. He loved to fly for relaxation, but it also allowed him to get quickly to the small towns across south Arkansas where Allied had exchanges. Wilbourn, who had moved to Sheridan to run that exchange when they bought it from Witt Stephens in 1947, moved to Conway to tend to the growing network in the northern half of the state.

Wilbourn earned his pilot's license the next year and bought a Piper Super Cruiser. From then on both Wilbourn and Miller managed their far-flung system by air. Since none of their telephone exchanges was in a city, they landed on dirt strips and pastures.

"I would call my man working in that territory and let him know that I was coming by," Wilbourn said. "I'd tell him, 'You drive out and park your car headed in the direction of the runway. I'll land right over your car or truck.' Now it might be a field. He might have got the farmer to cut a path, and I would fly over the car and land and then take care of business and fly out."[9]

Home Telephone

In 1957, Allied acquired its first sizable market, at least by independent standards: the Home Telephone Company at Fordyce in south central Arkansas, which had exchanges in the outlying towns of Bearden and Sparkman. Fordyce was a county seat town of forty-five hundred, more than twice as large as any other community in the Allied system. E. B. Rhodes, who had managed the company for most of the century and owned it with the

Holderness family, died in 1956. His son-in-law, a retail merchant, tried to run it for a while, but the families decided the demands of the company were too great and put it up for sale. Wilbourn and Miller, who had worked on the system, were eager to acquire it.

While Southwestern Bell Telephone Company officials urged the families not to sell to the upstart Allied company,[10] Miller and Wilbourn discussed trading Allied stock as part of the sale price. The families, however, considered stock in the little company to be of dubious value and demanded cash. Recognizing how important Home Telephone would be to Allied, Miller and Wilbourn agreed.

Fordyce, a thriving town in the heart of the wood belt, was the flagship of the Allied system for years. Home Telephone had upgraded from magnetos to common-battery switchboards, but the phones and switching equipment were still obsolete. Before long, Allied replaced the switching equipment and installed dial phones in all the exchanges.

Spreading Long Distance

Market pressures were not the only hostile influences on the owners of small companies. The state Public Service Commission at Little Rock was flooded with complaints from businesses and residents wanting reliable telephone service. The commissioners became virtual brokers for Allied and a couple of other expanding companies.

"My life really changed when I found out these little telephone companies could be bought," Wilbourn said. "They wanted out, most of them, but no one wanted them. We went to the Public Service Commission and made friends there with the commissioners, Lewis M. Robinson, Jim Malone, and John R. Thompson. The commissioners would call on the owners of some of these little companies, and they didn't give them much incentive to try to improve their systems on their own. They just said, 'We suggest that you get out of the business, or else we're going to take it away from you.' They had the power to take it away. It never happened, but they could be forceful. The commissioners wanted the companies off their backs because all they were getting were complaints."[11]

Charlie Miller poses with one of the planes he and Hugh Wilbourn used to travel easily to Allied's widespread telephone properties. *(Photo courtesy Meredith Bentley.)*

Allied had a reputation for improving service rapidly, and Miller and Wilbourn were not bashful about borrowing. By 1970, Allied's long-term debt totaled $26 million, of which $15.9 million was the principal on REA mortgages—and every year the company enlarged its capital budget.

From 1960 through 1974, Allied added another Arkansas telephone company to its system about every year, most of them tiny rural companies. "Hugh Wilbourn never met a telephone company he didn't want to buy," said Harry Erwin, an accountant who became an Allied board member in the early 1950s and who formed lasting relations with Hugh Wilbourn and Charlie Miller. "Allied had no money, but Hugh had enough vision that he would plunge straight ahead. We were basically buying a bunch of small telephone companies who had antiquated equipment. We'd buy them for whatever we could get them for and then borrow money from the REA for thirty to thirty-five years and remodel them. Hugh Wilbourn was an eternal optimist. He'd buy these companies that didn't have a damn thing in

William J. Moore, known as "Uncle Will," had been with the Boone County Telephone Company since 1914 and later became its president. Here, he sits with his two sons at the celebration of his one hundredth birthday and his retirement from the telephone industry. *(Photo courtesy Charles and Earlene Hinkle.)*

them. He'd pay what I considered an exorbitant price for them, but by golly, it worked."[12]

In 1964, Allied's annual income passed $1 million, and the company ranked among the top 125 independent telephone companies in the nation, but it served no city as large as five thousand in population and only a few as large as two thousand. Between 1965 and 1971, Allied acquired the territory and exchanges of three regional trade centers, which tripled the number of phones. In 1965, it acquired the Crossett Telephone Company, in the hometown of a giant Georgia-Pacific Corporation papermaking plant, and two years later it established one of the first Centrex systems for Georgia-Pacific. Allied Utilities Corporation was formed to provide service to the manufacturer and the city. In 1968, Allied acquired the DeQueen Telephone Company, which served the thriving wood-industry towns of DeQueen, Dierks, Horatio, and Lockesburg in southwest Arkansas.

Finally, in 1971, Allied acquired the Boone County Telephone Company in Harrison, in northwest Arkansas, the largest independent telephone company in the state that wasn't part of a holding company. Allied bought all the stock in the company in exchange for Allied convertible preferred voting stock.

William J. "Uncle Will" Moore had run the system in Boone County for most of the century. A teacher and rural mail carrier, Moore had acquired stock in the company in 1914, a year after a group of Harrison businessmen bought the exchange from Bell, which wanted to raise its rates by a third. Moore became the general manager in 1918 and ran the company until his one-hundredth birthday, the year Allied acquired it. "Uncle Will wanted a big birthday party, so Joe Ford and Hugh Wilbourn gave him a big party," said Charles Hinkle, who managed the Boone County company after Allied bought it. "That was one of the arrangements Uncle Will had made during the negotiations."[13]

Boone County had sixty-eight hundred phones and ninety-one employees. Its toll center was the largest in the state. The acquisition of Boone County, along with the purchase of the telephone companies in nearby Berryville, Marshall, Green Forest, and other towns along the White River, gave Allied a large presence in the Ozark highlands, a burgeoning tourism center, and a presence in the fastest-growing part of the state.

A Line of Talent

Miller, the cofounder and president of Allied, developed cancer in 1962 and died in November, keeping his illness a secret until not long before his death. His passing was a personal blow to the close family-held and family-operated company. The brothers-in-law and partners had brought complementary skills and personalities to the business. Both were strong willed, and they sometimes

THE EXPLOSION AT HARRISON

ONE OF THE LARGEST FINANCIAL commitments made by Allied and a prime example of how the company pulled together to solve a crisis was the $5 million construction and upgrade of the Boone County Telephone Company in Harrison, Arkansas, in 1979.

At 4:33 in the morning of January 16, 1979, an explosion destroyed the entire office building that served two local exchanges and held the local central office equipment and plant and engineering records. During the night, a crack in a natural gas pipe in the alley behind the building leaked gas into an underground vault of cables and wires and a tunnel into the building, and a spark from the electrical equipment or emergency batteries stored in the building apparently ignited it. A fireman and a radio operator who were at nearby City Hall were the only people injured, and they only slightly. The City Hall received major damage, and practically every business, church, school, and home within a ten-block radius was damaged.

"I had just sat down on the bed when I saw a bright white light and sparks like you see when fireworks go off," said Lee Mysinger, a former fire chief who witnessed the explosion from a few blocks away. "The light began to rise five to six hundred feet into the air. The shock waves broke a window and knocked some of my wife's fiftieth wedding anniversary gifts off the wall. The bed felt like it jumped two feet into the air."[1]

The city and environs were suddenly without any telephone service. Six thousand telephones were out of service. Allied sent executives and crews into the city for a super-human cleanup and restoration effort. Randy Wilbourn, son of Hugh Wilbourn and director of public relations for Allied, told the townspeople that day, "One thing about this, Harrison will have the most modern electronic telephone equipment known to man when we

A natural gas explosion in Harrison, Arkansas, reduced entire buildings to rubble, including Allied's office building (background). Allied employees, local businesses, and even out-of-state companies chipped in to help rebuild the center, which resulted in "the most modern electronic telephone equipment known to man." The new toll center featured a digital switching system (left), which seemed almost futuristic when compared to the old switching equipment (opposite page). *(Photos courtesy Charles and Earlene Hinkle.)*

rebuild." Within twenty-four hours, the company had restored telephone service to the hospital and fire and police departments. In another day, it had restored temporary service to businesses that depended on telephones.[2]

All records were destroyed in the explosion, so the company had no idea where the lines were or where they went. Four pieces of information that were essential to reconnect each line were missing. Three days after the explosion, Allied brought fifty employees to the site at 11 P.M. to assemble the material manually. But an engineer calculated that it would take that many people three weeks working twenty-four hours a day to gather and assimilate the information. Union National Bank, which had a computer system at Harrison, allowed Allied to use its computers to assimilate the information and choose a random order for restoring service to customers.

Four days after the explosion, Northern Telecom, Inc., a Canadian manufacturer, delivered a three-thousand-line digital switching system. The manufacturer had worked on the machine twenty-four hours a day for three days to complete it, and one worker had stayed inside the truck for a few hours after it was on the road to install the last of the equipment. Normal delivery time was thirty-six weeks from an order, but a Georgia telephone company that had ordered the equipment agreed to relinquish it to Allied. In one week, service had been restored to a fourth of the telephones in the area. Fifteen splicing technicians from Allied offices in Arkansas, Oklahoma, and Missouri worked for seventy-two hours nonstop, deploying cables into a cross-connect trailer that was moved onto the lot. Fifteen thousand wire terminations were made into the trailer along with several thousand other connections that had to be made into the switch. More than one hundred workers from other parts of the system arrived and worked in twelve-hour shifts to restore service.

In all, eight local, national, and international electronics and communications companies assisted Allied by providing crews or equipment. Within one month of the explosion, some kind of service had been restored to all six thousand customers, though some could call out but not receive calls, and many who formerly had private lines were temporarily put on two- and four-party lines.

Plans were quickly drafted for a new building. Ordinarily, all the equipment would have taken three years for delivery, but Northern Telecom promised delivery in seven months. Allied found a contractor that would construct the building in seven months.

Exactly a year from the explosion, the last temporary telephone connections were switched to the permanent equipment in the new toll center.

Left: Charles W. Miller (left), son of Allied cofounder Charles Miller, would go on to become ALLTEL's executive vice president. He and Joe T. Ford (right), future chairman and CEO of ALLTEL, worked together at Allied's airport office. (Photo circa 1960.)

Below: The younger Charlie Miller installs phone lines in Ecuador for the Wycliff Bible Translators Mission Center in 1972. *(Photo courtesy David Reynolds.)*

clashed over the direction of the company, but they always forged decisions that kept it on the right path.

The business was fortunate, too, that the families provided talent for succession. Miller's son, Charles W. Miller, born in 1935, was only twenty-seven when he stepped into his father's shoes. He had worked at the company as a youngster. Brainy and with a penchant for science, Miller attended Westminster College in Fulton, Missouri, and received a bachelor of science degree in electrical engineering at the University of Arkansas at Fayetteville. Miller brought a scientist's methodology to management, and as the executive vice president, he would help make the company a pacesetter in innovation. During his career, he would help guide Allied from a plain-vanilla wire-line telephone company to a high-tech company before leaving in the 1980s to start his own design engineering company. Miller also spent much of his time in Central and South America establishing communications systems for Wycliff Bible Translators.

Joe T. Ford, who would succeed Wilbourn as president of Allied and then lead ALLTEL during its vast growth in the 1990s, joined Allied in 1959 as a yellow-pages salesman after graduating from the University of Arkansas at Fayetteville and marrying Hugh Wilbourn's daughter Jo Ellen. Ford grew up in Conway, where he was a scholar and athlete. His father, Archie W. Ford, was the

state's top educator for a quarter of a century and an executive of legendary durability and resourcefulness. In 1953, Archie became the state commissioner of education, a political appointment that ordinarily lasted until the next governor, which usually was two or four years away. He would stay for more than twenty-five years, surviving the transfer of power from one governor to the next, serving, in all, five governors as the state's chief school officer. During all of that time, Archie Ford's position was in jeopardy only once. Segregationists in the administration of Governor Faubus and the legislature, unhappy that Ford had not backed the governor in his defiance of the federal courts in the integration crisis at Little Rock Central High School in 1957, tried to write

While he worked at Allied and ALLTEL, Joe Ford also held office as a state senator. Here he campaigns for the Arkansas senate in 1966.

Ford out of office in an appropriation bill for the education department. School administrators and teachers protested so vehemently that the sponsors backed down. Under succeeding governors, Ford guided the state through the full desegregation of the public schools. Arkansas desegregated its public schools in the 1960s more quickly and with less trouble than any other southern state.

The only one of Archie and Ruby Ford's three sons to live to adulthood (one died of spinal meningitis and another from eating poisonous wild berries), Joe inherited his father's ardor for public education and his remarkable political acumen. He defeated three other candidates for

the state senate from Little Rock in 1966. As a senator, he championed and helped pass some of the reforms advocated by his father: public school kindergartens, free textbooks, equal education for the disabled, modernization of school facilities, vocational education, major salary raises for teachers, and the significantly higher taxes that paid for the reforms. There was some talk of Ford running for governor, but he ended it by announcing his withdrawal from politics in 1982. Ford said he could not devote sufficient time to the widening demands of both the business and political office.

Calling on Innovation

From the time they were engineering for Southwestern Bell, Charlie Miller and Hugh Wilbourn had been fascinated with every breakthrough in communications technology. In their own little company, they were eager to find ways to keep up with Bell, although every changeover was more expensive and more complicated in the sparsely settled countryside and small towns than it was for Bell in the dense population centers.

By 1963, Allied had converted all of its approximately ten thousand stations to dial. But an early problem that frustrated callers in the expanding rural exchanges was a shortage of trunk lines to carry the rising volume of calls on the new dial phones. Wilbourn came up with a solution. A mechanism was installed that would limit local calls to nine minutes. After eight minutes, the customer would hear a warning signal so that the conversation could be brought to a speedy close. The connection would be automatically broken after nine minutes, thus freeing the line for other callers. The calling party could redial the number and continue the call in nine-minute segments.

In 1961, Allied became the first telephone company in the nation to supply customers with

Joe Ford and his wife, Jo Ellen, demonstrate Allied's new Tel-Touch push-button telephone in 1966.

direct long-distance dialing for station-to-station, person-to-person, collect, and credit-card calls. The system was installed at Fordyce, and it linked the outlying towns of Bearden, Sparkman, Thornton, and New Edinburg to the direct-dialing system. Governor Orval E. Faubus attended the ceremonies celebrating the event and dialed the first long-distance call over the system. It was placed to John Baker, a native of Paris, Arkansas, in the office of Secretary of Agriculture Orville Freeman in Washington, D.C.

The little company would establish other firsts in Arkansas. It was the first to install a Centrex telephone system (at the sprawling Georgia-Pacific Corporation wood-products complex at Crossett, in 1967) and the first to install push-button telephones. The old and new Allied

Allied's board of directors in 1963 consisted of (counter-clockwise from bottom left) Hugh R. Wilbourn Jr., his sister Marion Wilbourn Miller, Joe T. Ford, Charles W. Miller, and Harry C. Erwin.

executives took particular delight in beating Southwestern Bell.

Mobile telephones were first put into commercial use in St. Louis in 1946, but it would be many years before the technology reached most people. In 1964, Allied made mobile phones available in the territory of independents in Arkansas for the first time. The system served Fordyce and Sheridan, and it was expanded in the next few years to cover other Allied territory. In 1966,

Allied introduced its first push-button telephone, Tel-Touch, which made calling faster.

As fast as new technology was becoming available, the central task for most independent telephone companies was the same one they had faced after the war: replacing the long-obsolete handsets that required people to ring up the operator to make every call. In 1964, Allied installed dial equipment at the tiny Carthage and Leola exchanges in South Arkansas, making the company 100 percent dial, well ahead of other independent companies in the region.

But the greatest aggravation for rural dwellers was the multiparty line. Eight to a dozen families frequently had to compete for access to a single line. Allied was the first company in the region to offer four-party service throughout an exchange. Between 1963 and 1971, one- and two-party service grew from 30 percent to 52 percent of subscribers. The last of the old eight-party lines was replaced in 1977, and by then, the company was getting close to eliminating multiparty service altogether.

The Telfast Breakthrough

Wilbourn was absorbed with thinking of ways to make the business more efficient and how to make technological breakthroughs work for a rural telephone company. He once became so preoccupied with a technical problem while he was piloting his plane home from a business trip that when he landed, he realized with some terror that he had no memory of the flight.[14]

The problem of automating long-distance calls in Allied's small exchanges, where there were few operators, perplexed Wilbourn. Ever since the company had installed direct-distance dialing for station-to-station calls in the Fordyce exchange, he had wrestled with the possibility of further automating the calling to eliminate the need for operators altogether on long-distance calls. No telephone company had done that.

Sitting in a pew at the First Baptist Church in Conway for the worship service one Sunday morning early in 1962, Wilbourn couldn't keep his mind from wandering to the automation problem. Suddenly he had it. While the choir made joyful noises unto the Lord, Wilbourn scribbled

TELFAST

DDD IS HERE
Use Telfast DDD

For Fast-Accurate-Private
LONG DISTANCE TELEPHONE SERVICE
To Use, Dial These Access Codes:

Station-to-Station......82 *   ** Plus Number You Are Calling

Person-to-Person.......85 *   ** Plus Number You Are Calling

* Last digit of YOUR telephone number
** USE AREA CODES FOR ALL CALLS OUT OF ARKANSAS

An advertisement in the *Sheridan Headlight* on June 10, 1965, tells Allied customers how to dial long-distance calls with the short-lived Telfast system.

his formula on the back of offering envelopes. The next week, he talked to associates at Allied about it, then walked into the office of Ray H. Thornton Jr., the company's attorney and nephew of Witt Stephens, who had sold Wilbourn and Miller their first telephone exchange. He said he thought he had an invention that would allow people to dial their own long-distance calls without going through Bell operators. Thornton, later a United States congressman, president of Arkansas State University, president of the University of Arkansas, and still later justice of the Arkansas Supreme Court, said it sounded marvelous and arranged for them to confer with a patent lawyer in Chicago.[15] Wilbourn's Sunday morning woolgathering would set off a seven-year legal battle with AT&T and the Bell companies, give the little company a national profile, and set it on the course that would one day make it a national company.

Wilbourn's new technology, which he called Telfast (Telephone Fully Automatic Switching and Ticketing), was the invention of necessity. Direct-distance dialing had been in operation around the country. A customer could dial the access digit "1" and the area code and number and automatically get the station. Electronic equipment recorded the call and its duration on tape, which later was interpreted by a billing machine. But it worked only for station-to-station calls. For person-to-person or credit-card calls the customer had to go through an operator. Telephone people had been talking for years about making those calls automatic too. Everyone knew it could be done, but neither the Bell laboratories nor other communications companies had perfected it. At Fordyce, Allied's first sizable exchange, Wilbourn had already designed equipment that permitted long-distance dialing for person-to-person, collect, and special calls. At the center of each person's telephone dial were code numbers for station-to-station and other kinds of calls. Dialing the codes would bring onto the line an operator who would monitor the call until it was completed, provide any help the caller needed, record the credit number if necessary, and stay on the line to see if a collect call was accepted. But this system required operators around the clock, and that was not feasible at smaller exchanges.

Telfast solved the problem. The caller would dial the proper code and the area code and number, and automatic equipment would play a recording telling the customer precisely what he had dialed to avoid the possibility of an error. The preliminaries of the call would be taped automatically with periodic beeps to indicate that it was being recorded. When the caller got the person he sought on the phone, he dialed the number "2." This shut off the recorder, and conversation would proceed in private. The length would be timed and recorded on tape for billing.

Telfast would produce significant economies. It would take less time for a person to make a call, tying up trunk lines that much less. It would reduce the amount of operator labor required for long-distance calls, it would create more privacy, it would improve billing by reducing the number of calls that could not be charged, and it would eliminate the sneaky "code call," which was costing telephone companies millions of dollars in revenues a year. Code calls were long-distance calls prearranged by the caller and recipient to suggest a message by the use of the name of a fictitious person being called. People could communicate long distance without paying for it.

Wilbourn approached AT&T officials in Little Rock, Washington, D.C., and New York about manufacturing the device. An AT&T executive eventually wrote him in July 1962 that Bell researchers had studied the problem but that it was not time to introduce the technology into the Bell system because it was potentially confusing. "We would, however, be interested in learning the results obtained from any installations you might make of these facilities in your offices," the letter said.[16]

Wilbourn visited the Kellogg Division of International Telephone and Telegraph Corporation (ITT), a manufacturer for the independent telephone companies. Kellogg liked it, helped him get a patent, and agreed to construct it at Kellogg Laboratories in Corinth, Mississippi. ITT purchased from Wilbourn the nonexclusive rights to develop, use, and sell the device. Telfast was to be installed and tested at Allied's Sheridan exchange.

David versus Goliath

Telfast was bound to attract the attention of the Bell companies. Toll revenues were pooled and distributed among the Bell companies and independents based upon the degree to which each company's operators and lines were used. Because it bypassed Bell's operators, the device, if widely used, would shift a significant portion of toll revenues from Bell companies to independents like Allied. After Telfast was installed at Sheridan and as the company prepared customers for automatic calling in March 1963, Southwestern Bell informed Allied that it would not connect its long-distance facilities at nearby Pine Bluff with the new equipment at Sheridan. Allied terminated its agreement with Southwestern Bell and routed the Sheridan traffic so that it would connect with the Bell system at Allied's toll center at Fordyce, thirty-three miles south of Sheridan. Bell then petitioned the state Public Service Commission to prevent Telfast's use. Bell said Allied's device would "confuse" customers and that it would not be compatible with Bell's long-distance equipment. Ray G. Cooper, director of public relations and advertising for Allied, said the real objection was that it would not be compatible with Bell's pocketbook. It would reduce the toll charges going to Bell and enhance them for Allied.

The Public Service Commission conducted a hearing in July. Telfast obviously caused considerable alarm at AT&T. John M. Black, vice president for operations at Southwestern Bell, told the commissioners that Telfast was a radical departure from normal telephone operations and that if technological improvements were needed in the nation's telephone system, the Bell companies would invent them. An AT&T executive testified that the dialing system would confuse the people of Sheridan. AT&T asked the commission to prohibit Allied from even conducting a test of the equipment. The city of Sheridan intervened. Its city attorney said townspeople were offended that Bell considered them too unsophisticated to dial long-distance calls. The independent telephone industry intervened, saying that the device should be tested so that small telephone companies might have the technological advantages of Bell's city customers. An editorial in the weekly Sheridan newspaper castigated the telephone giant. "It is a sorry sight," the newspaper said, "for us to view the largest corporation in the world trying to prevent an independent Arkansas-owned company from providing modern service to the customers of the Sheridan exchange."[17]

But the commissioners ruled two to one in Bell's favor and ordered Allied to disconnect the equipment. They said the device violated the agreement under which Bell supplied the long-distance lines to Allied's exchange at Sheridan. Allied appealed to the Pulaski County Chancery Court, but in October 1964, the court upheld the regulatory agency. Allied appealed to the state supreme court, which upheld the decision on May 24, 1965, in a four to three vote. But in deference to Allied's argument that it was a federal interstate commerce issue beyond the reach of either the state regulatory commission or state courts, the supreme court said its decision and the regulatory ruling would not apply to long-distance calls originating at Sheridan and going to phones in other independent exchanges or to calls going outside Arkansas—only to long-distance calls to Bell stations in Arkansas.

Wilbourn went to Tennessee to see if the device could be modified to segregate calls that way, and it could. The modified device was installed.

On June 8, people in Sheridan began making fully automated calls outside the state or to independent stations in Arkansas, becoming the first people in the country to make such calls. Sheridan's two largest employers, West Bend Corporation and Rockwell Industries, could dial person-to-person calls to their headquarters in other states without the cumbersome operator procedure. Allied asked the supreme court the same day to reconsider its decision banning automated dialing and ticketing on other calls inside Arkansas.

Forty-eight hours later, Bell struck back in an extraordinary way. It interrupted all long-distance calls from Allied's exchanges in Sheridan and throughout south-central Arkansas. All the calls were routed to Bell operators in Little Rock, who told callers they could not dial long-distance calls of any kind from Allied telephones. They would have to give the numbers and other information to Bell operators, who would place the calls for them. Allied was out of the long-distance business altogether in much of its territory. Southwestern Bell said it needed to stop Telfast calls and that the only way to do it was to stop all calls because its equipment could not determine if a call went through a Telfast switch at Sheridan. A Southwestern Bell letter to the mayor of Fordyce, who had complained about the interruption of long-distance service to his community, said Bell did not object to the new equipment but that it took the unusual step of halting calls because there needed to be one uniform nationwide procedure for making long-distance calls.[18]

"I've been in this business thirty-two years and I've never heard of anything like this," Wilbourn declared.[19] The situation created an instant nightmare for Allied. Since the installation of Allied's automated long-distance innovation in 1961, about 75 percent of the calls going through Allied's toll center at Fordyce had been dialed. Most of the calls now weren't reaching Bell operators, so customers were instead dialing Allied operators to find out why their calls were being halted. The system was overloaded, and Wilbourn called on Allied customers to limit their long-distance calls to emergencies.

People in the small towns were outraged. A budding country musician penned a song called "I Can't Call You on the Phone Now, Pretty Baby." A sample of the lyrics hammers home the public's general opinion of Bell.

> *I can't call you on the phone now, pretty baby*
> *Unless it's an emergency call.*
> *Mr. Bell done messed up communications,*
> *And I can't talk to my baby at all.*
>
> *You see, I live down in Fordyce*
> *And my baby lives up in Prattsville.*
> *I guess if I wanna talk to my baby,*
> *I'll have to cut out to see her in my Coup de Ville.*

A forty-five-rpm record was cut, and disk jockeys on the small-town country-music stations kept it on the air. Wilbourn even sent every member of Congress a copy of the record, which included a radio voice narrative about Bell not wanting to permit the dialing and ticketing device because Bell Labs didn't invent it.[20]

Wilbourn filed an $18.4 million antitrust suit in federal district court in Little Rock against Bell, alleging that it used its monopolistic position to stop innovation by telephone independents. He asked the court to order AT&T not to interfere with long-distance calling from Allied exchanges.

The giant Bell system is trying to force free enterprise into submission at the expense of five thousand Arkansas customers. The time has come to demonstrate that the rights of the independent telephone companies don't require the prior approval of AT&T. AT&T's arrogant action in cutting off long-distance service without notice has no precedent. The public welfare has been jeopardized; Arkansas's com- *merce has been unjustly burdened; our citizens have been subjected to the monopolistic pressures of a gigantic corporation which can well afford to approach a problem legally and sensibly, but chose not to.[21]*

Wilbourn observed that the dial telephone itself was invented by an independent telephone pioneer soon after the turn of the century and that AT&T had tried for twenty years to block its use.

In the state and national press, the fight was characterized as a David and Goliath struggle: the largest corporation in the United States, with an operating subsidiary that serviced four hundred thousand telephones in Arkansas, squashing a little company with fourteen thousand phones.[22] Allied continued to suffer a legal drought, but it harvested a public-relations bounty. Until the Telfast battle, few people outside Allied's rural exchanges, even in Arkansas, had heard of the company. Now it was a hero to the independent telephone industry.

Allied considered taking the case to the Federal Communications Commission, and other elements of the telephone industry encouraged it, hoping the case might be the vehicle by which the FCC would end monopoly control of the telephone system. There were early signals that the FCC would entertain the case. But Allied had no experience in the thicket of federal regulation, and it pursued the judicial remedy instead. The FCC did accept a concurrent case from Texas in which the FCC would later establish the right of customers to connect non-Bell equipment

I CAN'T CALL YOU ON THE PHONE NOW, PRETTY BABY

45 RPM

ALLIED TELEPHONE vs BELL

A local radio station recorded a country-and-western song about Allied's battle with AT&T over Telfast, Allied's long-distance dialing and ticketing innovation. Wilbourn sent the record to members of Congress.

to the public phone network if AT&T could not prove that it would harm the network. The Carterfone decision, ironically, was handed down just as the Telfast case came to an end.

But in Allied's federal court case, the legal tide began to shift too, if slowly. Federal District Judge J. Smith Henley refused Bell's motion for a summary judgment in the antitrust suit and eventually transferred it to the El Dorado court of a new federal judge, Oren Harris, the south Arkansas congressman appointed to the bench in late 1965 by President Lyndon B. Johnson. Before leaving Congress, Harris, the chairman of the House Committee on Interstate and Foreign Commerce, had asked the FCC to investigate AT&T's attempt to stymie innovations that would help rural telephone consumers. While the case languished in a federal court with a big backlog of cases, the issue left the front pages and then fell from public view.

Quietly, in March 1969, AT&T and Wilbourn formalized a settlement, the terms of which were not publicly disclosed. Wilbourn sacrificed his invention—patent protections would soon expire and similar innovations would be developed by Bell—but the settlement was a milestone for the little company. Allied received options to purchase from Southwestern Bell extensive service facilities, mainly toll lines in North Arkansas. Allied bought from Bell, at almost book value, 129 miles of toll lines, a microwave system, numerous channels of carrier, and other long-distance terminating equipment. It would spend $3 million upgrading the toll complex. In exchange, Allied abandoned Telfast and dropped its antitrust suit.

That year, Allied acquired toll lines between many of its exchanges from Bell, which gave it a significantly larger share of long-distance revenues and increased its earnings for years to come. The company's revenues from long-distance services rose to $3.3 million in 1969, an increase of 61 percent in one year, for the first time almost matching its revenues from local service. Its plant investment that year increased from $19.8 million to $25 million.

Crossing the State Border

Investments every year in new toll centers and the upgrading of all the rural exchanges to direct-distance dialing during the 1960s also con-tributed to rising long-distance revenues. Allied spent nearly a million dollars a year running lines to new neighborhoods and to rural communities that were getting phone service for the first time. Revenues and net income were rising by double-digit percentages every year. In a single year, 1966, operating revenues increased 35 percent.

Its stature raised by the bout with Bell and its earnings bounding, Allied found independent companies willing and eager to become a part of the company that had bearded the giant. Allied had become a holding company in 1967 and reorganized its holdings into three operating subsidiaries: Allied Telephone Company of DeQueen, Inc.; Allied Utilities of Crossett, which also operated the cable television system for the city; and Allied Telephone Company of Arkansas, which operated some thirty-five other exchanges across the state. But the company then began to look for growth beyond the state's borders.

On December 1, 1967, Allied acquired an option to buy the stock of the Oklahoma Automatic Telephone Company in Kiowa. In May 1968, Allied exercised the option, and the first exchanges outside Arkansas became a part of the Allied system. The eleven exchanges added two thousand main stations to the Allied system. In October 1968, Allied assumed management of four independents in Missouri: Triangle Telephone Company in Dixon, Stover Telephone Company in Stover, Swan Lake Telephone Company in Mendon, and Madison Telephone Company in Madison. The next year, the four companies merged with Allied to become Allied Telephone Company of Missouri, adding 6,600 stations to the system. In the next five years, through 1973, the company acquired twenty more companies outside Arkansas, including the first ones in Texas, Kentucky, and Tennessee. In July 1969, it added 9,700 stations, the largest acquisition in its history, with the purchase of the family-owned Holt companies in Missouri and Oklahoma: the Milan Telephone Company, Stilwell Telephone Corporation, Vian Telephone Company, Holt Telephone Company, and J. W. Holt Investment Company. It acquired Milan for 54,422 shares of Allied common stock and the others for $6.6 million in cash. The acquisition in January 1972 of the Echo Telephone Company of Shepherdsville, Kentucky, on the outskirts of Louisville, gave the company its first fast-growing suburban territory. At the end of 1971, the company had doubled the number of telephones in its base in only two years. The purchase of the Powell Telephone Company near Knoxville, Tennessee, in December 1973, which added ten thousand customers and four exchanges, completed the round of acquisitions.

At the beginning of 1974, Allied had only 142,000 telephones, compared with the Bell system's 119 million, but Allied's stock was selling at an earnings multiple almost twice that of AT&T's, and it had become the eleventh-largest independent telephone company in the United States.

Smart Shopping

Though Allied's acquisition policy was aggressive, it was not reckless. Wilbourn said the company was not out knocking on doors so that it could expand for the sake of being larger. The central criteria of the policy were that the new company would help maintain Allied's 9 percent to 15 percent yearly profit growth and that the addition should at least break even in the first year and contribute to consolidated earnings the second year. Allied looked specifically for possibilities of consolidated operations, where neighboring exchanges could merge their operations.

In one bidding war, Allied bid $2.2 million for a small company, another competitor bid under $2 million, and the winner bid $3 million. It was fortunate for Allied. The winner met only half its profit objectives after the acquisition, and Wilbourn calculated that it would take five years for the new operations to break even. "It hasn't necessarily been the acquisitions we have made that have made us successful," he said. "It's been the ones we haven't made."[23] What Allied was willing to pay for an acquisition depended on its potential earning power and ranged from as little as a few hundred dollars per station to as much as $1,000 per station in high-growth areas.

The acquisitions posed another risk called regulatory lag, particularly in fast-growing areas. The purchase of small companies, which typically had obsolete equipment, involved considerable inflationary construction costs. The company spent $1.9 million on capital improvements in 1966 before it launched the fast-paced expansion into other states. By 1971, the capital budget had grown to $6.6 million, and by the end of the decade Allied was spending $20 million a year on plant improvements. The bottom line was lower operating costs, higher productivity, better service, and greater profits. But in fast-growing areas like Louisville and Knoxville, where the number of stations was expanding at the rate of 15 percent a year, rate increases couldn't keep up with the inflationary costs. When a utility company grew at more than 15 percent a year, long lags in revenue relief could be catastrophic. Wilbourn and Ford looked critically at the regulatory climate in a state before they moved.

During this period of exponential external growth, Allied's internal expansion was running about 8 percent a year, well above the national average. Times had changed sharply since the early 1950s, when Hugh Wilbourn and Charlie Miller were knocking on doors trying to persuade people they needed a telephone and succeeding with only about one in three. By the mid-1970s, nearly everyone wanted a phone, and Arkansas was far behind the rest of the nation. Nationally, there were sixty-two telephones for every one hundred people. In Arkansas, forty-three in every one hundred had a phone, and those were mostly in the cities.[24] The rate was somewhat higher in the other states of the Allied system, but the market potential was great everywhere.

No Ivory Towers

By 1963, the company had outgrown its headquarters in the industrial district around Adams Field, the Little Rock municipal airport, and, besides, it needed a better profile. It acquired a portion of the capital stock of Mart, Inc., which was building a sleek, brown-brick office building on Cantrell Road, one of Little Rock's two east-west arteries, in the renovated Riverdale section immediately west of downtown. Allied's business occupied six thousand square feet, which was less than half of the top floor. By the time Allied moved from the Mart building to the river-bend site four blocks away that would become the sprawling campus of ALLTEL years later, it

sharing pension plan. Employees over the age of twenty-five who had five years with the company could contribute 3 percent of their wages, and the company would match it at the rate of up to 10 percent of the employee's earnings. Later in the decade, it implemented a stock-purchase plan, an employee communication program, and other benefits. Every annual report lavished praise on the company's workers as the keys to all the year's successes. Wilbourn would tell publications that he had a rigid policy never to hire people who were not smarter than he was. In 1967, the company established the first technical training center at Sheridan, where employees and new linemen received classroom instruction and practical training.

Moreover, Allied continued to instill a sense of family and commitment in its employees. David Reynolds, who began working at Allied in 1955, remembered fondly his experiences with Allied's top executives over his thirty-three-year career. "I truly appreciate Hugh Wilbourn giving me an opportunity to work for him," Reynolds said. "I had a good relationship with Hugh, Charlie Miller [son of cofounder Charlie Miller], and Joe Ford through the years. They truly did things for me that were beyond what I would have expected." When Reynolds was hospitalized in 1988 for heart problems, both Miller and Ford came to the hospital to visit him. "Charlie stayed in the hospital with me

occupied all of the building except for a small portion on the main floor.

Like his counterpart in Ohio, Weldon Case, Wilbourn would maintain that the company's real strength was not farsighted management but exceptional employees, although the two assets, at least in the case of these companies, were clearly not mutually exclusive. Allied regularly gave employees incentives and recognition. In January 1963, it inaugurated a profit-

over and over, and he'd offer to do anything he could to help my wife. Joe followed up. He'd call me at home. They're all great people."[25]

Elsie Johnson began her forty-year-long career at Allied as a supervisor over the data processing division in the mid-1950s. "Some days it was like a family picnic," she said. "Other days it was just serious, hard work, but everybody pitched in and helped everybody else. At billing time, even Hugh Wilbourn stopped and helped stuff envelopes if the deadline was close."[26]

And as Allied grew larger, it managed to maintain the local viewpoint that Wilbourn and Miller had so prized. As the company expanded across the Midwest and its management burgeoned, it sent its top executives out to live and work in selected operating territories for a period. "This helped sharpen our perspective about the business by getting us out there on the firing line," said Robert L. Shults, Allied's financial vice president. "We can't afford to exist in an ivory tower."[27]

Mid-Continent was devoted to providing top-quality telephone service to rural areas throughout Ohio. Here, a Mid-Continent crew uses one of the first corner-mount diggers in Elyria, Ohio, in the early 1960s. *(Photo courtesy Barbara Mansfield.)*

CHAPTER FIVE

THE MID-CONTINENT WAY: A RECIPE FOR SUCCESS

1960–1977

[M]ost people are motivated to make some recognizable contribution to the world around them. This philosophy holds that all persons are deeply concerned with their place in life whether business or personal, in terms of some form of recognition.

—Weldon W. Case[1]

WHILE THE BELL COMPA-nies had enjoyed serving half the nation's territory and nearly all its lucrative urban markets since the turn of the century, the great residential expansion and considerable industrial growth in the last half of the century would be in the burgeoning suburbs and countryside served by a couple of thousand independent telephone companies. The earnings growth of the nation's independent companies, as a whole, was outstripping that of Ma Bell by about half. The potential for these independents was without limit, but the hazards were formidable.

Consider the playing field of independent utilities like those run by the Case brothers in northern Ohio in the transforming year of 1960. The geographical territory of a regulated utility was circumscribed so that it was not allowed to grow by offering service in a neighboring area assigned to another monopoly. It could improve its bottom line by operating more efficiently, but if the economies came at the expense of the customers' quality of service, the government would step in. Utilities could ask the government, typically a state public utilities commission, for permission to charge their customers more for their monthly service or for installation of new service. But before they could seek the higher rates from customers, they first had to raise and spend sub-

stantial amounts on better equip-ment and then justify earning a modest return on that investment. Regulatory commissioners, more-over, were either politically appointed or elected and were under either statutory obligations or political pressure to hold utility rates down to levels that assured utilities received only the lowest possible return on their investment while still maintaining basic financial health. Since telephone and electric companies were monopolies, the government was not apt to allow them the robust earnings that an energetic entrepreneur might capture in an unregulated marketplace. A department store might gross annual sales four times its total investment, and a manufacturer's revenues might exceed one and a half times its assets. But the gross annual sales of a solid telephone company would not exceed a fourth of its assets, and a telephone company that appeared before a regulatory commission seeking higher rates more than once every half-dozen years usually encountered an agitated public and a hostile commission.

In 1960, a group of Ohio independent telephone companies—including Western Reserve, run by Weldon Case, and the other Case brothers' operations—merged their companies to form Mid-Continent Telephone Corporation.

That was the business environment for a utility. Even a regulated and protected monopoly will have trouble attracting investors when it needs capital if it shows consistently stagnant returns for its shareholders. And to keep up with the furious pace of communications technology in the last half century, a telephone company always needed capital.

To Buy or to Sell

Like Hugh Wilbourn and Charlie Miller in Arkansas and hundreds of other independent managers, Weldon Case saw acquisition as the only clear option for generating profits and a perpetually increasing return on investment for shareholders. Independent telephone companies could not sit still. If the managers had squeezed out all the company's possible economies, they had to acquire other territory and then reap all the economies of scale that could be had from aggressive management and technology.

Every independent telephone company in the country faced the same dilemma: either buy or sell. A fresh technological revolution in the communications industry was coming at least twice a decade now, and customers everywhere wanted and expected the marvelously swift and trouble-free telephone connections they knew were available in other jurisdictions. Rudimentary dial service had taken half a century from its invention to become universal, but there was no such patience in this age.

For the small companies that served suburbs and rural communities, the pace of change was too fast, consumers and government too demanding. The companies couldn't raise the capital, couldn't command the engineering know-how, or couldn't muster the management skills needed for a modern communications company. The same family, or the same manager, sometimes had run a company for most of the century and was simply superannuated. For the operators of very small companies, the biggest incentive to sell sometimes was the need for vacations and leisure weekends, respite from the around-the-clock responsibilities of operating a telephone exchange. Pressure from businesses, residential customers, and sometimes government regulators helped persuade them to sell.

Mid-Continent Emerges

In the spring of 1960, Weldon and Nelson Case, who ran the Elyria and Western Reserve companies to the west and south of Cleveland, talked about their operating problems. Their needs were about the same, beginning with ready, affordable capital and lower administrative overhead. Separately, progress would be made at a snail's pace. But if they could consolidate some functions and assemble a pool of managerial and technical expertise, both companies could install innovations faster and more efficiently and thus raise earnings.

Weldon and Nelson expanded the conversations that summer to include officers of three other Ohio independents: the Chardon Telephone Company near Cleveland, run by brother Baxter; the Home Telephone Company in Fairview; and the Citizens Telephone Company in Coolville, which together served parts of eight counties in southeastern Ohio. Each was going to have to raise substantial capital in the next few years to convert to new technology and to provide new service, but none knew if it could raise the capital on reasonable terms without diluting the equity of the companies' owners. The prospects looked better if they pooled their interests. Volume buying, machine billing, equipment modernization, and other consolidated administrative functions could hold down costs and rates.

Larger companies were suitors of each, but the experience of some other Ohio independents was not cheering. Their companies had been swallowed up, new managers and key employees brought in, and boards replaced by absentee ownership. The owners and managers of none of these five companies wanted to surrender the local identification and local interests. The question was whether they would have to give up the community interests of local ownership to achieve

Opposite: By the 1970s, Mid-Continent was appealing to businesses as well as individuals as a prime telephone provider in Ohio. "Who else can offer so much, and still be so close at hand, always ready to solve your problems?" asked this company brochure. "Mid-Continent of course. Answering the call of business."

Answering The Call Of Business.

the efficiencies of large corporate ownership or whether they could somehow have the advantages of both.

A lawyer named George McConnaughey, who would later serve on the new company's board of directors and as general counsel and secretary, helped the brothers put together what was to become Mid-Continent. He remembered Weldon Case's rationale behind the decision to form a holding company. "Weldon said to his brothers, 'You know, we can sell out, be millionaires, and never work a day in our lives. Or we can try to be part of this movement and put together a system and run it the way we think it ought to be run.'"[2]

In June 1960, the five companies formed what they thought was a new kind of telephone holding company. Case wanted to name the company the Mid-America Telephone System. He asked American Telephone & Telegraph if it minded. It most emphatically did, AT&T replied, so the new company was named Mid-Continent Telephone Corporation. It opened a headquarters in Elyria. Weldon Case, the principal author of the new concept, was president. Mid-Continent issued two mil-

lion shares of common stock, and more than one million shares were issued on an exchange basis to the shareholders of the five companies.

The five charter companies, which served fifty thousand customers, empowered Mid-Continent to assemble a central staff of specialists in engineering, finance, accounting, purchasing, labor relations, advertising, merchandising, law, traffic, and marketing. The operating companies were to retain a strong measure of autonomy, including their management, employees, and boards of directors, and the central experts were to keep each company supplied with information on new developments. The experts were to be available to the operating companies for recommendations and direct assistance, but without exception they were never to give line instructions to the managers.

Mid-Continent was to be the servant, never the master. To guarantee that role, every purchase agreement would carry two stipulations—that each operating company would retain its board of directors and that Mid-Continent executives were never to serve on the boards of the operating companies. The operating companies were contracting with the holding company to help them provide the most efficient and modern telephone service available in the land and to help them do so at a good profit.

That would later form the Mid-Continent creed. Case would call it "Quality Communications," and for two decades it would be the corporation's philosophy and its major selling point to independents in the eastern half of the United States. The central idea was that independent telephone companies could provide their customers the most advanced service and equipment at least as soon as the Bell companies did, if not sooner, and that customers of the independents were willing to pay a reasonable price to get them. Neither half of the theory was universally accepted. Independents had generally lagged well behind Bell in technology. And it seemed dubious to many that customers of rural companies, who were generally less affluent, less urbane, and not as demanding as their urban counterparts, would obligingly pay the freight to be in the forefront of communications.

But in the next two decades, a period of phenomenal growth for the little northern Ohio holding company, its exchanges would frequently be the first in the state or in the nation to offer new services. Both the hybrid corporate relationship with operating companies and the philosophy of top-drawer communications services would prove amazingly workable, although it was not clear whether the concepts themselves were intrinsically successful or whether the extraordinary personality and gifts of Weldon Case made them work.

A Likely Leader

No longer general manager of an operating company but a big-picture man, Case nevertheless kept a personal relationship with the growing central staff and with affiliates. He was always challenging people to think about ways to innovate, economize, and improve service. One day the central office engineers had assembled the plant managers from all the affiliates for an all-day meeting and asked Case to step in and say a few words. Case spoke for about twenty minutes. In the first ten, he said he was a little disappointed at the condition of many of the trucks and that they should see that the vehicles

were kept in the best state of repair, including their appearance. Then he spent ten minutes saying vehicle maintenance expenses were running too high and that they should look for ways to economize. Son Tom lingered behind and overheard one plant manager murmuring to another: "He spent ten minutes telling us to fix up our trucks and another ten telling us to reduce vehicle expenses. How can we do that?" In the car afterward, Tom related the conversation to his father and asked how they could possibly do what he had asked them to do.

"The heroes will figure out a way," Case replied.[3]

As Mid-Continent's president, Weldon Case had a special mission: to scout the countryside for promising acquisitions for the company. Case was already widely known in the telephone industry in both Ohio and the Midwest. He was active in the Ohio and United States associations of independent telephone companies. He was twice the president of the Ohio Independent Telephone Association and its youngest president ever. He would be a leader of the national association, its president, and for many years chair of the Separations and Settlements Committee, which affected the earnings of every independent telephone company in the nation because it negotiated with Bell and AT&T on the distribution of long-distance revenues. Wherever he was known, he was liked. Gregarious, solicitous, and talkative, Case formed friendships and trusts easily and cultivated them forever. He grasped the economic movement of the region—where there were prospects for fast growth down the line and where it would be slow.

A longtime banker friend and board member many years later would describe Case's mind as the most analytical he had encountered.[4] Case, he recounted, could sit down with the management and stockholders of a company and, after a good discussion, grasp all the elements of the business situation for both sides and sum up all the conclusions that could be reached. Pulling an old slide

A Mid-Continent crew replaces a telephone pole that was hit by a dump truck in Northfield, Ohio, in the late 1960s. *(Photo courtesy Barbara Mansfield.)*

rule from his pocket and dazzling everyone with his legerdemain, he would reach the bottom line and sketch the full terms of a business proposal. Then, to the dismay of attorneys, he would suggest that everyone consummate the deal with a simple handshake and go home. The Case handshake would become famous in the industry.

A Good Provider

In the year after the merger, Mid-Continent acquired three more modest-size affiliates, in Geneva, Kenton, and Ashtabula, and in 1962 a fourth, Delta Telephone Company. To demonstrate the fruits of affiliation with Mid-Continent, the holding company instantly doubled Ashtabula's capital budget to $800,000, which resulted in a new central office building and modern switching equipment. "Mid-Continent, as a parent company, was able to build up resources, technical and otherwise, and had a good idea of what companies might need those resources," said Bob Bonnar, who was an accountant for the Ashtabula company when Mid-Continent acquired it. Bonnar retired in 1986 as ALLTEL's senior vice president and controller.[5]

Mid-Continent introduced new push-button telephones in Chardon in 1961 and quickly moved to make them available throughout the system. Each button on the dial sent a specific tone pulse into the central office, which translated the tones into transistorized circuits and sped the call to its destination. The company's engineers came up with another device called the electronic "register-sender," a solid-state switching system that allowed Mid-Continent to use the new electronic push-button technology and old rotary dial phones without relegating its older central office equipment to the scrap heap. Central offices could be expanded to match community growth without taking more space, which kept costs down while enabling the company to serve many more customers. Mid-Continent also introduced an IBM punch-card billing system throughout the operation.

Mid-Continent's acquisitions were not exactly abundant during the first three years, but in 1964 it acquired its first subsidiaries outside Ohio, the Kittanning Telephone Company of Kittanning,

Pennsylvania, and the Eastern Rowan Telephone Company of Granite Quarry, North Carolina.

The Case handshake acquired something of a legendary status after the North Carolina deal. As Case would later relate it, he and Arnold Snyder were matched in a round of golf during a telephone convention at Miami Beach that summer. While he was lining up putts, Arnold told Case about negotiations to sell his North Carolina company to a Minnesota firm. Learning that the deal hadn't been consummated, Case suggested that they talk about a deal. Snyder was agreeable. Case took a band of experts from Mid-Continent to Salisbury, North Carolina, where they looked at the Eastern Rowan property and were entertained luxuriously at a columned mansion. Then he sent a plane to North Carolina to bring Snyder's people to Hudson. After two days of conversations, lawyers prepared a stack of papers to carry out optional proposals for acquiring the southern company. Case arose and made this offer:

> Gentlemen, we have been to North Carolina, viewed your company, and met your people. And we have been so completely impressed with what we saw.
>
> We've talked about an exchange ratio that is fair to both of us, and I think we pretty well know what that is. So, if you like what you've seen in the last two days as much as we liked what we saw when we visited your place, I'm going to suggest we all stand in the center of the room, each placing his hand on the others'. When everyone involved has extended both hands, then we have a deal.

The head of the North Carolina company followed:

> Mr. Case, I want you to know three things. First, this is the first time I have ever been in an aer-o-plane. Second, this is the first time I have ever been north of the Mason-Dixon line. And third, to my complete astonishment, I find that you people in Ohio are exactly like us people in North Carolina.
>
> If you are prepared to stand as you suggest in the center of the room, placing hand upon hand, we are prepared to join you.

And they closed the deal. The lawyers told Case afterward that he had no deal at all, but Case insisted it was finished. It went through precisely as they had agreed.[6]

A key selling point was that the management and the board of Eastern Rowan would remain in place. Case persuaded them that the affiliation would raise the level of service for customers and provide financial advantages to the owners, who would own marketable securities.

In 1965, Mid-Continent listed its stock on the New York Stock Exchange for the first time, which allowed it to aggressively pursue acquisitions outside of Ohio. The company also expanded its footprint into New York and Illinois with the acquisition of the Red Jacket Telephone Company of Shortsville, New York; Finger Lakes Telephone Corporation of Marcellus, New York; the CT&N Telephone Company of Casey, Illinois; and the Champaign County Telephone Company of Champaign, Illinois. Two smaller Ohio companies, Hoopeston Telephone Company and Thermal Belt

On January 18, 1965, the Case brothers hold a stock tape reflecting the first trading of Mid-Continent Telephone Corporation common stock on the floor of the New York Stock Exchange. Mid-Continent stock had formerly traded over the counter. From left: Weldon Case, Nelson Case, Baxter Case, and Theodore Case.

Telephone Company, also joined the system. In five years, Mid-Continent had tripled the number of telephones served and ranked among the nation's dozen largest telephone systems. Case remarked in a report that year that it had been done without disrupting local autonomy in a single case and while improving earnings and significantly strengthening employee benefits, including a group health insurance plan and a systemwide pension program that permitted retirement as early as age sixty. All fifteen operating companies did all of their own hiring and firing—completely. "Of what other telephone system company can that truly be said?" a company pamphlet that year asked.[7]

How to Grow Good People

Case wrote a lengthy treatise for the *Harvard Business Review* entitled "People: The New Philosophy of Acquisition," which described the success of an acquisition philosophy that seemed peculiar. The critical factor in approaching an acquisition and its ultimate success was not financial but human—the people who were already running the company. In evaluating a company for acquisition or merger, he naturally examined the purchase price, the capital investment needed to bring it up to Mid-Continent standards, and the foreseeable growth in the territory. But the crucial and difficult consideration was the capacity of the middle management to run the company autonomously while using some expertise from the central office. The company's recent earnings record might not be salutary, but that could be because the environment wasn't favorable. The task sometimes required instilling fresh zeal into old management.[8]

"The technique of redeveloping old management in new acquisitions," he wrote, "stems from the fundamental belief that most people are motivated to make some recognizable contribution to the world around them. This philosophy holds that all persons are deeply concerned with their place in life whether business or personal, in terms of some form of recognition. Each wishes to become an entity, recognized as such by his fellow man." Case described the example of an assistant manager of one company who was responsible for the company. His pay was poor and his daily responsibilities heavy, but he didn't have the authority to make progressive changes. His suggestions for small improvements were usually disapproved. After Mid-Continent's acquisition, he was given the title of manager and given full charge of the company along with a pay raise and new benefits. He was made an officer of the company and a member of the board, which gave him status in the community. He instituted numerous cost savings and streamlined operations, which led to long-overdue rate increases and rapid growth, and the affiliate became one of the corporation's best producers.[9]

"The total approach to the people factor in acquisitions stems from the belief that the parent system should not ask what its subsidiary can do for it but what it can do for its subsidiary," Case wrote, borrowing a literary construction from President John F. Kennedy's inaugural. "In these terms frequently the best thing the parent system can do is to develop the current work-force, to seek out their strongest qualifications and give them the freedom and the tools which permit these talents to be fully utilized."[10]

Overall success also involved solicitous attention to employees in general, not just to management. Everyone, including the custodial worker, was important to the company's success and profited from encouragement. On a day when delicate merger or acquisition negotiations were to occur in the central office, the condition of the executive boardroom and the offices became suddenly vital to the company's future. The custodial worker's efficiency was arguably as critical that day as anyone's in the company.

Weldon Case (left), Hugh Wilbourn at Allied, and Joe Ford, who became ALLTEL's chairman and CEO, all received the Distinguished Service Medallion of the United States Independent Telephone Association (above), the organization's highest honor, for their leadership in the industry.

Case was a stickler for neatness anyway. He considered it important for morale and efficiency that the offices had the aura of a professional environment. "He didn't like material all over his desk," remembered Anne O'Herron, who served as Case's administrative assistant for nearly thirty years. "We put all of the material away at night, every night. When you walked in that office, it was a clean-desk policy, and everybody cleared their desks off at night."[11] Son Thomas Case recalled going with his father to exchange headquarters after hours. Finding files strewn across desktops and on file cabinets, Weldon would sweep it all onto the floor with a brush of his arm. When the staff opened up the next morning, it appeared that burglars had ransacked the offices, but they knew that Case had been there. One visit per exchange was all that was needed.[12] Mid-Continent offices always looked like they were ready for inspection by the general staff.

Throughout the Mid-Continent enterprise, employees benefited from Weldon Case's leadership. "He was my hero as far as the way he handled his business," said O'Herron. "He was so fair.

He let me rise to my full potential. Everybody who he came in touch with ended up having a wider perspective on life and business than they did when they went in. You did your job, and he took care of you."[13]

Ask and Receive

Ready and affordable capital was a universal problem for telephone independents, which found themselves perpetually needing to make major expenditures for new switching equipment, cable, and other capital assets to meet new customer demands and rapid technological advances. Such needs provided inducement for small companies to sell. The holding company could raise the money more readily and cheaply, at near prime rate, and distribute the risk.

The Rural Electrification Administration's mortgage program for rural telephone companies had been a godsend for many small independents, including Allied in Arkansas, because it offered long-term loans at 2 percent, a particular salvation in a capital-poor state like Arkansas. But Western Reserve and Elyria had never used REA. The Cases had managed to raise money in the commercial market. While REA money was much cheaper, the government mortgages and REA rules placed restrictions on the borrower. The

After the Case brothers formed Mid-Continent, the Western Reserve headquarters (below) were retired, and the company opened a new office in Elyria.

improvements had to meet REA specifications, and the REA restricted dividends to the company's investors during the life of the mortgage.

With the formation of Mid-Continent in 1960, Weldon Case needed capital fast to fulfill the expectations of the affiliates. Case made an appointment with a loan officer at Chase Manhattan Bank in New York and asked for a loan. He told the loan officer he was starting a telephone holding company and needed money. The loan officer finally told him that the little company didn't meet the requirements for a loan—something about insufficient collateral and earnings. Case asked how a person got a loan from Chase Manhattan Bank. Loans even of the magnitude Case wanted, the officer said, would have to go to the chairman of the board. "Well, let's go meet with him," Case said. The loan officer said it wasn't that easy. "Well, let's try," Case insisted. To his astonishment, Case found himself a while later in the Chase Manhattan boardroom. He told the chairman his plans for the new company and its creed, they had a warm chat, and Case walked out of the bank with a check for $5 million in his vest pocket.

"When he got home," Case's son, Tom, said, "He realized that he had never signed a note. Dad always said it was one of the most amazing things that had happened to him."[14]

Eight years later, on September 10, 1968, after scores of acquisitions and phenomenal earnings growth, officers of major U.S. banks toured Mid-Continent, a visit that resulted in a $20 million line of credit with eleven major banks and $3 million with local banks.[15] The company was issuing prime-rated commercial paper as well.

Mid-Continent never had trouble raising capital. Between 1960 and 1967, nearly one thousand of the thirty-three hundred non-Bell companies disappeared into holding companies, which were producing major economies by consolidating purchasing, accounting, and engineering. Bell companies controlled eighty million telephones, and the largest independent was General Telephone and Electronics Corporation, which had about eight million phones. Another eight million were divided among the other twenty-three hundred or so smaller independents. But the growth percentages of the independents—a result of extending systems to people who had never before had service—far outstripped those of the Bell companies.

The Acquisition Roll

For Mid-Continent, the pace of acquisition picked up in the late 1960s. In 1968 it acquired the historic Jamestown Telephone Corporation of Jamestown, New York; the Meadville Telephone Company of Meadville, Pennsylvania; and the Home Telephone Company of Ridgeway, Pennsylvania, in an exchange of stock. Mid-Continent exchanged 1.4 million shares of its common stock and 246,000 shares of new preferred stock with a total value of about $44.2 million. The companies operated more than a hundred thousand telephones in western New York state and northwestern Pennsylvania, which made Mid-Continent the sixth largest independent company in the United States, with 427,000 phones in ten states. The merger brought Frederick J. W. Heft, a career telephone man from Jamestown, into Mid-Continent as operating vice president, and Pierce Bray as vice president and treasurer. In all, fifteen companies joined the Mid-Continent system in 1968.

From 1967 through 1968, Mid-Continent diversified its holdings by purchasing cable television operations in Ohio and other states.

The decade of the sixties was a story of astonishing business success. While absorbing a crop of acquisitions of historic proportions, in both number and size, and investing record sums every year in capital improvements, the company still increased its net earnings and earnings per share substantially every year through 1968. The pace finally caught up with the company in 1969, although it had acquired operating companies that year in Florida, South Carolina, Pennsylvania, Indiana, and Michigan. Owing to the frantic pace of acquisitions in the previous two years, construction requirements were 46 percent greater in 1969 than in any previous year, but, perversely, interest rates soared to their highest in U.S. history up to that point. The company had to absorb the higher costs without immediate rate relief. Pretax earnings that year declined by $200,000.

In 1970, Mid-Continent added nine more companies and another cable television system.

In its first ten years, Mid-Continent had increased the number of telephones served eleven times, its operating revenues twelve times, and its gross plant fifteen times. Its earnings per share had risen 167 percent, and its common stock dividend rate had risen 83 percent. It served 535,000 telephones in eleven midwestern, eastern, and southern states, making it the fifth-largest independent telephone company in the nation. By the end of 1982, before it began negotiations to merge with Allied Telephone Company in Arkansas, Mid-Continent had acquired ninety operating telephone companies.

While it was modernizing equipment and service in each of the new exchanges added to the system, it responded to customers' appeals for more convenient service. People in suburban Cleveland and surrounding towns petitioned Mid-Continent and other companies for direct local service, rather than long-distance service, between their communities and Cleveland proper. Other companies protested, and the case went to the Public Utilities Commission and eventually to the Ohio Supreme Court. Mid-Continent decided it was an opportunity rather than a burden and provided extended area service in the first communities in 1967. Case said wide-area telephone service enhanced suburban living and in the long run was good for the company.

Mid-Continent modified its acquisition policy in 1970. With more than a half-million phones in service, the company was large and diverse enough to provide steadily ascending profits, at least as long as the regulatory environment didn't change dramatically. It would continue to acquire companies, but it would not consider those that would significantly dilute earnings or necessitate disproportionate immediate investment in facilities at high interest costs. Companies would be examined if they presented high growth potential and would generate increased profits in the fairly short term.

But the new policy was only partly voluntary. The pressure of steadily mounting competition among holding companies to acquire independents had driven the purchase prices higher and higher until they had reached the point, Case told security analysts in Cleveland in October 1969, that they were "just plain uneconomic."[16]

Mid-Continent had bought fifteen operating telephone companies in the nationwide buying spree of 1968, and most of the truly desirable crop of acquisitions that year were marketed at thirty to forty times their annual earnings. At the same time, the stocks of the holding companies were selling on the stock exchanges at about half the equivalent price-earnings ratio. The result was predictable: Every major acquisition accomplished by an exchange of stock diluted the holding company's earnings per share and stockholders' equity values. If the holding company accomplished the sale in whole or in part with cash rather than stock, the interest cost in the money market was extraordinarily stiff. Either way, the aim was to slow the furious pace of acquisitions and force an industry-wide reassessment of acquisition policies.

Working with Regulators

Mammoth investments in capital facilities during the last half of the sixties began to return better earnings as the company obtained rate increases from state regulatory commissions. It was the need to invest and the uncertainty of state regulation that had encouraged many companies to sell. In Arkansas, Hugh Wilbourn and Joe Ford had examined the regulatory climates warily before venturing into other states. A couple of chary or politically inspired utility commissioners or a headstrong or incompetent regulatory staff at a state capitol could depress a company's earnings significantly.

Mid-Continent found the utility commissions generally hospitable. The rate increases it won from state utility commissions in 1971 alone represented twenty cents a share of company earnings for each of many future years. And rate cases that were in progress at the end of that year would yield an annualized value of another twenty-two cents a share. Customers of most of the companies had not experienced a rate increase in more than ten years.

But the climate was not uniformly hospitable; it varied in time and place. Because the country was under loose federal price controls during the inflation spike of 1972 and 1973, it was not a particularly propitious time to seek to recover a utility's investment, although phone rates had lagged far behind the rising price levels of the U.S. economy. Roaring inflation and skyrocketing borrowing costs, which skirted the government price controls, would keep Mid-Continent in the same dilemma for much of the decade.

A company might also find itself hostage to a quirky regulator or boisterous local politics. Andy Coulter, vice president for operations at ALLTEL and in the 1970s a Mid-Continent executive, recalled his experience trying to improve the company's earnings in a couple of southern states. Two small Mid-Continent operating companies in Alabama, Elmore-Coosa and Leeds, were seeking rate increases from the Alabama commission after making substantial investments to modernize service to the rural communities. The commission had hired a new entry-level analyst who had a Ph.D., and it dispatched him to the companies' offices to audit the books in preparation for the rate hearing. He stayed six weeks. Coulter would later divine that the staff director had sent the man there to get him out of the staff's hair. He kept coming back to the companies and finally wrote a report that, among other eccentricities, accused the companies of having ghosts on their payrolls. During a meeting between Coulter and the regulatory staff at Montgomery, the analyst barged in, yelling that Mid-Continent was involved in a conspiracy and threatening to call the police and the attorney general of Alabama. The commission eventually fired the man, he sued the commission for mistreatment, and Coulter was subpoenaed to testify at the trial. The by then politicized rate proceedings dragged on for months, and the company ended up getting not a penny from the case.[17]

Still, Mid-Continent's regulatory success was extraordinary. The industry sought faster recovery of its mammoth capital investment, but it was not until 1984 that the Federal Communications Commission authorized accelerated depreciation of capital assets. Nevertheless, earnings during the 1970s, a decade of harrowing inflation and recessions, were impressive. For the decade, Mid-Continent's earnings-per-share growth was the highest of all the telephone companies listed on the New York Stock Exchange.

On the Cutting Edge

As Case had promised in the Quality Communications creed, Mid-Continent introduced the latest technology, which usually brought not only faster and more reliable telephone service but operating economies as well. When Stromberg-Carlson developed a fully electronic hybrid central office, Mid-Continent was the first company to install it. It was put in the Hinckley, Ohio, exchange of the Western Reserve Telephone Company in November 1970.

Mid-Continent had been establishing toll-free service from its exchanges in the countryside and the small cities around Cleveland to central Cleveland, which was in the Bell system, and this was giving telephone engineers fits. Mid-Continent was faced with installing common control equip-

As president of Mid-Continent, Weldon Case was devoted to providing customers with the latest telecommunications technology and to treating customers, business associates, and employees with the utmost respect.

ment in the central office that was not compatible with equipment in Hinckley. It seemed to require multiple machines to translate all the rotary and push-button signals, which would be costly and troublesome and would consume large amounts of space. The electronic crossbreed central office met all the demands, and it meant a 40 percent reduction in space and a subsequent reduction in future building costs. The seven hundred lines filled all the immediate needs and could be expanded to two thousand lines without requiring more building or much more expense.[18]

In 1974, Mid-Continent installed the first stored-program electronic switching system in the United States. It was put in the North Ridgefield exchange west of Cleveland.

The computer-controlled central office's seventy-two hundred lines routed telephone calls at speeds and efficiency levels unmatched by earlier generations of switching equipment. Its miniaturized components meant that the switching equipment occupied only half the space of conventional systems, which meant less building space and maintenance. By the end of the year, six more systems were under construction in Mid-Continent exchanges.

Mid-Continent was in the vanguard of the digital revolution in communications. The digital, computer-driven switches handled traffic and processed calls far more efficiently than the old electromechanical equipment. They monitored their own operations, spotted trouble, and provided repair by remote control. Digital systems allowed the company to change a telephone number at a faraway home remotely by changing it at the Mid-Continent service center. Exchanges could be converted without new brick and mortar. The new calling features also provided the company a new source of local revenue and slashed operating costs.

In 1977, Mid-Continent became the first telephone company in the nation to offer local digital telephone service to its customers. The first digital switching center was installed at the Fort White office of the North Florida Telephone Company. Economics made the area, with its sixty-five miles of farm country and a growing farm population, ideal to introduce digital equipment. Mid-Continent installed digital switching in six other central offices in 1978. By the end of 1979, the company had twenty-four digital and twenty-one electronic offices. Another sixteen offices were converted to digital in 1980, and by the end of that year, a fourth of all of Mid-Continent's customers were using digital or electronic equipment to make calls.

Mid-Continent would be the first telephone company to offer transistorized service that could answer an absent subscriber's calls and take messages. In 1970, the company installed the first videophone in the system headquarters building. Mid-Continent would field-test the phone for a marketing program aimed, the company said in its 1970 annual report, at establishing a commercial beachhead in the business community.

Staying in the forefront of technology, which was a highlight of nearly every annual report, was excellent promotion for the company. Technology always made service faster or more reliable, or both, and often it lowered the cost of service to consumers. Technology uniformly made the company more efficient, too. It was one reason, although not the sole one, that Mid-Continent consistently led the telephone industry in productivity. In 1979, the company had the largest number of telephones per employee of any major telephone company in the United States. Weldon Case would attribute the extraordinary efficiency rating to the company's management style ("We try to be approachable as well as professional," he said) and to the motivation and dedication of the company's forty-five hundred employees. ("People working together, investing their time, energy and resources, ready to respond to the challenges of the world, whatever the time or place—it's as simple as that."[19])

As Allied and Mid-Continent adapted to evolving competition, both companies continued to focus on providing rural residents with quality phone service by updating existing systems and building out new ones.

CHAPTER SIX

COMPETITION EMERGES

1970–1980

We at the Commission are driven by the winds of change created by the accelerated rate of technical innovation and complexity previously unknown to mankind.

—FCC Commissioner Robert E. Lee, 1974

New Invention Gives Voice Privacy and Permits Better Telephoning

A new invention called the Hush-A-Phone is rapidly supplanting the unsatisfactory booth in modern banks, brokerage offices, it is on the desks of purchasing agents, credit men, accountants, lawyers and executives in every business or profession.

Use this Coupon

HUSH-A-PHONE

TRADE MARK

PAUSING AT A SHOP WINDOW on his lunch break in lower Manhattan one day in the late 1940s, a lawyer for AT&T spotted an advertisement for the Hush-A-Phone, a mechanical device that fit over the mouthpiece of a telephone and magnified the speaker's voice, assuring a measure of privacy from eavesdroppers in a busy office.[1] A person could speak softly and be heard on the other end of the line but not across the room. The lawyer bought one and hustled back to the AT&T offices with it. The contraption was just a tiny megaphone that had been in use since 1921, but AT&T thought it was a new gadget that invaded the company's lines, and the company filed a complaint with the FCC contending that the Hush-A-Phone could potentially cause a massive failure of the telephone system and that its sale should be prohibited. The FCC ruled in AT&T's favor—as it had many times since an 1899 Bell agreement prevented non-Bell equipment from being "interconnected" to its equipment—to protect both the network and the economics of the telephone system.

Hush-A-Phone appealed the FCC's judgment, and in 1957, the U.S. Court of Appeals for the District of Columbia concluded that the device was harmless and that the Bell companies—or any other company for that matter—could not prevent the attachment of the gadget to telephones, all of which at the time were owned by the telephone companies. Henceforth, AT&T and the Bell companies could block use of an interconnecting device only by proving that it actually harmed or endangered their equipment or degraded telephone service. Competition was about to open up.

Hush-A-Phone was inconsequential in its immediate effect on AT&T, but the decision was a warning shot across the whole telephone industry. It was the first decision to open the tightly regulated and protected telephone market to competition, and it furnished a precedent for regulatory and judicial decisions that would have more ripple effects. Allied Telephone and other independents had often chafed under the Bell companies' efforts to control innovation and the distribution of long-distance revenues. Now, however, due to the rapid improvements in technology and changes in the regulatory environment, they more often than not would find themselves siding with the giant in trying to stave off some of the unjust aspects of the new competition or in shaping the new competitive terrain.

The Hush-A-Phone opened the way for competition among telephone companies after an appeals court ruled that it could legally be attached to telephones.

As electronic and digital advancements picked up speed, the tightly regulated monopolies like the telephone companies found themselves handicapped in competing with entrepreneurs who faced neither the large capital needs nor the heavy regulatory burdens that the larger companies were saddled with. The new unfettered competitors could pick off the more lucrative sectors of the communications market, particularly large commercial users.

How telephone companies responded to the challenges of competition and then of deregulation would determine if the companies would continue to grow or stagnate and would also shape the telecommunications world at the century's end. At Mid-Continent in Ohio and Allied in Arkansas the angst would turn into ingenuity. Hush-A-Phone and succeeding decisions on competition felt like blows to the solar plexus, but by the end of the 1970s, these decisions would turn out to be perhaps the best thing that ever happened to the two companies.

Serving a Just Public Purpose

The changes in technology and the regulation environment created a horizon on which Allied, Mid-Continent, and other telephone companies could see the end of the intense postwar growth if the competition siphoned off the most lucrative markets. The sharpest signal was not the Hush-A-Phone case but its spawn, the Carterfone. Carter Electronics of Dallas made a coupler that permitted direct conversation between two-way radios and telephones without need of an electrical connection. Carter wanted to interconnect private mobile radio systems with the nationwide exchange and toll network of AT&T and the independent telephone companies. Following the doctrine of the Court of Appeals in the Hush-A-Phone decision, the FCC in 1968 struck down the tariffs that prohibited the connection and ruled that AT&T and other companies had to prove that a device would harm the network before its connection with the system would be restricted. Thus was the interconnect industry born.

Even more daunting for the traditional companies was the prospect that the landline telephone network that they had built could be bypassed altogether. The railroads had experimented in 1948 with their own private microwave systems for long-distance service, and in 1959 the FCC allowed other industries to form their own microwave networks that bypassed AT&T—but only as long as they were merely for internal use.

This had proven useful for large corporations with far-flung operations, but a two-way radio service in Joliet, Illinois, had a new idea. Its radios had a range of only about fifteen miles, but its truckers' routes extended beyond that range to Springfield and St. Louis. With the current system, dispatchers at each end could not keep in touch with their truckers for long.

Jack Goeken, owner of the Joliet company, wanted to build enough repeater stations along the route to facilitate constant communications, which of course would mean that he could sell a lot more radios and also potentially provide long-distance service without building a landline infrastructure. But Goeken had to get an FCC license to do it, so he and four partners formed Microwave Communications Inc., later MCI, put up $3,000, and set out to get the license. AT&T strenuously opposed the license, but it had to show that MCI's microwave network would be too costly to build and that, therefore, the prices it would have to charge to serve the public would not be competitive.

As AT&T was the only authority in the country on the costs of long-distance service, its testimony was highly regarded and seemed irrefutable. Goeken heard a rumor that AT&T's confidential study showed that the network would be much less costly than its officials had testified, and he flew to AT&T's New York offices and gulled an unwitting AT&T employee into granting him access to the library copy of the study.[2] He submitted the study to the FCC, and six years later, in 1969, the FCC granted the license. Then, MCI began offering long-distance service to small users. Wilbourn and Case observed the

Opposite: In 1968, the FCC reaffirmed the appellate court's findings in the Carterfone case, ruling that AT&T must prove that a device would harm the network for it to be prohibited. Here, Weldon Case (right) visits with Ralph Nader (left) and Tom Carter (middle) of Carterfone fame.

MCI and Carterfone cases and the flood of new license applications with some chagrin, and they were in a good position to share their views.

Allied and Mid-Continent were two of the best-performing independents in the country, and Weldon Case and Hugh Wilbourn were perhaps the most influential, honored, and outspoken leaders of the United States Independent Telephone Association (USITA). Case led the permanent negotiations with AT&T over the division of toll revenues,

steadily enhancing the independents' share. For six years, Wilbourn was chair of the organization's Legislative Committee, which determined USITA's stance on legislation and regulatory policy. In 1970, he had received the association's first Pacesetter Award, given for exceptional and effective service to the industry. In October 1973, as the FCC was handing down ruling after ruling, granting licenses and expanding the scope of the competitive doctrine in the 1969

MCI decision, Case became president of USITA. A year later Wilbourn would assume the presidency. Both men traveled the country expressing the industry's dismay at regulatory rulings that they said had the potential of driving up the costs of telephone service for most people while large consumers got the breaks from competition. They did not so much oppose competition as appeal for an even playing field for regulated companies that had to serve everyone.

In a Mid-Continent publication upon his election as USITA president, Case said the independent telephone industry had to formulate a policy on interconnection that would protect the country's communications system from poor equipment and services. The policy should also permit telephone companies to price their product and services to com-

pete with the new interconnect companies. "Our industry's rate structure has been designed to help accomplish a basic social purpose of extending the availability of telephone service to almost all citizens, including those of low income and those in sparsely settled areas," Case said. "The competitive elements of interconnect force us to revise our policy. Interconnect will raise the price of phone service rather drastically."[3]

But Case could be sanguine about the competition. "Things are changing," he told *Telephony* magazine in an interview upon his election as president in 1973. "Ten years ago, who would have given any thought to interconnection, who would have given any thought to the possibility of telephone companies being run out of the cable television business? Yet these things are fact today."[4] Both Mid-Continent and Allied had bought cable television franchises at the turn of the decade, but the FCC had held that telephone companies had to stay out of this lucrative

Both Mid-Continent and Allied had long prided themselves on superior upkeep and maintenance of their lines, but with the wave of competition rulings, the companies feared they would be forced to charge more for service to residential customers.

and fast growing market. They had to divest ownership of the CATV properties.

Wilbourn was more alarmed about the impact of the competition rulings on residential telephone customers, especially those in rural areas. The effect of the rulings, he feared, was to end the traditional value-of-service pricing that both the FCC and most state regulators used.[5] That doctrine considered that the telephone might be of more value to one user than another. Since businesses gain the most from telecommunications, they should pay a higher price for it. Business and industry in effect subsidized residential customers, particularly rural ones who could not afford telephones if they had to bear the full cost of the service. The unit price of putting a phone in a rural home was many times greater than serving a high-volume commercial user such as a hotel. It cost only $200 to serve a business but from $1,200 to $1,800 to serve a remote home.

When the FCC gave new companies the authority to sell telephone equipment to hotels and other high-volume users and to provide them low-cost long-distance service with microwave transmissions that bypassed the wireline networks, it potentially meant that the telephone companies would have to sharply lower prices to the big users if they were to compete for their business. They would then have to make up the difference by raising the monthly price of residential service to a level closer to its actual cost. This would put the companies in a vice before state regulatory commissions attuned to the concerns of residential phone customers. The interconnect businesses and microwave networks had no such worries. Unless the telephone companies were allowed by regulators to reduce their rates for the big customers to compete for the business, the non-regulated companies could pick them off, leaving the traditional phone companies with reduced volume and high-cost customers.

How did it happen? The telephone companies, Wilbourn said in an interview with *Telephony* magazine, had been so busy putting telephones out into the countryside that they had been unable to introduce all the technology that was being so rapidly developed.[6] Instead of throwing the market open to interconnect equipment companies, he said, the FCC should have prodded the tele-phone companies to supply the specialized equipment that businesses wanted. The telephone companies could have met the demand as cheaply, with less confusion, while maintaining the integrity and quality of the network service, he said.

Wilbourn expounded his view in a speech to the Alabama and Mississippi independent telephone company executives at Birmingham: Competition from the hardware merchants and private-line carriers like MCI would lead to higher telephone rates for residential customers.[7] Suppliers and customer-owned equipment and firms that offered intercity private telephone lines were forcing utilities to meet the competition by slicing revenues from commercial accounts, which inevitably meant raising the price of residential service. The historic subsidy of residential service by commercial customers had served a just public purpose, he said. Wilbourn had hoped to see the day when every rural home in the country would have one-party telephone service, but he feared that the competition rulings would postpone that reality.

Wrestling Match

As for the specialized common carriers like MCI that were entering the long-distance market, the FCC had created a nightmare for the independent telephone companies, which would have to deal with several long-distance carriers. "I think the independents have pretty much caught the backlash of the FCC's dealing with AT&T, and they really can't do any different for us than they do for them," Wilbourn told *Telephony*. "I think it was a strong push to keep [AT&T] in line ... from the FCC's standpoint, and this rubs off on the independents. But I would hope that the complexion will change and that during the coming years we're going to see a different ball game at the FCC."[8]

But the game didn't change at the FCC. In fact, at USITA's convention in 1974, after high-decibel criticism of the regulatory changes, FCC Commissioner Robert E. Lee let it be known in a talk to industry representatives that the regulatory climate had changed forever.

The recent concern within the telephone industry that the newer policies of the commission are

IN GOOD COMPANY

BEFORE THEY MERGED TO BECOME ALL-TEL, both Allied and Mid-Continent had become virtual melting pots of smaller telephone companies. Following is a year-by-year record of the companies Allied and Mid-Continent merged with or acquired, from their formations until they became ALLTEL in 1983.

Mid-Continent Acquisitions and Mergers from 1960 to 1983

1960: Formation of Mid-Continent Telephone Corp. with five charter companies in Ohio: Elyria Telephone Co. of Elyria; Western Reserve Telephone Co. of Hudson; Chardon Telephone Co. of Chardon; Citizens Telephone Co. of Coolville; and Home Telephone Co. of Fairview

1961: Kenton Telephone Co. of Kenton, Ohio; Geneva Telephone Co. of Geneva, Ohio; and Ashtabula Telephone Co. of Ashtabula, Ohio

1962: Delta Telephone Co. of Delta, Ohio

1964: Eastern Rowan Telephone Co. of Granite Quarry, North Carolina, and Kittanning Telephone Co. of Kittanning, Pennsylvania

1965: Red Jacket Telephone Co. of Shortsville, New York; CT&N Telephone Co. of Casey, Illinois; Thermal Belt Telephone Co. of Tryon, North Carolina; and Champaign County Telephone Co. of Champaign, Illinois

1966: Finger Lakes Telephone Corp. of Marcellus, New York; Hoopeston Telephone Co. of Hoopeston, Illinois; Eastern Illinois Telephone Co. of Rantoul, Illinois; Denton Telephone Co. of Denton, North Carolina; Neapolis Telephone Co. of Neapolis, Ohio

1967: Mooresville Telephone Co. of Mooresville, North Carolina; Oswego County Telephone Corp. of Fulton, New York; Calhoun Telephone Co. of Homer, Michigan; Whiteford Telephone Co. of Lambertville, Michigan; Midstate Telephone Co. of Manlius, New York; South Penn Telephone Co. of Waynesburg, Pennsylvania; South Penn Telephone Co. of West Virginia; and Reade Telephone Co. of Glasgow, Pennsylvania

1968: Jamestown Telephone Corp. of Jamestown, New York; Meadville Telephone Co. of Meadville, Pennsylvania; Home Telephone Co. of Ridgway, Pennsylvania; West Branch Bell Telephone Co. of Muncy, Pennsylvania; Lawrence Telephone Co. of Lawrence, Michigan; Citizens Telephone Co. of Bridgman, Michigan; Aurelius and Vevay Telephone Co. of Mason, Michigan; Rural Telephone Co. of Stockbridge, Michigan; Inman Telephone Co. of Inman, South Carolina; Commerce Telephone Co. of Commerce, Georgia; Florence Telephone Co. of Prentiss, Mississippi; Paulding Telephone Co. of Paulding, Ohio; Danforth Farmers Telephone Co. of Illinois; Morrison Telephone Co. of Morrison, Illinois; and Majenica Telephone Co. of Markle, Indiana

1969: North Florida Telephone Co. of Live Oak, Florida; Citizens Telephone Co. of Lexington, South Carolina; Ogemaw Telephone Co. of Rose City, Michigan; Hopedale Telephone Co. of Hopedale, Ohio; Carbon Telephone Co. of Lansford, Pennsylvania; and Uniondale Telephone Co. of Uniondale, Indiana

1970: Byron Telephone Co. of Byron, Georgia; Cairo Telephone Co. of Cairo, Georgia; Carroll Telephone Co. of Delphi, Indiana; Deer Creek Telephone Co. of Deer Creek, Illinois; Emden Telephone Co. of Emden, Illinois; Glenn Telephone Co. of Glenn, Michigan; Citizens Telephone Co. of Rock Creek, Ohio; Kershaw Telephone Co. of Kershaw, South Carolina; Key Mutual Telephone Co. of Key, Ohio

1971: Cutler Telephone Co. of Cutler, Indiana

1972: Newark Telephone Co. of Newark, Ohio

1974: Old Town Telephone Co. of Winston-Salem, North Carolina, and Empire Telephone Co. of Comer, Georgia

1975: Elmore-Coosa Telephone Co. of Eclectic, Alabama

1976: Leeds Telephone Co. of Leeds, Alabama

1977: West Ohio Telephone Co. of Covington, Ohio; Morenci Telephone Co. of Morenci, Michigan; Parma Telephone Co. of Parma, Michigan; and Clearfield and Cambria Telephone Co. of Coalport, Pennsylvania

1978: Sandhill Telephone Co. of Aberdeen, North Carolina

1979: Telephone Utilities of Pennsylvania of Export, Pennsylvania; Brookville Telephone Co. of Brookville, Pennsylvania; Enon Valley Telephone Co. of Albion, Pennsylvania; Huntington and Centre County Telephone Co. of Warriors Mark, Pennsylvania; Midway Mutual Telephone Co. of Midway, Pennsylvania; Murraysville Telephone Co. of Export, Pennsylvania; Mountain State Telephone Co. of Hundred, West Virginia; Preston Telephone Co. of Masontown, West Virginia; Telephone Utilities of Marlington, West Virginia; Newark Telephone Co. of Newark, Ohio; and Home Telephone Co. of Middlefield, Ohio

1980: Clymer Telephone Co. of Clymer, New York, and Tygart Valley Telephone Co. of Mill Creek, West Virginia

1981: Kingsville Telephone Co. of Kingsville, Ohio, and Westford Independent Telephone Co. of Jamestown, Pennsylvania

Allied Acquisitions and Mergers from 1947 to 1983

1947: Hugh Wilbourn Jr. and C. B. Miller purchase Grant County Telephone Co. of Sheridan, Arkansas

1948: Southwest Arkansas Telephone Co. of Glenwood, Arkansas

1950: Felker Telephone and Oil Co. of Mulberry, Arkansas, and Southwest Arkansas Telephone Co. for Glenwood, Amity, Norman, and Mt. Ida, Arkansas

1951: Quitman Telephone Co. of Quitman, Arkansas

1954: Formation of Allied Telephone Co.

1955: Murfreesboro Telephone Co. of Murfreesboro, Arkansas

1956: Public Service Corp. of Tuckerman and Swifton, Arkansas

1957: Home Telephone Co. of Fordyce, Arkansas

1960: Standard Telephone Co. of Marshall, Arkansas

1961: Dalark Telephone Co. of Dalark and Leola Telephone Co. of Leola, Arkansas

1962: Carthage Telephone Co. of Carthage, Arkansas

1963: Wilmot-Parkdale Telephone Co. of Wilmot, Arkansas

1965: Berryville Telephone Co. of Berryville, Arkansas, and Crossett Telephone Co. of Crossett, Arkansas

1966: Okolona Telephone Co. of Okolona, Arkansas

1967: DeQueen Telephone Co. of DeQueen, Arkansas

1968: Rural Telephone Co. of Elaine, Arkansas; Oklahoma Automatic Telephone Co. of Kiowa, Oklahoma; Triangle Telephone Co. of Dixon, Missouri; Stover Telephone Co. of Stover, Missouri; Swan Lake Telephone Co. of Mendon, Missouri; New State Telephone Co. of Roosevelt, Oklahoma; Madison Telephone Co. of Madison, Missouri; and Alma Telephone Co. of Alma, Oklahoma

1969: Nocona Telephone Co. of Nocona, Texas; Vandalia Telephone Co. of Vandalia, Missouri; Green Forest Telephone Co. of Green Forest, Arkansas; Holt Telephone Co. of Poteau, Oklahoma; Stilwell Telephone Co. of Stilwell, Oklahoma; Vian Telephone Co. of Vian, Oklahoma; Milan Telephone Co. of Milan, Missouri

1970: Boone County Telephone Co. of Harrison, Arkansas; Southern Telephone Co. of Purdy, Missouri; Liberal Telephone Co. of Liberal, Missouri

1971: Doniphan Telephone Co. of Doniphan, Missouri, and Echo Telephone Co. of Shepherdsville, Kentucky

1972: Verona Telephone Co. of Verona, Missouri, and Indian Grove Telephone Co. of Indian Grove, Missouri

1973: Powell Telephone Co. of Powell, Tennessee; Elmore City Telephone Co. of Elmore City, Oklahoma; and Myrtle Telephone Co. of Myrtle, Missouri

1974: Wickes Telephone Co. of Wickes, Arkansas

1980: White River Telephone Co. of Elkins, Arkansas

1981: Montague Telephone Co. of Montague, Texas

1982: ComPath Office Communications Systems of Oakland, California *"experiments" which the commission has under-taken in one of its lighter moments is not war-ranted. We at the commission are driven by the winds of change created by the accelerated rate of technical innovation and complexity previously unknown to mankind.*[9]

Lee found little credibility in the telephone industry's alarm that either the burgeoning inter-connect industry or the competition for long dis-tance from microwave companies would cause great economic harm to the traditional telephone industry. He cited recent earnings and growth figures of both the independents and AT&T and suggested that there was little evidence that the regulatory policies were hurting the industry.

And the dismantling of the old regulatory order continued. In 1977, the FCC in the Execunet case allowed customers to dial up the alternative carri-ers from any residential or business telephone, which allowed MCI and any other new carriers to expand their service. Soon afterward, the FCC handed down its Resale and Shared Use decision, which allowed the unlimited sale and sharing of all interstate telephone service, including switched ser-vices, a move that allowed anyone to buy long dis-tance and retail it to end customers. Research by USITA predicted huge losses to independent tele-phone companies from the Execunet and other interconnect decisions by the FCC—on the order of $4.75 per telephone by 1985.

Joe Ford, who was Allied's president at the time, would recall the era as a scary period for the telephone companies. The FCC had mandated the companies to sell service to MCI at a discount of about 56 percent.

"If you're going to have competition, let us compete," Ford said. "But the FCC said, 'We're going to mandate you to sell those facilities that are below your cost to subsidize so that they can stay in business and compete.' Well, that's not competition." On the other side, the traditional telephone companies were tightly restricted by state and federal regulators concerning the cus-tomers they could serve and the rates they could charge.[10] The FCC saw AT&T and the indepen-dents as giants competing against tiny upstarts who needed a little government assistance; the telephone companies saw themselves as being told to wrestle a wiry competitor while having one arm strapped to their sides.

Diversifying into Supplies

Over time, Allied and Mid-Continent would adapt better than the others to the new environ-ment, first as separate companies and after their merger in 1983 as ALLTEL. By the end of the 1960s, the pace of acquiring small independent telephone companies had slowed sharply for Mid-Continent and came virtually to an end for Allied. The scarcity and high cost of capital made bor-rowing problematic, and managers were reluctant to further dilute earnings by going to the equity markets to finance acquisitions and improve-ments. The pell-mell consolidation of independents during that decade slowed everywhere. Those conditions, added to the government's determina-tion in the last half of the decade to introduce competition, on fair grounds or not, made future earnings prospects for the traditional telephone business look less and less rosy. Diversification was the answer.

One attempt to diversify into cable television was cut short before companies like Allied and Mid-Continent really got the chance to run with it. In the late 1960s, both companies had entered the fledgling community antenna television (CATV) business in a handful of communities. It was a market that required low capital investment and was not labor intensive. The profit potential was great, and it was a natural fit for telephone compa-nies. Allied had begun CATV service through a subsidiary in Crossett, Arkansas, in the 1960s. About the same time, Mid-Continent had begun to operate cable franchises in New Bethlehem and Kittanning, Pennsylvania, and Hoopeston, Illinois. But by 1972 the FCC thwarted that initiative by ruling that telephone holding companies could not provide CATV service in communities their tele-phone subsidiaries served and that they had to sell such properties by June 30, 1974. So in 1973 Allied sold its CATV properties to Communications Systems of Dallas. Mid-Continent disposed of its three cable subsidiaries in 1972 and 1973.

In the wake of this ruling, again Wilbourn's concern was for the rural, small community cus-tomer. The FCC's stance seemed particularly per-

In addition to providing telephone service to rural areas in Arkansas, Missouri, and Oklahoma, Allied offered customers a variety of phones to choose from. Bill Geater mans the Allied booth at the Berryville/Carroll County Fair.

verse to Wilbourn, who told the editor of *Telephony* magazine in 1974 that the ruling that barred telephone companies from providing cable television and telephone service in the same communities would make cable television economically impractical for many small towns and rural communities for a long time.[11] The FCC had told independent telephone companies they could provide cable television to small communities because the cable companies were not profitable, but once the telephone companies had built the cable companies up, they were told they had to divest. "The telephone companies would have been able to put in the service using our poles, facilities, and people and thus provide CATV to the public," Wilbourn said. "But the FCC said we had to sell those CATV facilities, so we sold and got out. Many areas do not have CATV today because it's not economically feasible for a company to go into some of the small towns and do it, whereas we could have done it."[12]

Before the FCC's action, Wilbourn, Joe Ford, and Charles W. Miller at Allied explored how the company might diversify into a related field and enhance its earnings. Eight hundred miles away,

in Hudson, Ohio, Weldon Case was talking to the top management at Mid-Continent, Frederick J. W. Heft, Pierce Bray, Robert Bonnar, and Norman R. Weston, about the same strategy. Almost simultaneously, the two holding companies entered the communications supply business.

In June 1970, Mid-Continent acquired all the common stock of the Buckeye Telephone and Supply Company, headquartered in Columbus, Ohio, which had been in business almost fifty years. Case described the acquisition in his report to shareholders at year's end as "an important step toward profitable diversification."

Buckeye was a major distributor of equipment and materials to independent telephone companies and other utilities throughout the United States. It had distribution agreements with nearly all the major manufacturers of communications equipment such as key systems, cable, carrier equipment, telephone instruments, and PABXs. It was also a distributor of cable television equipment and supplies, and it manufactured hospital signaling systems at its Columbus headquarters. Buckeye had warehouses in Columbus, Ohio; Rock Hill,

In 1970, Allied and Mid-Continent began diversifying into communication supplies. By 1991, ALLTEL Supply offered more than ten thousand telecommunications and data products from more than three hundred manufacturers. *(Photo by Eric Myer.)*

South Carolina; and Las Vegas. When Mid-Continent purchased it, the telephone company's subsidiaries got an internal supplier of all their equipment needs on very favorable terms. Moreover, they gained profits from the burgeoning sale of equipment and supplies to other independent telephone companies across the country.

While Buckeye's contribution to Mid-Continent's earnings in 1970 was small, Case calculated the prospects for future growth as bullish. He was right. Net income after taxes from Buckeye's sales in 1970 totaled $319,578. By the end of the decade, it would reach $2.2 million.

In August 1970, Allied too made an acquisition that provided it with well-stocked warehouses of communications equipment for its customers. The company completed the purchase of Southern Telephone Supply Company in Atlanta, a newer company but one similar in size to

Buckeye. It served small and medium-sized independent telephone companies and Bell operating companies in twelve southwestern and southeastern states. The acquisition was accomplished by an exchange of Allied common stock for the capital stock of Southern.

Founded in 1961, Southern marketed a wide range of cables, supplies, telephone instruments, and other equipment to the telephone industry and to CATV companies. It also sold a line of electric utility industry supplies. Southern's vendors included Stromberg-Carlson, Northern Telecom, ITT, Anaconda, General Cable, Siemens, Miltel, 3M Corporation, and Essex.

Allied would add financial support and operational guidance to Southern's management group and sales force. Ford said his company knew what telephone and cable companies expected from suppliers and could help the supply company expand its market and better serve customers. He expected Southern to contribute substantially to Allied's earnings per share.

Modern, efficient storage facilities allowed both Buckeye and Southern to keep sensitive communications equipment stocked in dry, clean environments. Inventories of cable, wire, carrier, electronics, and switching equipment were stocked at all the warehouses and, by the end of the 1970s, linked by computers that provided instantaneous stock availability, sales histories, current pricing information. and cross-references on the capabilities of alternative products.

Over the next ten years, the supply company grew faster than Allied's basic telephone business. Sales would grow an average of 28.3 percent a year over the decade, contributing 21 percent of Allied's total net income by the end of the decade, despite sales slumps during the economic stagnation in the mid-1970s. Southern's sales totaled $5.3 million in 1970; by 1980, they had soared to $64.6 million. By decade's end, Southern was marketing its products in all fifty states and had opened warehouses in Dallas; Los Angeles;

For Hugh Wilbourn, shown here in 1977, the 1970s was a decade of dramatic change, the likes of which he had not seen since he founded Allied Telephone in the 1940s.

Fort Wayne, Indiana; New Brunswick, New Jersey; and Lincoln, Nebraska.

Beating Them at Their Own Game

Despite misgivings about the interconnect market, Allied had decided to dive into the competition for this burgeoning market that transmitted business information through analog, video text, or the new digital technologies. In 1980, Allied formed Allied Telecommunication Systems as a subsidiary of Southern Telephone Supply to market advanced telecommunications systems and a wide range of information technologies to businesses in major markets. William Moore, a senior vice president of Southern, was made president of the new division.

Mid-Continent, too, joined the competition. In 1978, Mid-Continent Communications Corporation was formed to sell and install digital terminal equipment to businesses that wanted to own their own PABXs, key systems, and other terminal equipment rather than lease it from the telephone operating companies. The reputation of Mid-Continent's extraordinary management and technical teams gave it another avenue for diversifying—putting its expertise at the disposal of foreign companies. It formed Mid-Continent Telephone Service Corporation to provide overseas consulting, and in 1979 it contracted with the Telephone Organization of Thailand to install a management information system at Bangkok, a twenty-month project. In 1980, it was hired by a telephone company in Saudi Arabia to provide management and technical expertise for operating and maintaining a telecommunications system in the new industrial city of Yanbu, in northwestern Saudi Arabia. Mid-Continent's decision to diversify enhanced its business, and it emerged as a strong company amid the challenges of regulations and competition.

While Hugh Wilbourn and Weldon Case had disavowed any interest in marketing interconnect equipment themselves early in the decade, by its end they had bowed to the realities of this booming market and made it work to their advantage.

The telephone industry saw a technological revolution in the early 1980s, but that didn't curtail the need for surefooted linemen.

CHAPTER SEVEN

A BREAKUP AND A MARRIAGE

1981–1983

*Our continuing goal will be to keep ALLTEL abreast of the telecommu-
nications leaders in applied technology, business communications systems, and customer service.*

—Joe T. Ford[1]

**NOBODY SAID
WE HAD TO.**

The merger that made us one
of America's leading telecommunications companies was
dictated by good judgment.
Not by a judge.

ALLTEL made synergistic
sense. A geographic, strategic
and philosophic intertwining of
two historically growth-oriented
companies: Mid-Continent Telephone Corp. and Allied Telephone Co.

For a fuller orientation, write
for our first annual report.

ALLTEL
CORPORATION
102 Executive Parkway, Hudson, Ohio 44236

FROM THE WINTER OF 1876, when Alexander Graham Bell and Elisha Gray disputed each other's claims of having invented the telephone and earned the patent rights, legal questions have troubled the development of the industry, particularly its domination by Alexander Bell's commer- cial descendant, American Telephone and Telegraph (AT&T). The government and eventually the courts granted Bell the broadest possible patent, covering the whole principle of transmitting speech by electricity.

For almost a century, the government recog- nized the Bell System's hegemony and protected its turf from competitive invasions that the com- pany said could violate the integrity of the tele- phone system. But from time to time, the govern- ment also was bothered by the giant system's market power and domination and at least feinted at curbing it. During the first two decades of the twentieth century, the federal government's alarm over AT&T's acquisition of independent companies resulted in a formal consent by the corporation to end the practice and also to give the independent companies access to the Bell long-distance wires.

Then in 1949, the U.S. Justice Department filed an antitrust suit against AT&T and Western Electric accusing them of conspiring to monopolize the telephone equipment market. The Department of Justice tried to force AT&T to divest the equip-

ment manufacturer, but a consent decree seven years later only restricted AT&T to regulated telephone service and Western Electric to the making of equipment.

On November 7, 1974, the Justice Department of President Gerald Ford filed another civil antitrust suit against AT&T, accusing it of conspiring to sup- press competition. The arguments were similar to those raised in the 1949 suit.

The 1974 suit alleged that AT&T and subsidiaries Western Electric and Bell Telephone Laboratories violated antitrust laws by conspir- ing to monopolize the supply of telecommunica- tions services and equipment. Again, the Justice Department asked the court to separate Western Electric and AT&T and to separate some or all of AT&T's Long Lines Department. It recommended severing the regional exchange carriers as well. The intricate case dragged on for years in the court of U.S. District Judge Harold H. Greene.

Meanwhile, the business and political climate had been changing. A powerful movement was in full swing to open heavily regulated American indus- tries, particularly segments of the transportation

---

After the merging of Allied and Mid-Continent, the newly
formed ALLTEL Corporation published ads in national and local
publications to familiarize people with the new company.

and banking industries, and it was supported by elements of both major political parties. Reacting to the rapid pace of technological change in the communications industry and to irrepressible entrepreneurial activity, the FCC was already forcing competition upon the telephone industry. As the antitrust case moved slowly along in the U.S. District Court of Washington, D.C., it became evident that the legal foundations of the great Bell system were crumbling.

At the end of the government's case in September 1981, Judge Greene said he would issue an order by the following July. President Ronald Reagan said that if Congress enacted a law opening the telephone industry to competition, he would direct the Justice Department to dismiss the lawsuit before the judge ruled. In October 1981, the U.S. Senate approved by a vote of ninety to four a sweeping bill to end federal regulation of many areas of telecommunications, although events soon afterward would forestall its passage by the House of Representatives. The bill would have permitted AT&T to sell unregulated products such as data-processing equipment, although only through a subsidiary that did not use money from telephone subscribers.

The prospects of revolutionary change were not lost on the executive offices of Mid-Continent and Allied, or on other independents. The national communications network was so integrated and interdependent that they could not be immune from whatever fortunes befell AT&T. The independents had both competed and collaborated with Bell. They had chafed as the government sided with Bell on occasions when the competition begged for judicial or regulatory refereeing, as in Allied's battle with AT&T in the 1960s over Telfast. Now they found their interests—and in their minds their customers' interests—integrally linked with those of the Bell system. Almost any kind of breakup of the Bell system would affect the independents, and some changes potentially could serve them worse than Bell would fare.

Will Staggs, ALLTEL's vice president for federal and state regulatory affairs, headed Allied's regulatory department at the time of the AT&T breakup. "We kept reading the trade presses," Staggs recalled. "Everybody was saying that the Bell breakup would only affect the regional Bell operating companies, that it wouldn't affect the independents, when in reality it was like water cascading. It had to affect us. We all knew in the back of our minds that it would, and there was a big effort to try to get ahead of the curve that was leading to deregulation."[2]

An Even Playing Field

A month before the Justice Department filed against AT&T, the editor of an industry magazine asked Hugh Wilbourn at Allied, who was the new president of the United States Independent Telephone Association, about rumors of government action to dismember AT&T and perhaps even other large telecommunications companies. Wilbourn replied:

I'm a staunch believer that big is not necessarily bad, and unless some company does something that's totally wrong—and I know of no such case—I see no reason to break up any company. There would be no stopping place because, after all, in the eyes of my neighbors I'm big, and yet I'm a grain of sand compared to AT&T. I think that when you have a monopoly, a regulated monopoly, and the regulation is good, there is no reason it will not do this country more good to keep it like it is than to start trying to break it up.[3]

To Wilbourn and Joe Ford at Allied and to Weldon Case at Mid-Continent, it was more than a philosophical question. The possible breakup of AT&T posed unanswerable questions about the economics of the independents as well. After World War II, both the Bell companies and independents like Allied and Mid-Continent had their hands full extending telephone service to those who previously could not afford it or else could afford only the most troublesome multiparty service. Wilbourn and Case had talked about their dreams of achieving universal telephone service in their lifetimes, by which they meant single-party service to every home. Scientific innovations had seemed to advance that dream. Vast improvements in transmission and maintenance during the four decades after the war made long-distance service more affordable. The regulatory policy of the country, eagerly assented to by the industry, was to use long-distance revenues to subsidize expensive local exchange service. For Allied, the policy was especially advantageous because it enabled the company to extend and upgrade telephone service to tens of thousands of rural families who could not have afforded rates based on the actual cost of the service. It seemed inevitable that a court-ordered severing of AT&T's long-distance lines from the local exchanges would produce a telephone rate system that would be too costly to people in rural areas.

Looking at the antitrust case in 1974, Wilbourn was especially rueful about what was in store for the industry and its customers unless deregulation and divestiture took into account the problems that would confront the telephone companies. It was an anxious industry that awaited the decision of the district court.

In September 1981, after Judge Greene refused an AT&T motion to dismiss the suit, AT&T concluded that the risk was too great. Perhaps Judge Greene would order a more sweeping remedy than the company had imagined. Then too, AT&T was none too eager for Congress to dictate a competitive structure. Thus the company negotiated a settlement with the Justice Department, which was announced in January 1982.

Eight months later, Judge Greene signed what became known as the Modified Final Judgment, the most sweeping and complex restructuring in the history of American business. By January 1, 1984, AT&T would spin off its twenty-two telephone companies, which would continue to provide local exchange service. Subject to the court's approval, the regional holding companies, the "Baby Bells" as they were called, would be allowed to enter nontelecommunications businesses. AT&T would keep its manufacturer, Western Electric, along with its research division, Bell Laboratories, and its Long Lines Department, which comprised the embedded base of terminal equipment and the assets to provide long-distance service between exchanges. AT&T also would control a new subsidiary that would sell computerized products and services.

Wilbourn's concerns nearly ten years earlier about the breakup of AT&T and the introduction of new forms of competition in the long-distance market were about to be realized. As the subsidy from long-distance revenues was phased out, the cost of local telephone service would go up. Once considered a luxury or a mechanism reserved for emergencies, the speed and ease of long-distance calling had made it an everyday household necessity, and its usage multiplied. By 1982, long-distance tolls accounted for 56 percent of the revenues from telephone operations at Mid-Continent and nearly 64 percent at Allied. Revenues from long-distance settlements with AT&T were rising by as much as 33 percent a year (in 1982) for Allied and Mid-Continent in the three years or so immediately preceding the AT&T divestiture. The two companies, or rather their successor, would not see those kinds of increases again. As the breakup approached, AT&T announced that it would reduce long-distance charges by 10 percent since the toll revenues would no longer subsidize local exchange service. MCI and other competitors in the market, whose rates were already lower, quickly matched AT&T.

In October 1982, only two months after Judge Greene had issued his modified judgment in the AT&T case, GTE, the largest of the traditional telephone companies, announced that it was acquiring long-distance and satellite operations from Southern Pacific Communications Corporation and that it planned to compete vigorously for long-distance business. GTE, which also had been sued by the Justice Department, entered into a consent decree in 1983 to provide "equal access" to other long-distance companies. This meant that other local telephone companies, including Allied and Mid-Continent, had to provide all the competing long-distance carriers equal access to their customers and to modify their switching equipment so that long-distance providers could access the local networks. Equal access allowed customers to dial 1, an area code, and a seven-digit telephone number to reach a phone anywhere in the United States. Then began the administrative and logistic nightmare in every company: asking each customer to select a primary long-distance carrier.

Since the old system of settlements—dividing long-distance revenues between the long-distance company and local exchanges on a formula based on the share of their plant costs assigned to interstate service—was no longer usable, the FCC created a new method of assessing rates with its National Exchange Carrier Association (NECA). Phone companies were to charge each customer a fixed "subscriber line charge" or access charge to cover the costs associated with providing interstate service. At the outset it was to be $2 a month for each residential customer and $4 for businesses. NECA collected the line charges from the companies and redistributed them to companies based on a formula that recognized that some companies served high-cost areas. The FCC theorized that customers would be compensated for the extra local fee by the declining cost of their long-distance calls, which was true of the person who typically made many toll calls.

"Before the AT&T divestiture, the Bell companies performed a lot of different functions for us," noted Americo Cornacchione, ALLTEL's senior vice president, Accounting and Finance, who began working as an accountant for Mid-Continent in 1970. "The Bell companies carried the long-distance calls, and they compensated us based on a couple of different methodologies that were accepted by the industry. In many cases, they were doing our recording for us. We were more like partners in those days than we were competitors. After the divestiture, we transformed the business from what I term a partner arrangement to a competitive environment."[4]

After equal access and the subscriber line charges were imposed, the advantages that MCI and the other new unregulated long-distance companies had enjoyed began to disappear. Now all companies paid the same price.

Bold Moves Pay Off

By the spring of 1983, the U.S. telephone industry found itself in a universe that seemed light-years away from the familiar world in which it had thrived since the Great Depression. Telephone companies had been flourishing in the greenhouse of government regulation since the Communications Act of 1934. They were protected from outside competition, and they created a vast sophisticated telecommunications network that enabled 93 percent of American households to have telephone service by 1983. With the breakup of AT&T, protection vanished and telephone companies found themselves braving the winds of competition as cold and fierce as those encountered by any segment of American business.

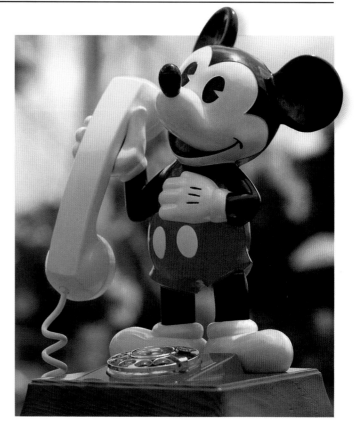

Mid-Continent's "conversation stations" sold novelty phones, like this Mickey Mouse model, which were particularly popular with children.

Although deregulation had looked scary in the late 1960s, when the courts and the FCC declared that people could hook almost any kind of equipment onto the local telephone lines and that businesses could manufacture and sell equipment without the telephone companies' assent, some telephone executives in 1983 could look back more philosophically, recognize the inevitability of deregulation, and see potential in it.

Allied and Mid-Continent expanded their products and services and, as a result, saw their earnings rise. The key to understanding the need for deregulation, Allied said in a lengthy discourse on the new business environment that it sent to shareholders in 1983, was to understand the revolution in telecommunications technology:

It is difficult to think of anything that has been more radically changed by developments in modern technology than the telecommunications field.

Digital electronics and microelectronics have transformed telecommunications equipment, giving these devices speed, compactness, "intelligence" and relatively low price tags. Similarly, the transmission of message—whether by copper wire, coaxial cable, long trunk lines over land or sea, airborne satellites, or optical fibers—has undergone major technological changes and breakthroughs. Whether it is voice, video, or data—combining technologies in telecommunications, television, and computers—great progress has already been made and more is on the way. These advances are not merely an American phenomenon, but a worldwide development.[5]

The change in the business environment seemed abrupt for some of the traditional telephone companies. However, both Allied and Mid-Continent had begun to diversify into unregulated telecommunications fields by 1970, first by buying and developing telephone and electronic supply companies. When the government ruled that customers could own their own terminal equipment, Mid-Continent quickly opened "conversation stations," where it sold or leased a variety of telephones and other terminal equipment to customers. Another way the company anticipated the changes was the creation of a new subsidiary, Mid-Continent Communications Corporation, that in 1978 began selling and installing PABXs, key systems, and related equipment to businesses that wanted to own terminal equipment rather than lease it from Mid-Continent or another telephone company. (A PABX, or Private Automatic Branch Exchange, is a telephone switch in private ownership that connects extension telephones to each other and to the public network via exchange trunks.) Allied took a similar approach.

In 1982, Mid-Continent gave its energetic and innovative executive vice president and chief financial officer, Pierce Bray, full responsibility for all the holding company's nonregulated activities, including its burgeoning international consulting. Mid-Continent entered the discounted toll market after the FCC ruled that companies could purchase Wide Area Telephone Service (WATS) and other services from the Bell system and resell the long-distance service at a lower cost than AT&T's direct-dial rates.

Mid-Continent also began offering a new service called Valu-line, a high-quality, discounted long-distance service. Whether they were in Mid-Continent's operating territory or not, Valu-line users could call anywhere in the continental United States from their homes or businesses and save an average of 20 to 25 percent. In July 1982, with comedian George Gobel as celebrity spokesman, Valu-line launched a multimedia advertising campaign in the Cleveland-Akron area that later expanded into Pittsburgh and other cities. But the fledgling enterprise did not prove terribly profitable.

Another Mid-Continent subsidiary moved into the growing unregulated market for residential and small-business security alarm systems. It sold a wireless alarm system that looked like a stereo receiver and could detect burglaries, fires, and smoke and summon emergency help. It offered the option of constant alarm system monitoring through another Mid-Continent subsidiary, Answering Service Inc.

Early in 1983, Mid-Continent moved into new territory by investing $10 million in Argo Communications Corporation, a new satellite-based domestic and international telecommunications carrier. The investment gave Mid-Continent 10 percent ownership of Argo and linked it with a digital satellite carrier. Argo's network would connect fifteen major metropolitan areas and offered voice and data transmission. Argo entered into an agreement with France Cables et Radio, an entity of the French government, to help provide businesses with international telecommunications services between the United States and Europe. Though the results would prove disappointing for the next three years and the company would take an after-tax writeoff of the investment in 1985, Mid-Continent was boldly moving forward.

At the conclusion of his 1982 message to shareholders, Weldon Case was almost exuberant about facing the new winds of competition:

Change is now a constant. America's rapid entrance into the Age of Information challenges all of us. Mid-Continent foresees a broadening array of opportunities to serve its customers, to gain new ones, and to do so at profitable levels for the benefit of the company's shareowners.[6]

Allied Telephone likewise made a bold move into diversification, by forming Allied Telecommunication Systems, which sold and installed terminal equipment to businesses that wanted to own their own equipment rather than lease it. In 1982, it made another move that enabled it to penetrate the affluent and rapidly expanding West Coast market. Allied acquired ComPath Office Communications Systems, the oldest and largest marketer of office communications systems in California and well known for its innovative solutions to communications problems. ComPath, founded in 1969 in Oakland as a marketing and service business, employed 450 people, including communications consultants, customer service specialists, and

manufacturer-certified technicians in fifteen sales offices throughout California. The company was noted for its innovative solutions to communications problems. Becoming a wholly owned Allied subsidiary allowed it to take full advantage of financing through Allied's Telecommunications Credit Corporation and the capabilities of its telecommunications supply company, Southern Telephone Supply. ComPath gave Allied a chance to penetrate the affluent and rapidly expanding West Coast market.

A few days after the stunning announcement in 1982 that AT&T had signed a settlement with the Justice Department to break up the Bell system and that the FCC had rendered a fresh decision throwing the industry open to further competition, Joe Ford penned a lengthy analysis of the developments and the opening of competition and what it meant for the future of the company. In the annual report to shareholders, he mapped

Joe T. Ford stands in front of Allied Telephone's new headquarters on the Arkansas River in Little Rock in the spring of 1983.

the company's strategy in the same optimistic overtones that characterized Weldon Case's message to his stockholders in that watershed year:

The next few years will challenge the industry with a major transformation in the way telephone companies operate.... Allied management believes we can maintain superior performance by emphasizing our competitive strength, marketing expertise, and adaptability to fundamental changes in telecommunications technologies and markets. At Allied, we have been anticipating these changes for several years and have taken steps to strengthen our management team and to prepare our employees to meet these competitive challenges.[7]

Ford outlined the company's strategy, emphasizing the need to be responsive to customer demands, to stay on the cutting edge of technology, and to cultivate a responsive field organization and middle management. He listed the factors supporting long-term growth prospects:

We have (1) telephone service territories with strong demographics and economics, (2) a young and experienced management team, (3) a marketing subsidiary to capitalize on the move toward increased competition in a variety of telecommunications markets, (4) commitments in hand to finance our construction program for several years, and (5) operating costs that are substantially below the industry average.

We see a very challenging future ahead for the Company, and it is our firm intention to remain competitively viable and growth oriented in the new environment that is unfolding.[8]

Despite the uncertainties about the composition of the postdivestiture and postregulation world and despite a period of roaring inflation that drove borrowing costs into the stratosphere, followed by the steepest economic downturn since the Great Depression, the five years leading up to the AT&T split-up of January 1, 1984, were especially prosperous ones for the two regional holding companies.

Maintaining their profiles as high-growth companies, Allied and Mid-Continent consistently increased their earnings per share. Allied's earnings per share, which rose every year between 1964

and 1980, grew at a compounded rate of 19.3 percent annually over that period, which included two recessions. Mid-Continent, which was still buying companies and spending $120 million or more a year to upgrade its exchanges with new digital switching equipment, managed dividend increases twice a year through most of the decade of the seventies. Mid-Continent's earnings per share during the decade were the best of all telephone companies listed on the New York Stock Exchange. (Allied's stock would not be listed on the NYSE until December 2, 1981.) Rapidly rising toll revenues were a major factor, but the companies obviously were doing quite well in their first ventures into the unregulated marketplace. During the decade of the 1970s, for instance, Southern Telephone Supply, the Allied subsidiary that marketed telecommunication products, grew far faster than the telephone service segments. Sales grew an average of 28.3 percent annually, and the subsidiary's net income rose at the spectacular annual rate of 38.1 percent.

In 1982, Allied moved its headquarters to a $7.5 million building on a picturesque bend in the Arkansas River near downtown Little Rock, the site of what would become the sprawling campus of ALLTEL. The splendid building, which enjoyed a commanding view of the mammoth rock bluff that was the first outcropping of the Ozark Mountains, was a fitting backdrop for a company that was soon to achieve its national ambitions.

The Merging of Great Lines

Allied and Mid-Continent analyzed the business environment, exploring and maximizing opportunities early. Keeping up with the high costs of rapidly changing technology would place many midsize regional companies like Mid-Continent and Allied at an increasing disadvantage because of the almost perpetual demands for capital and renewal. Just as the independents searched for buyers after World War II when they realized they needed help, Allied's last annual report to stockholders for 1982 telegraphed the message that Allied itself should examine the possibility of a merger. "Since the independent telephone industry is highly fragmented, it is logical to expect further consolidation in the industry," it said.

"The smaller companies will find it beneficial to merge with or be acquired by the larger independents in order to gain the financial backing to operate and market effectively. Acquisitions and further diversification will take place in the larger companies when profitable opportunities and markets arise."[9]

For more than five years, Allied's executives had been talking to Mid-Continent executives from time to time about such an opportunity, though they had never reached a serious stage. Wilbourn and Ford at Allied and Weldon Case and Pierce Bray at Mid-Continent had been friendly for a number of years, all having observed each other's work through their leadership of the industry's national association. But there would be a few fruitless attempts at mergers first before the perfect match would be made.

As early as 1969, Case told shareholders that the company might consider becoming a part of a larger communications company. That year, the Mid-Continent board weighed a merger offer from United Utilities, the country's second-largest independent telephone holding company. After several months, United abandoned the plan.

A more serious effort three years later also failed. The Mid-Continent board accepted a merger proposal from Continental Telephone Company, which Case recommended, but Continental backed out when the proposal reached its board. Years later, Philip F. Searle, an Ohio banker who was a member of the Mid-Continent board of directors in 1972, would recall the negotiations with Continental and its president, Charles Wohlstetter. Searle was a great admirer of Case and thought the man who built one of the best-performing telephone companies in the country should be an important part of the management of the merged company. Case thought the deal was a good one for Mid-Continent shareholders and recommended it, although he would be, in Searle's words, "falling on his sword." Searle was going to be in New York and arranged lunch with Wohlstetter to get a reading on the company that would be swallowing his company and the man who ran it.

I remember the meeting clearly. We met at one of the most fashionable, high-profile restaurants on Wall Street and sat at Charlie's regular table.

He ordered an expensive imported vodka in an acorn glass (chilled, no ice) and had as the main entree steak tartare (raw beef). In the course of the conversation, I mentioned my admiration for Weldon and for the outstanding company he had built. Charlie allowed as how Weldon certainly was a good telephone man and that, with his homespun ways, he could find a useful and rewarding role out among the properties in the less populated areas.

I was totally underwhelmed by the entire episode, but I did not argue with him, for I was not a part of the negotiations and I, too, believed that the prospective exchange ratio would be in the best interests of the company's shareholders.[10]

One member of the Mid-Continent board, unidentified, had vague misgivings about the deal. When Continental Telephone's board of directors was unwilling to take the negotiated terms, the companies withdrew from further negotiations. The director's hunch, Searle said, was vindicated. Searle continued:

A few years later, Weldon was seriously injured in an automobile accident. This mishap started the directors thinking more urgently about the management succession situation in the company. When pressed on the issue, Weldon often mentioned an independent telephone company headquartered in Arkansas, led by a very capable young president. His strategy was, of course, to acquire the company and successor management all in the same transaction. The knowledge most of us possessed about Arkansas at that time was limited to hawgs and to Orval Faubus [the state's segregationist governor of the 1950s and 1960s], and we therefore gave this particular succession/acquisition strategy little chance of success. So much for trying to outstrategize Weldon Case.[11]

In the spring of 1983, in the face of the onrushing Bell divestiture and deregulation, Joe Ford told Merrill Lynch Capital Markets, which happened to be the financial adviser and investment banker for both Allied and Mid-Continent, that the time might be right to pursue seriously the often-mentioned idea of merging the companies.

On October 25, 1983, Weldon Case (left), who became chairman and CEO of the new company, and Joe Ford, who became president, sign the merger agreement that formed ALLTEL Corporation.

Case was called, and the management teams worked out the details in a single week in June and performed the ritual Weldon Case handshake. On June 30, the directors of both companies unanimously (one Mid-Continent director was ill) approved the merger and announced the definitive merger agreement, which was subject to the approval of shareholders, the FCC, and a couple of state utility commissions in Allied's territory. The new company, as yet unnamed, would be based, at least for the time, in Hudson, Ohio, Mid-Continent's headquarters.

One impulse for the merger on Mid-Continent's side was the concern about succession. Weldon Case was sixty-three, and most of the senior managers and operating presidents were about the same age, approaching retirement. Mid-Continent board members had broached the succession issue with Case from time to time. But there also was a recognition at both companies that the new competitive environment required greater financial power and national resources. The considerably smaller Allied had management talent that complemented Mid-Continent's. Youth was only one factor. Allied had more financial management—some fifteen CPAs.[12]

"We had expressed some concerns at Mid-Continent about the depth of its management," said Mid-Continent and retired ALLTEL board member William Zimmer. Zimmer's company, Cincinnati Financial Corporation, had a healthy investment in Mid-Continent and was wondering if that investment would continue to pay off. "We were originally going to get out of our investment prior to the merger," Zimmer said. "But after meeting Joe Ford and his officers, we were so impressed that instead of getting rid of the Mid-Continent stock, we bought more."[13]

The merger of the regional companies, the fifth and thirteenth largest telephone companies in the country, would produce a company with a national presence. Based on the closing prices on June 30, 1983, in New York Stock Exchange composite trading, they had a combined market value of $409.4 million. Mid-Continent stock closed that day at $23.25 a share and Allied at $25.50.[14] The new company would operate telephone systems in nineteen states—the thirteen of Mid-Continent and six of Allied—but in nonregulated fields it operated in all fifty states. The combined company would have assets of $1.3 billion. Net income from telephone operations the previous twelve months totaled $52.7 million on revenues of $412 million. The companies had 842,000 customer lines, served 1,344,000 telephones, and employed 6,300. They would become the nation's fifth-largest telephone company, although it would slip to twelfth after the breakup of AT&T and the formation of the regional Bell holding companies.

The terms of the merger were simple. Each share of Mid-Continent and Allied stock would be exchanged for one share of the new company. Shareholders of the two companies approved the merger on October 24.

Case, who would be chairman and chief executive officer of the new company, said in Ohio that the merger represented a significant opportunity for Mid-Continent because Allied served different parts of the country from Mid-Continent, primarily fast-growing Sun Belt areas. "Moreover," he said, "the infusion of additional management talent makes it possible for us to position ourselves even more advantageously in the changing and challenging environment of the future."[15] The combined marketing and financial strengths of the two companies would be greater than either could achieve independently, he said.

"The potential of this combination goes well beyond size," Case said. "It is an excellent fit from many perspectives, but particularly geographics, business mix and management philosophy."[16] The merger would enable the company to better compete after the changes dictated by the AT&T divestiture and the steps taken by the FCC to deregulate telecommunications. "This gives us the opportunity to be in six more states, some of them in the Sun Belt with faster growth rates than Mid-Continent's states," he said.[17]

Choosing a New Name

As much hard deliberation went into the choice of a new name as into the terms of the merger, as the name would be important to marketing. To help the company settle on a new name, a consulting firm was hired to study the needs, problems, markets, corporate strategies, and objectives of the companies. A corporate identity committee was formed to establish criteria and to evaluate names. The winning name would need to be unique, upbeat, memorable, easy to spell, pleasing to the ear, and short enough to make a fetching logo. It also would have to reflect the nature of the company's operations without being so restrictive that it could not embrace future diversification. Another consideration was that it should not be offensive to other cultures, owing to Mid-Continent's already firmly established overseas consulting ventures.

Six weeks after the merger was announced, they settled upon and announced the name, ALLTEL. Case was compelled to explain to Mid-Continent employees why the company name would not bear any resemblance to "Mid-Continent." It was not, he said, simply the first letters of Allied's name but a description of the new company. "Mid-Continent" no longer described the company geographically, and neither was the entity to be simply a telephone company. "ALLTEL" suggested that the company was engaged in "all" aspects of telecommunications and across much of the country.[18]

Joe Ford, who would become president and chief operating officer of ALLTEL, said, "The wide world of communications is our charter, from the Middle East to Florida to California."[19]

"It is vital that we take the long view of the unprecedented change now occurring in the telecommunications industry," he said in a statement. "Our continuing goal will be to keep ALLTEL abreast of the telecommunications leaders in applied technology, business communications systems, and customer service."

The merger was hailed on Wall Street. "Mid-Continent will have the expertise of Allied for moving more aggressively into the new equipment and new technology side of the business," Elliott L. Schlang of Prescott, Ball & Rurben told *Crane's Cleveland Business.*[20] Analyst William S. McKeever of Dean Witter Reynolds in New York called it "a good move for Mid-Continent" because it was merging with one of the fastest-growing telephone companies in the nation.

The officers and directors of ALLTEL would embrace the top management of both companies. Pierce Bray of Mid-Continent became the executive vice president and chief financial officer. Max E. Bobbitt of Allied was elected the executive vice president for nonregulated operations. Nelson H. Case of Mid-Continent became executive vice president for telephone operations. And Charles W. Miller of Little Rock, the Allied chairman and son of the company's cofounder, was elected executive vice president. The other officers were Robert D. Bonnar of Mid-Continent, senior vice president and controller; Frank G. Skedel, vice president and treasurer; Steven J. Caldwell of Mid-Continent, vice president for Marketing; Harley R. Ferguson of Mid-Continent, vice president for Information Services; Tom Orsini of Allied, vice president; and George C. McConnaughey of Mid-Continent, secretary.

All five Allied board members joined the ALLTEL board: Ford; Miller; Emon A. Mahony Jr. of Fort Smith, Arkansas, president of Arkansas Oklahoma Gas Company; Carl H. Tiedemann of New York, general manager of Tiedemann/Karlen/Partners; and Hugh R. Wilbourn Jr., the founder and former chairman and CEO of Allied. In addition to Weldon Case, Bray, and McConnaughey, seven Mid-Continent directors joined the first ALLTEL board: James G. Callas of Kittanning, Pennsylvania, a partner in Callas & Graff, Attorneys; Alfred E. Campdon of Johnston, Pennsylvania, former president and treasurer of L.C.S. Corporation;

T. H. Davis of Winston-Salem, North Carolina, founder and chairman of the executive committee of Piedmont Aviation; Frederick J. W. Heft of Bemus Point, New York, a consultant and former Mid-Continent executive; John H. McConnell of Columbus, Ohio, chairman and CEO of Worthington Industries; Harold G. Payne of Atlantis, Florida, a former telephone executive; and Philip F. Searle of Orlando, Florida, chairman and CEO of Flagship Banks of Miami.

Carl Tiedemann, who had been on Allied's board since 1980, remembered that the newly meshed board members "all got along pretty well right from the start.... I was really sorry to leave that board because it was really sort of like a family."[21]

On October 25, 1983, a day after shareholders of both companies overwhelmingly approved the union, the merger was concluded. Prudential-Bache Securities gave the new stock a strong buy rating, the same that it had given the premerger Allied. (Mid-Continent had a slightly lower "hold" recommendation.) Financial analysts talked about the synergy of the marriage—the likeminded business philosophies, how the telephone operations and the nonregulated activities complemented each other, how the new company was positioned to move aggressively in the burgeoning competitive fields. Case, the new chairman, was buoyant in a message to employees of the company:

Max Bobbitt became executive vice president for nonregulated operations in the new company.

The ALLTEL board of directors after the merger in 1983. From left, seated: Pierce Bray, Carl H. Tiedemann, John H. McConnell, Weldon W. Case, Harold G. Payne, and Hugh Wilbourn; standing: Joe T. Ford, James G. Callas, Frederick J. W. Heft, Alfred E. Campdon, Emon A. Mahony, Charles W. Miller, T. H. Davis, George C. McConnaughey, and Philip F. Searle

not all companies will meet the challenges or grasp the opportunities. ALLTEL will meet these challenges because it is strong—strong in management, strong financially, strong technologically, strong in marketing. These strengths will enable us to vigorously compete in the telecommunications business.[22]

Deregulation and the breaking up of American Telephone & Telegraph have thrust the industry into a new era—an era marked by intensive competition in a less-regulated industry. Competition will bring a wave of technological advances, and

Completely changing the names of two old and established companies is a treacherous undertaking under the best of conditions. Familiarity is gone, and loyalty and trust are put at risk. At Mid-Continent there was some disappointment with the name because it seemed to reflect no vestige of a

company of which the employees were so proud. Outside the nineteen states in which they operated, Allied and Mid-Continent were not household names, and "ALLTEL" enjoyed no familiarity and no loyalty anywhere.

The first task was to overcome the internal doubts and to quickly establish the new name and an image. A fetching corporate identity is a tangible corporate asset. Especially in the competitive environment in which the new company was sprouting, a company needed to somehow stand out from competitors, and the corporate name and logo were an important way to do it. At ALLTEL, leaders were convinced they had found

a name that connoted an advanced technological and high-growth company. They quickly developed a national advertising campaign to familiarize the business world with the ALLTEL name and logo and its mission, "a stronger voice in telecommunications."

But the familiar universe of highly regulated business was rapidly vanishing in the fall of 1983, and gaining familiarity with a new and dynamic name would not make the future any less uncertain. All that was predictable about telecommunications was that each generation of technological change would roll over not in decades now but every few months.

In 1989, ALLTEL tested the use of fiber optics in the Piper Glen development near Charlotte, North Carolina, to provide enhanced communications services. *(Photo by Eric Myer.)*

CHAPTER EIGHT

NEW TECHNOLOGY AND THE DAWN OF WIRELESS

1984–1989

Years later, we looked back at our first business plan for cellular, and we laughed at how far we had underestimated the revenues and profits.

—Joe T. Ford[1]

EXECUTIVES OF TRADITIONAL regulated telephone companies in the fall of 1983—awaiting the impending breakup of AT&T and watching the waves of deregulation hurtling toward them—could have easily felt disheartened about the future. Revenues from the ever expanding long-distance market had helped underwrite the great expansion of modern telephone service into millions of homes, but now long-distance and local service would each have to stand alone, which meant that companies like ALLTEL would have to raise their local exchange rates. By doing so, they faced the potential for both ratepayer rebellion and reluctant state regulators.

The independents also faced what they considered to be a more serious peril, a concept called "bypass." Businesses, like homeowners, would be able to own their telephone equipment rather than lease it from the telephone company. A large business, government agency, or institution could bypass the telephone company and purchase and operate its own sophisticated communications system if it were willing to forego the service and reliability provided by the telephone company. The loss of such lucrative business for the telephone company would further heighten the pressure on the telephone rates of residential and small-business customers. Someone, after all, had to bear the freight of the embedded cost of telephone service. A sur-

vey by the United States Telephone Association that was submitted to the FCC indicated that bypass could reduce the revenues from toll settlements between long-distance and local exchange companies by $10 billion, or 36 percent. It reported that 40.5 percent of businesses and 21.2 percent of residential customers were potential customers for bypass.

A company like ALLTEL that served mainly suburban, small-town, and rural areas was not quite as vulnerable as companies that served high-density industrial areas, but still ALLTEL projected in 1984 that if all its business customers for whom it was economically feasible bypassed ALLTEL and installed their own private telephone exchanges, the company could lose $11 million a year. The more customers who left the telephone system, the fewer who were left to pay the embedded cost of the network. Consequently, the higher the rates that the remaining customers had to pay, the more they were impelled to leave and build their own

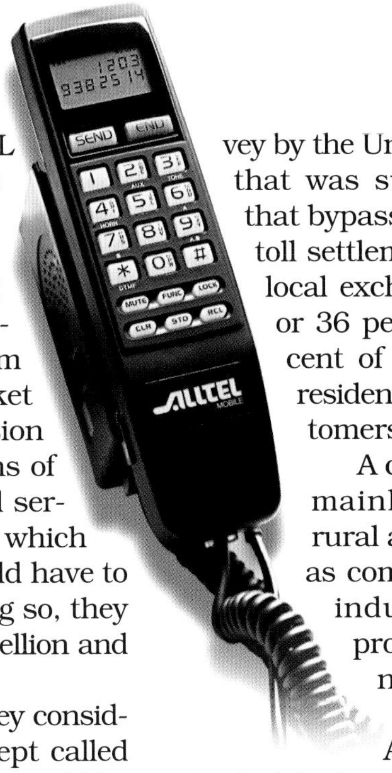

Cellular industry predictions made in 1983 predicted 1.5 million customers by 1990. By early 1989, there were already 2 million cellular customers.

system. It was in many ways a dispiriting time for telephone managers.

On the other hand, the telephone executive who could somehow peer through the haze of deregulation and divestiture might visualize the dizzying opportunities that would lie ahead. The early moves to open the communication markets to competition had already provided a shot of adrenaline to the scientific laboratories. Communications technology that formerly might have taken decades to travel from the drafting board to homes, automobiles, shops, office towers, and factories was now sometimes coming on line within months—technologies like new generations of digital switches, pagers, mobile telephones, laser technology, custom calling devices, and all sorts of office automation products that were the spawn of the digital revolution. The visionary executive could see the pace of change quickening and realize the business opportunities for those who could forecast and develop the markets.

ALLTEL's predecessors, Allied and Mid-Continent, were industry leaders to a considerable extent because they had been ahead of most everyone else, often even the AT&T network, in developing communication innovations on their own or putting new technology to work ahead of the others. In the winter of 1983–84, as the mammoth realignment of the telephone industry creaked into place, the rhetoric from the newly realigned executive suites at ALLTEL was anything but mournful. Weldon Case and Joe Ford talked more about new horizons and opportunities than about the perils facing the industry. Fortified by the merger, they said, the company had the financial strength and perfect positioning to prosper in the new competitive world. But they also said ALLTEL would have to compete more vigorously in the future than the two companies had competed in the past.

Mid-Continent and Allied had led the independent industry in growth because their rate base had grown so rapidly and because they had been successful in keeping their costs low and winning relief from regulatory agencies, all of which provided a steady growth in the rate of return on their investment. Though it might still be rudimentary in some places, telephone service in the past decade had become nearly universal in the United States, even in the remotest Arkansas countryside. But now, Case told stockholders and employees, the rapid expansion of the company's rate base was ending and future growth of telephone service might be little more than a reflection of housing starts. To make matters worse, Ford said, the company faced a chance that the rate base—the aggregate of plant and equipment—might actually decline as people and businesses purchased their telephone equipment.[2]

With the loss of the long-distance subsidy and the prospects of a stagnant or declining rate base in the regulated business, ALLTEL needed to find ways of shielding and even enhancing the revenue stream. This new revenue would have to come largely, though not altogether, from the unregulated sides of the company. The predecessor companies' diversification of the past dozen years was about to pay off.

Bypassing Bypass

Bypass was a particularly troubling issue for ALLTEL. Starting in the late 1970s, significant numbers of large business customers, especially those with far-flung operations, had bought their own microwave systems or fiber-optic and satellite networks to handle their communications. The rapid improvement in microwave and fiber-optic transmissions was an incentive for the move, but the overriding factor was the rising cost of telephone service, particularly long distance.

The chief remedy that would offset bypass—ALLTEL insisted to the FCC, state regulators, and Congress—was some form of cost-based pricing of local telephone service so that telephone companies could offer communications packages for business customers that would be competitive. FCC and state regulators, however, were nervous about the political repercussions from the AT&T divestiture and deregulation. The FCC recognized that bypass was a serious peril to the finances of telephone companies and that there needed to be a universal access charge to local telephone customers to pay for the connection of local phones to the long-distance network, but feeling pressure from Congress, the FCC hesitated about imposing the charge. Ford said in December 1984 that the regulatory bodies and Congress were reacting to

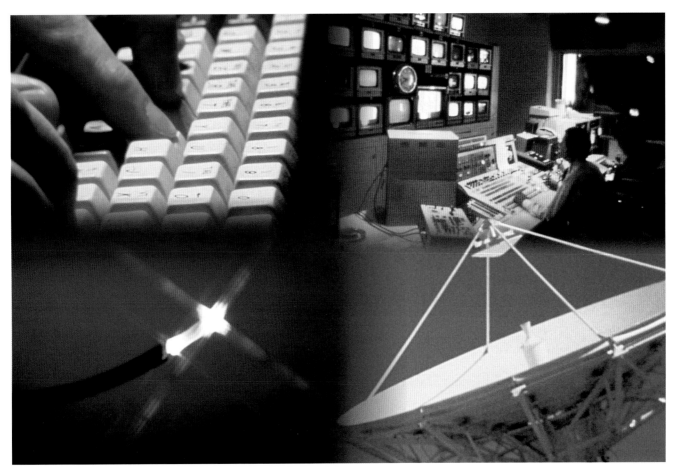

short-run political fears rather than considering the long-term best interests of consumers. An access charge that reflected the cost of service, he said, would remove most of the economic incentive to bypass the companies' networks.[3]

In June 1985, the FCC finally took the first small step: a $1 monthly "subscriber line charge" on residential telephone bills. (In 1983, it had directed companies to collect a $6 charge on larger business customers.) In the spring of 1986, the residential subscriber charge was raised to $2 a month, which helped offset the loss of revenues from long-distance settlements.

Then the FCC took the last step and deregulated all equipment inside a customer's premises, removing all of it from regulatory pricing effective December 31, 1987. Two of the telephone industry's three parts—terminal equipment and long distance—were now competitive. Only the dial tone part remained stringently regulated. Telephone companies had to decide whether to stay in the telephone leasing business at all, and many chose to

The decade of the 1980s saw ALLTEL evolve from a regional telephone company into a national high-tech company.

abandon it. ALLTEL opted to stay in leasing and offer customers a chance to buy its equipment, but it could now price the equipment competitively.

ALLTEL countered the bypass threat in another way too. It began educating business customers about the realities of bypass: If they owned their own telephone networks, they were responsible for maintaining them, including line repair. Because technology was advancing so rapidly, the system they were buying probably would be obsolete in a few years. They would have to make expensive modifications or buy another system entirely, a substantial risk for a business. If a business concluded that it ought to construct its own bypass system, ALLTEL offered its engineering and maintenance service to help customers build their own systems. In that way, ALLTEL could continue to supply its customers with telecommunication services and partially offset the losses in toll revenues.

ALLTEL also offered a succession of sophisticated business services to customers as an alternative to bypass. The company developed an integrated business network (IBN), which was an enhanced Centrex service, for major business customers. In April 1987, MRC Bearings/SKF Aerospace in New York, a world leader in manufacturing and supply of precision aircraft ball and roller bearings for nearly every kind of aircraft from 747s to fighter planes and the U.S. space program, became the largest company to contract with ALLTEL for the central office–based service. In 1989 ALLTEL developed the ALLTEL Digital Centrex, a highly flexible system for voice and data communications that gave businesses all the advantages of a PBX (private branch exchange) without having to buy their own system. The all-digital switching equipment, a state-of-the-art service for business customers, was located in ALLTEL's central offices and maintained twenty-four hours a day. In addition, the company developed the ALLTEL Message Center, a form of central office-based voice mail, and Ring Plus, which used a coded ring to indicate which member of a household or office a caller was trying to reach.

Fiber Optics Roots

When the FCC moved to decouple long distance and the highly regulated local telephone service and to open long distance to competition, it set off a competitive free-for-all never imagined in the industry. It also unloosed more technological innovation in two decades than the communications industry had experienced in the first eight decades of the century. Though the merger of Mid-Continent and Allied produced a company that was still small among the giants left by divestiture, ALLTEL recognized the revolutions in the making and decided, whatever the risks, to be a pacesetter in introducing new technology such as fiber-optic cable. Owing to that decision, by century's end it would be the one company that would be heavily invested in all facets of the telephone business—wireless, local wireline service, and long distance—and with a footprint that would stretch across most of the country.

The concepts behind fiber optics—that glass can be spun into fibers and that messages can be transmitted by light energy—had been around for centuries. A Frenchman, René de Réaumur, made spun glass fibers in 1713, and in 1880, three years after he patented the telephone, Alexander Graham Bell invented an optical telephone system, which he called the Photophone. Bell theorized that signals could be sent through the air, but the earth's atmosphere would not transmit light nearly as reliably as wires transmitted electric signals. Bell didn't pursue the technology and gave his Photophone to the Smithsonian Institution. It would be almost ninety years before the problems of optical transmission would finally be resolved and the two technologies—Réaumur's flexible glass fibers and Bell's telephone—merged.

Medical researchers, hoping to peer inside the body, were most interested in the science of transmitting light through flexible objects, and research to turn the technology to communications use didn't begin until the 1920s. The research turned on the idea of total internal reflection—confining light in a material, such as glass, that is surrounded by other materials with a lower refractive index.

The invention of the laser in 1960 stimulated a more urgent interest in fiber communications. Scientists at the Corning Glass Works announced in September 1970 that they had made single-mode glass fibers that would transmit signals with an extremely low fiber loss. Within weeks, Bell Laboratories and a team at the Ioffe Physical Institute in Leningrad (now St. Petersburg) made semiconductor diode lasers that emitted continuous waves at room temperatures, thus opening the door to fiber communications.

A couple of other developments stimulated interest in the new fiber technology. With an abundance of new technologies that promised to make long distance cheaper, the FCC, in a succession of decisions, threw the long-distance market open to competition. The expanding sophistication of computers

Opposite: ALLTEL worked constantly to maintain and improve its telephone network. By 1987 more than half of the company's customers were served by digital switching.

created mammoth demands upon the communications network for transmitting data as well as voice. But here was a technology that could transmit vast amounts of data and messages far more reliably than anything the industry had ever imagined. Not only could it transmit vast quantities of information simultaneously, but it was largely unaffected by the usual atmospheric interference that had plagued the industry since 1876. There would never be the crosstalk that aggravated subscribers. By the early 1980s, the laser had progressed sufficiently in life expectancy and price, and fiber had been developed with a sufficiently low attenuation that the technology could be applied on a wide scale.

Transmission of messages by fiber optics followed the same premises as the original Bell telephone. Information was beamed from one point to another from a light source rather than being carried by electrons, the method used with copper cables. Semiconductor lasers, smaller than a grain of salt, transmit the light, or signals, which travels through optical fibers that are as thin as a human hair. A coder at the transmitting end converts sound or data from electrical pulses into light signals, and another coder, or detector,

Unlike copper wires, which transmit information with electrons, fiber-optic cables transfer messages using light.

at the receiving end converts the light back into electrical pulses. The detector allows the transmitted data to be called up on a computer screen.

Early Endeavors

The significance of the scientific developments had not been lost on the executives at Allied and Mid-Continent, who were looking for new ventures and new ways to improve the efficiency of their service. "Early on, we recognized that the digital world was upon us," said Frederick Heft, who retired as Mid-Continent's executive vice president for operations in 1980 and who served on the ALLTEL board until 1991. "We knew we had to make progress as quickly as we could. We had to wade into fiber optics, well before some of the other companies, in order to get the productivity and provide the service that our customers really wanted at a rate they could afford."[4]

In the winter of 1981–82, Mid-Continent, which had been looking for a suitable application for a year, made its first use of fiber optics, stringing a cable eleven miles through utility ducts between Ashtabula and Geneva, Ohio, in the company's Western Reserve district. It was among the first

uses of fiber optics in Ohio and the longest fiber-optic system in the state at the time.

The fiber-optic cable solved a threefold problem. First, it provided additional trunk lines, which were much needed because the screened cable that had been installed in 1976 was already reaching its capacity. Second, the optical cable would handle four hundred times the communication of the conventional copper wire. Finally, fiber optics solved interference problems. Northern Ohio suffered unusually harsh winters from the howling storms that roared off Lake Erie, and heavy industrial activity along the lake caused electrical interference with the conventional wires. The atmospheric conditions between the two offices made a microwave system impractical.

In the summer of 1982, Mid-Continent strung another fiber-optic cable into the nearby nuclear power plant at Perry, thus completing the first fiber-optic subscriber loop in the United States. A fiber-optic cable at a power plant was especially important because a mechanical failure in the transmission line could cause a fault in the ground system, and copper telephone wire would act as a conductor and carry the current back to the central office or to someone working on the cable. A fiber-optic glass cable, however, isn't conductive and is therefore safer.

A year later, in the fall of 1983, as Mid-Continent and Allied were merging, ALLTEL began converting a subscriber system to fiber optics at the Mid-Ohio Telephone Company's Newark exchange. The fiber cable tied the digital remote offices of the company to the central office at Newark. That winter, ALLTEL installed a fiber-optic cable on a ten-mile span from Manlius to Cazenovia, New York, and the company would continue to install fiber-optic links in high-growth areas throughout the system.

Investing in Long Distance

The magnificent technology of fiber optics, combined with deregulation, created a boom in the long-distance market. Scores of long-distance ventures sprang up, but high risks were inherent. ALLTEL sought to capture its share of the nation's multibillion-dollar toll market without incurring the costs of building its own network. By the beginning of 1988, the company had established a 34 percent ownership interest in LCI Communications, Inc., whose LiTel network served key markets in the Midwest, and a 20 percent interest in Microtel, a long-distance company serving the heavy toll areas of Florida and Georgia.

In June 1988, when Microtel announced it was merging with Advanced Telecommunications Corporation (ATC), an Atlanta-based long-distance company, ALLTEL found an opportunity to enhance its investment profile. The merger, which gave ALLTEL approximately 14 percent interest in the new company, enhanced Advanced Telecommunications Corporation's growth prospects by combining two of the nation's most profitable and productive regional long-distance companies. It also enhanced the company's market share, giving it a total of more than 150,000 commercial and residential customers in a ten-state area of the southeastern and southwestern United States—a market

that enjoyed one of the highest concentrations of intercity toll volume in the country.

To maximize the growth opportunities that the merger represented, ALLTEL sold its 34 percent interest in LCI to an investor group and purchased an additional 2.7 million shares of Advanced Telecommunications Corporation common stock. ALLTEL ended up owning a 32 percent interest in Advanced Telecommunications Corporation.

ALLTEL's interest in ATC positioned it for higher profits. The long-distance market was one of the fastest-growing mature markets, but ALLTEL knew that it could not afford on its own to build a fourth network that could compete profitably with AT&T, U.S. Sprint, and MCI. Instead it invested in ATC, which served business customers in ten Sun Belt states.

ATC's fiber-optic and digital network was suited for transmitting data fast and efficiently. ATC had expanded its market share in 1989 by issuing 6.5 million shares to acquire Galesi Communications, Inc., and its Telus, Inc., long-distance subsidiary. The Telus acquisition reduced ALLTEL's position in ATC from 32 percent to 23 percent, but it added one hundred thousand customers in Florida and gave the company 9 percent of the booming Florida market.

Fiber optics remained a somewhat expensive technology, but its installation brought both efficiency and economies, and ALLTEL looked for new applications for the fiber-optic cables. In September 1989 it began field trials at its Matthews, North Carolina, exchange to determine whether fiber-optic cables could be not only used to link central offices but also run to the curb of subscribers' homes. Running fiber-optic cable all the way inside the home, the perfect scenario, would remain too expensive because it would involve complicated terminal equipment, but if the cable could be run to the curb, it would be an advancement. The traditional twisted wires or coaxial cable

An ALLTEL representative shows schoolchildren a fiber-optic cable in Matthews, North Carolina. In Matthews, the company set up field trials to test whether fiber-optic technology would be feasible in people's homes in addition to businesses. *(Photo by Eric Myer.)*

could carry the transmission from the network at the curb into the home. Don and Debbie Whelchel in the Piper Glen subdivision near Matthews became the first people in North Carolina to place a call over a fiber-optic cable that linked their neighborhood to the network. Moreover, ALLTEL's Piper Glen application was the first in the world to carry fiber to the customer's curb rather than the customer's door, which made fiber-optic technology more practical by eliminating the need for expensive connecting devices.

By the turn of the century, ALLTEL would have more than fifteen thousand miles of fiber optics interconnecting its far-flung wireline properties.

Building Blocks

Nothing the company did would prove to be more provident than the other gamble it took by entering the bidding for wireless telephone markets. Wireless would dramatically alter the character of the company, giving it a truly national footprint. In less than fifteen years, income from ALLTEL's wireless operations would surpass every other sector of the company's business, but in 1983, when ALLTEL was making plans to launch its first cellular markets, no one was quite sure what was in store. Wireless communications were uncharted waters in a particularly turbulent sea. The commercial potential of the technology seemed limitless, but there was no structure for the market, and since wireless communication used the public airwaves, the government obviously would have to erect some kind of structure.

A cellular, or wireless, phone transmits low-energy radio waves to a local antenna, which connects the caller to a landline or wireless location and sends signals back to the caller. A computerized system monitors the calls to be sure that each one receives the strongest signal that is available wherever the caller travels.

The basic wireless technology had been around for most of the century, but it was of little practical commercial use. Radiotelephone systems were useful for oceangoing ships, but when a few police departments tried them in the 1920s, they proved to be impractical. The necessary equipment was too bulky. Topography and buildings also were an impediment to radio signals until 1935, when Edwin Armstrong discovered frequency modulation (FM). The bulky equipment for AM (amplitude modulation) transmission was no longer required, and FM transmission was of better quality.

The need for portable two-way battlefield communications during World War II created a powerful stimulus to develop FM technology. Products developed by Bell Laboratories, Motorola, and General Electric for the war effort would have peacetime uses. Mobile telephone systems were established in a few cities in the 1940s, but they could accommodate only a few subscribers. A city like New York could have only twelve users at a time. It obviously was not an inviting market. More often than not, customers would get busy signals when they called, and signals carried no more than seventy-five miles.

In 1947, AT&T discovered that it could use the limited airwaves more efficiently by scattering transmitters throughout a metropolitan area and handing off calls from transmitter to transmitter as a car made its way through town. More people could have access to the system simultaneously by reusing the same radio frequency as they moved from one "cell" into another. Still, it was not until the 1970s that the hand-off technology advanced sufficiently and Motorola developed a compact radiotelephone set.

In 1977, the FCC issued two licenses for experimental wireless systems, to AT&T in Chicago and to Motorola and American Radio Telephone Service in the Baltimore-Washington, D.C., corridor. Then the FCC began to consider how it might grant commercial licenses for cellular service nationally. AT&T argued for a single wireline company in each market, while other companies wanted a competitive marketplace. It was clear by then that a monopoly would not be the solution. Finally, in May 1981, the FCC settled on a regulatory scheme. The country was divided into 305 metropolitan statistical areas (MSAs) and 428 rural service areas (RSAs), with the metropolitan areas covering three-fourths of the population. The FCC then issued two licenses in each market—a nonwireline carrier and a wireline (local phone) company.

The FCC issued its first commercial license to AT&T in Chicago on October 6, 1983, but by then the agency clearly had a problem. For just the thirty markets ranked sixty-first to ninetieth in size, the FCC received 567 license applications. It would take years to evaluate all the applications, hold comparative hearings, and issue licenses. So two weeks later it announced that lotteries would be used to award licenses in all but the thirty largest markets. It spent another six years adjusting the lottery process as hundreds of thousands of applications were filed.

Ground Floor Partnerships

At the time the FCC announced its regulatory plan in 1981, John Dunbar, vice president for technical services at Mid-Continent, was already studying the prospects for wireless telephone. But in the early 1980s, cellular didn't have many champions inside the phone businesses. It was exotic and expensive technology that few people believed would ever have universal appeal. Dunbar, however, had high hopes for the rapidly improving technology. "It was kind of a gut feeling," he said years later. "Entrepreneurial endeavors are not always based upon specific research, and I guess I just sensed that if I could be someplace and talk to somebody whenever I needed to, then I would appreciate that—and other people who were out there trying to make a living would appreciate that."[5]

Dunbar was persistent in his belief that cellular would catch on, and after a number of visits to Weldon Case's office he finally got permission to lead a team to pursue it. Dunbar set up an office and hired Dan Thompson, another believer in the future of cellular, to help with the market research and FCC filings.

Dunbar and his team then began the grueling process of filing for licenses with the FCC. "We were on the road all the time," Dunbar said. "I was out of the office four or five days a week. We were up all night. We worked all weekends. The filings were very difficult because they required detailed engineering and marketing studies, but we were excited. We were involved in something unique—a pioneer sort of thing—and the adrenaline propelled us."[6]

Mid-Continent and nineteen other wireline telephone companies announced joint plans in June 1982 to offer cellular telephone service to twenty-nine major metropolitan markets if they won

John Dunbar was the first president of ALLTEL Mobile Communications. His efforts went a long way toward helping the company become a leader in cellular services.

licenses from the FCC. They sought licenses to provide advanced mobile phone service to three primary markets—Detroit, Cleveland, and Pittsburgh—and twenty-six secondary markets. The FCC had warned companies that without a joint effort they would face long delays in gaining license approval for cellular service in markets with more than one wireline carrier.[7]

"It was obvious that a lot of people were filing for the same markets," Dunbar remembered. "So with the okay of the Federal Communications Commission we began to negotiate. It was really difficult to get the markets even after you filed for them because every independent in the country was interested in some way or another in the markets.

But I was the only person from any company who did not have to go back to corporate to get permission to make a decision in the negotiation process. Even the AT&T people had to go back and talk to somebody else who wasn't at the meeting."[8]

Dunbar's hard work in the negotiations paid off. In the summer of 1983, a few months before Allied and Mid-Continent merged, the FCC authorized Mid-Continent Mobile Phone Corporation (the name of Mid-Continent's new cellular subsidiary), GTE Mobilnet, and Ameritech Corporation to construct a mobile phone system to serve Cleveland and the surrounding area. It issued a separate license for the Pittsburgh area to Mid-Continent, Bell Atlantic, and the North Pittsburgh Telephone Company. Mid-Continent would be a 10 percent partner in Cleveland and own 3.6 percent in Pittsburgh.

At that time, Allied had yet to file any licenses with the FCC, though it was interested in pursuing cellular. When ALLTEL was formed that fall, the new company inherited all of Mid-Continent's cellular endeavors, and Dunbar became the founding president of ALLTEL Mobile. Mid-Continent's cellular venture would, in fact, be a major contribution to ALLTEL. Dunbar began working with Allied's Donald E. Steely, who helped put in place the systems that would run ALLTEL Mobile, and Randy Wilbourn, son of Allied founder Hugh Wilbourn, who performed market research and connected the mobile division to advertising agencies. Dunbar also worked with Tom Orsini, who had been Allied's treasurer and a vice president and who became a vice president of ALLTEL. Orsini helped Dunbar develop budgets and made sure the expectations for cellular were kept conservative.[9] ALLTEL forecast spending $35 million on cellular and paging businesses, but eventually it would spend $56 million in the Charlotte system alone.

As the merger was taking place, the FCC licensed the Mid-Continent joint venture in Detroit with Ameritech and GTE Mobilnet. ALLTEL's minority position there would be 4.1 percent. Later, ALLTEL would be a limited partner in joint ventures in Syracuse (45 percent), Rochester (15 percent), Jacksonville, Florida (23 percent), Akron (10 percent), Canton, Ohio (10 percent), Youngstown and Warren, Ohio (6 percent), Greenville and Spartanburg, South Carolina (3 percent), and Flint, Michigan (3 percent).

But ALLTEL's major venture, approved by the FCC in February 1984 and launched in April 1985, would be the Charlotte-Gastonia, North Carolina, market, where it would be the operating partner. Charlotte-Gastonia was the sixty-first-largest metropolitan statistical area in the country. After intense negotiations, ALLTEL won 70 percent ownership of the venture, BellSouth Mobility 23 percent, GTE Mobilnet 2 percent, and United TeleSpectrum 5 percent. The company's goal was to have seven hundred customers there by the end of the first year and thirty-five hundred after five years. ALL-

TEL met the goal of seven hundred customers in the first year with a couple dozen to spare and exceeded the five-year plan in only the second year. In three years, the company had more than nine thousand customers in Charlotte and Gastonia, and the growth afterward was exponential. The story would be repeated in the other metropolitan markets that ALLTEL entered as the managing partner in the years ahead—Little Rock; Jackson, Mississippi; Ocala, Florida; and Gainesville, Florida —except it exceeded the business plan earlier each time.

With the Charlotte-Gastonia business off the ground, ALLTEL applied to the FCC in 1985 to provide cellular service to the Little Rock and Jackson metropolitan areas. Business operations began in both cities the following year. At Jackson, the company partnered with Mobile Communications Corporation of America and BellSouth Mobility. And at Little Rock, ALLTEL formed a partnership with Century Telephone Enterprises of Monroe, Louisiana, and Perco Telephone Company of Perryville, Arkansas. The Little Rock joint venture served Pulaski, Saline, Faulkner, and Lonoke counties. The other two wireline companies in the Little Rock metropolitan area, Southwestern Bell and General Telephone Company, did not participate in the partnership, which expedited the construction permit for the six-cell system.

Paging Service

ALLTEL offered wide-area paging as a complementary service to mobile telephones, but it was directed at a slightly different customer profile: hospital administrators, doctors, nursing supervisors, repairmen, plumbers, electricians, salespeople, and key people in large factories. ALLTEL began to apply to the FCC for licenses to provide paging in twenty-seven cities where it was, or hoped to be, the operating partner or a limited partner in cellular systems. In the spring of 1984, the FCC granted the company its first construction permit for a paging system, in Binghamton, New York. It won permits for the other cities as well. According to Dunbar, it was paging, not cellular, that first brought revenue to ALLTEL Mobile.[10]

Pagers had been large, unwieldy devices, but they had been slimmed down by 1983 and were far more versatile than the old beepers. Tone-alert pagers emitted a tone that signaled the wearer to call home or the office. Silent vibra pagers signaled a call by vibrating silently. Display pagers provided the calling party's telephone numbers. Alphanumeric pagers flashed numbers and a written message over a small screen on the paging unit.

The mobile telephone passed swiftly from luxury to necessity, as illustrated by these construction workers.

ALLTEL was one of the first companies to offer the alphanumeric portable message center to business executives. In August 1984, the company opened its first paging sales office, in northeastern Ohio, competing with Ohio Bell, which offered paging in twenty-one cities across the state. In January 1985, ALLTEL Mobile began offering digital paging in Little Rock, and on December 12, 1985, ALLTEL bought MCI Airsignal's northern Ohio radio paging system, adding six thousand paging customers.

Selling Cellular

At first, ALLTEL saw cellular as primarily appealing to business people, doctors, lawyers, construction supervisors, salespeople, real estate agents, and others whose work required them to commute out of the office, "although some residential customers will find cellular systems attractive."[11] As more and more people realized the benefits of cellular phones, the company had to shift its marketing strategies to appeal to the wider segment.

In early 1985, ALLTEL moved the headquarters of its cellular operations, ALLTEL Mobile Communications, from Hudson to Little Rock, and Thomas W. Case, son of the Mid-Continent founder, became its president. (Dunbar shifted his talents back to the traditional wireline business to become president of ALLTEL's southern region.) Case had arrived at ALLTEL by a circuitous path. In May 1984, ALLTEL Systems merged with the business communications subsidiaries of CP National

From its earliest days, ALLTEL Mobile used white floors in its installation centers to demonstrate the quality and attention to detail each customer would receive.

Corporation and Pacific Telecom in a new marketing venture to be known as ComPath National. ComPath marketed business communications systems in thirteen western states, along with Texas, Minnesota, Georgia, Arkansas, and Kentucky. Case, formerly executive vice president of CP National Business Communications Division, was named president of the partnership. A year later, in early 1985, he would move over to run ALLTEL's burgeoning cellular properties.

"When talking about the growth of the industry," Case said, reflecting on the period a decade later, "many people overlook the fact that the vast majority of the sixteen million cellular phones in use today were sold one at a time—one salesperson, one customer, and one phone—all in just ten years."[12]

In the early days of cellular, everyone was a salesperson. Case himself sold hundreds from his desk in ALLTEL headquarters. Few people had heard of a cellular telephone, and those who had learned about mobile telephones over the years had heard about their difficulties. Selling was as much a novelty as the device.

Gary Kiser, one of ALLTEL's first sales representatives in Charlotte, remembered that he had trouble explaining the concept of the cellular phone to his family and friends. "My wife didn't know if cellular was a bone disease or a skin cream," he said. "When she heard that I was going to work for straight commissions, she asked, 'What are we supposed to eat on?' I told her, 'Honey, cellular service is something that a lot of people in Charlotte are going to want.'"[13]

The phones cost $1,500 to $2,000 in those days, a prohibitive cost to most people. The price of the service ran about 35 cents a minute. "When we started in Charlotte, we had zero name recognition," remembered Randy Wilbourn. "Less than 2 percent of our target audience could give you a definition of our product, and we knew for sure that knowledge of the price of the product was a deterrent for anyone to purchase it. It was probably four years before we ever put price in an ad. We talked about the product benefit, the quality of the product, its use, etc. The last thing the salesman was supposed to say was, "Oh, by the way, this thing costs $1,500."[14]

Despite the hefty price tag, salespeople were selling about twenty a week at the outset. Kiser

ALLTEL developed wide-area paging around its cellular markets. The paging service was directed toward professionals such as doctors and supervisors.

recalled that when they hit fifty a week they received a big basket of fruit from the corporate headquarters with a note saying "You did it." Another basket arrived when they hit one hundred a week.

"There are many cellular companies in the country that can't boast of comparable results," Thomas Case said in 1994 about the first decade of cellular. "The reason for our success is we were able to assemble an outstanding group of people, most of whom are still in important positions with the company. They were able to consistently hit the center of the bullseye in terms of identifying the market and delivering the products and services to maximize market share and development. They also have had the backing of a great company, which placed a tremendous amount of faith in all of us in those early years."[15]

Still, delving into the wireless arena wasn't always easy. ALLTEL's people had to make the jump from operating in the traditional, regulated wireline monopoly to the competitive enterprise that was wireless. In essence, they were working in a duopoly—not pure competition but not a pure monopoly either. "When we organized the cellular business, our wireline and our wireless structures worked separately," explained Jim Kimzey, ALLTEL's senior vice president for networks. "On the one hand we had the wireless business that was very entrepreneurial, very quick on its feet, driving, driving, driving. Now on the wireline side, we were driving as well, but we were slow and methodical. We didn't make decisions without all the facts and without understanding all the issues."[16]

The mixture of competition and regulation was a major change to ALLTEL's culture, but the company adapted quite well. "Our people, who came from wireline backgrounds and other backgrounds, adapted to the new culture very quickly," said James Gadberry, executive vice president, Administration. "They were successful, more so than others, in operating in a duopoly."[17] ALLTEL, in fact, would be one of the first telecommunications companies to converge its wireline and wireless franchises.

Wireless Tendrils

Despite the exponential sales growth at Charlotte and in nearly every other market that ALLTEL entered as the managing or limited partner, the total mobile properties would not show a profit until 1992. While individual systems would report a profit after two or three years, the company entered new markets every year, where the start-up costs always were high.

In the last half of the decade, the company acquired majority and managing interests in other smaller metropolitan areas. ALLTEL and the Missouri Telephone Company formed a partnership in 1987 to provide wireless service to the Springfield, Missouri, area, with ALLTEL initially owning a 51 percent interest. In 1988, it acquired a 45 percent interest in the Aiken, South Carolina-Augusta, Georgia, system, and the next year it bought the remaining interest from Cellular America and a private investor. Also in 1989, it purchased a 40 percent interest in the Wichita, Kansas, wireline cellular system from the Kansas Cellular Telephone Company.

Starting in 1987, the company had begun to reposition itself in the expanding national wireless market, a strategy that it would follow for the rest of the century. It began systematically to divest itself of minority interests in paging and wireless properties in the Rust Belt regions and trade them for or purchase interests around its booming Sun Belt markets. In the spring of 1987, ALLTEL sold its 3.97 percent interest in a Detroit wireless system to Ameritech. In October, it sold Independent Cellular Network its wireless interests in Johnstown and Altoona, Pennsylvania; Wheeling and Parkersburg, West Virginia; and Steubenville and Marietta, Ohio.

The next month it obtained another 2 percent interest in the Charlotte market and 100 percent of the Ocala, Florida, system from United TeleSpectrum. To complete the deal, ALLTEL exchanged cash, its 4.94 percent interest in a Youngstown, Ohio, system, and its 3.05 percent interest in the Greenville and Spartanburg, South Carolina, partnership. In 1988, ALLTEL exchanged its 3.13 percent interest in a Jacksonville, Florida, wireless system for BellSouth Mobility's 70 percent interest in an Albany, Georgia, system, which made ALLTEL the builder and general partner. The company also purchased 16.65 percent of a Chattanooga, Tennessee, cellular system.

In 1989, ALLTEL acquired interests in 2.6 million wireless POPs—the term for the potential customers in a system—in rural service areas. ALLTEL was fairly aggressive in picking up the RSAs that were attached to its metropolitan statistical areas. "That gave us an edge-out strategy from our MSAs so that we had the largest possible footprint," explained Randy Wilbourn. "We did that through partnerships, many of which we later came back and purchased. The partnerships gave us a branding advantage over isolated systems because if we managed the wireless service under our own brand, even if we were a minority partner, then we had a brand advantage over our competitors. Those rural service area partnerships have been a very successful part of our edge-out strategy."[18]

ALLTEL turned on its first rural wireless system in 1990, in Hot Springs, Arkansas. Shortly after, the RSAs gave ALLTEL 6.4 million POPs, nearly all in the high-growth Sun Belt regions.

As the last decade of the century approached, ALLTEL had established itself as one of the most successful wireless providers in the country, and it was about to reap the profits. The company had made a couple of strategic decisions. Though its regional definition would change dramatically in the next decade, for now it would try to position itself in the most lucrative markets in the eastern half of the Sun Belt. To control costs and achieve efficiency, it would cluster its rural service areas around its metropolitan systems. To hold down selling costs, it employed an aggressive commission-only sales force. While it could

have chosen to compete on the basis of price, it instead positioned ALLTEL Mobile as the quality provider of mobile service. It developed its own engineering, maintenance, and construction forces. And it developed upscale retail and installation facilities that emphasized customer service. Overall, ALLTEL set out to create a public identity as the quality service provider in each community, just as it had with its telephone exchanges in hundreds of communities from Texas to New York.

ALLTEL Mobile used a variety of innovative ways to introduce wireless service to new markets. "Micro Man" was a popular guest at the company's retail stores. *(Photo by Eric Myer.)*

CHAPTER NINE

BEST IN THE BUSINESS

1984–1989

Quite frankly, I believe that we're better than anyone in the business.

—Joe T. Ford, 1987[1]

WRITING TO SHAREHOLDERS in ALLTEL's 1983 annual report, the first after the merger of Mid-Continent and Allied, Weldon Case and Joe Ford, the chairman and president respectively, described the newly formed company as "one of the country's leading telecommunications firms." Separately, they had run a couple of the country's best-performing regional telephone companies. Owing partly to the merger but also to the pressures and opportunities of a revolutionizing marketplace in the 1980s, ALLTEL in November 1983 obviously was something more than simply a substantially larger regional telephone utility. Even as the merger was occurring, Mid-Continent and Allied were gingerly exploring ventures that a few years earlier would have been considered harebrained for a public utility. Fortified by its new financial power, ALLTEL had plunged headfirst into the hectic competition for the new wireless and paging markets and had invested in fiber optics and the suddenly competitive long-distance field.

The company was infected by a certain entrepreneurial aura. Writing in the 1984 annual report, the first report that covered a full year of the new company, Case and Ford concluded their message to shareholders with the question, "Is ALLTEL now a public utility system—or a high-tech growth company?" They answered their own question: "We believe we are both."

Local telephone service was a mature industry with diminishing prospects for the kind of extraordinary growth the companies had separately achieved during the previous two decades. Thus ALLTEL was branching into riskier but potentially high-growth technology fields. Still, ALLTEL was at heart the local telephone company. While two of the three fundamental functions of the telephone industry—terminal equipment and long distance—were now largely deregulated and competitive, the diversified company was built around the third function, the still regulated local dial tone.

ALLTEL's local telephone operations in 1984 accounted for 77 percent of the company's revenues and sales. Five years later, local service and network access would account for only 47 percent, and the local revenues would continue to decline as a share of the company's business. But until the 1990s, when the company's footprint would cross the country, ALLTEL continued to develop around its core business—the telephone systems—from New York to Michigan and from Texas to Florida.

In 1983, the company formed ALLTEL Supply, which offered customers a large array of telecommunications equipment.

The company developed cellular and paging in the territory it knew best, and if it did venture into far-flung country with those partnerships, it would trade the territory for markets near home. And despite the entrepreneurial spirit, Case, Ford, and the rest of the management insisted on performing like a sound, old-line company: lean, efficient management and low overhead.

Responsible Growth

ALLTEL was far more conservative about acquiring telephone properties than it had been in the days when Hugh Wilbourn at Allied and Weldon Case at Mid-Continent were snapping up almost any independent company that was willing to sell, but it continued to enlarge its telephone operations. The companies had to be in fast-growing regions, preferably near existing ALLTEL systems, and at a good price.

It would come across four such opportunities in the decade. In December 1985, ALLTEL announced that it was acquiring two small Pennsylvania telephone companies, Beallsville Telephone Company and Centerville Telephone Company in Camp Hill, Pennsylvania. Together they added about 1,000 customer lines to the ALLTEL system, and they were contiguous to the company's exchange at Waynesburg. That August, ALLTEL acquired The Heins Company of Sanford, North Carolina, in central North Carolina, which expanded ALLTEL's customer base by 19,000. (It had previously bought 39.5 percent of the company's common stock.) Then, in February 1988, ALLTEL acquired the St. Matthews Telephone Company, with 3,500 customers, just southeast of the company's Lexington, South Carolina, operations.

The most significant acquisition, however, was CP National, a diversified telecommunications and energy company based in San Francisco that had 1,800 employees and served more than 150,000 customers in California, Arizona, New Mexico, Nevada, Oregon, Utah, and Texas. ALLTEL closed the sale for $300 million in stock in December 1988.

CP National's 65,467 telephone customer lines gave ALLTEL a presence in the rapidly growing western states, formerly served only by its product

distribution network, and brought its total customer lines to 1,084,283 in twenty-five states. It also provided natural gas to 67,900 customers in California, Oregon, and Nevada and cable television to 5,700 customers in California and the Navajo Indian Reservation.

ALLTEL subsequently sold the gas and cable properties, which were outside its core business. "At the time [of the acquisition], we were looking at another way to become more diversified," explained Jerry Fetzer, ALLTEL's vice president of shared services. "We thought we were going to get into the natural gas business." Indeed, ALLTEL had filed for an exemption to the Public Utility Holding Company Act (PUHCA), which normally would not allow a holding company like ALLTEL to own such diversified subsidiary businesses. "We filed for the PUHCA exemption, but after a few months, it was rejected," Fetzer said. "So we had no choice but to divest ourselves of the natural gas business."[2] Stephens Inc., the Little Rock investment firm started by W. R. "Witt" Stephens, would play a role later in finding a buyer for the gas properties.

While CP National gave ALLTEL access to key growth markets in the West, the acquisition also made ALLTEL a much larger company, swelling its assets to $2.2 billion and its annual revenues to $1.1 billion. Moreover, it gave the company a large presence in a new field: air-traffic-control communications equipment and naval command systems and electronics.

The Switch to Digital

It had been a hallmark of ALLTEL's forebears to give customers in the rural areas state-of-the-art technology, sometimes ahead of the Bell companies in the cities. Mid-Continent, in fact, was the first telephone company in the United States to offer local digital telephone services. (Built in 1977, the digital switching center served customers in Fort White, Florida.)

But technology advanced so rapidly in telecommunications in the last quarter of the century that it would overtake the financial ability of the industry to keep pace. Allied and Mid-Continent were in the midst of converting their exchanges to electronic switching when the development of digital switching technology made the electronic exchanges obsolete. In the 1980s, ALLTEL would commit from $160 million to $200 million a year for equipment, the largest share of it for central office digital switches. The goal was to convert the entire system to digital by the early 1990s.

The older analog switches transmitted messages through the network electronically. But analog signals, which faded over distance, required frequent amplification, and they picked up other sounds that interfered with the message. Digital switches transmit signals like a computer. They take the continuous electric current that corresponds to the sounds of the message and convert it into sequences of the digits "1" and "0." The digital switches duplicate the sequences of digits as the signals move through the network and then convert them back to voice or data for the recipient. A fully digital system maintains the purity and strength of the message over great distances and dramatically raises the capacity of the network to handle data communications.

Digital switching was imperative to any telecommunications company that expected to compete. Besides elevating the quality and reliability of telephone service, digital switching made possible all kinds of office automation products. ALLTEL could offer revenue-producing calling features like touch-tone, call waiting, call forwarding, teleconferencing, and other advanced custom-calling features, which ordinarily were not available in small communities. Digital switches monitored their own operation, diagnosed trouble, and provided repair by remote control. They required a heavy capital investment, but they reduced operating and repair costs dramatically by automating traditionally labor-intensive functions.

Through computerized remote testing, ALLTEL employees were able to pinpoint and correct service problems from central offices without expensive service calls. The company could process far more calls with fewer employees and with fewer service interruptions and other maintenance problems. So reliable was the digital system that the frequency of customer trouble reports and the response times tumbled as more central offices converted. ALLTEL and its predecessor companies had always enjoyed the highest productivity rates in the industry, and

the rate continued to improve in step with the conversion to digital.

Increasing Productivity

The potential of digital technology to make management leaner was not lost on the company either. In the half-dozen years after the merger, employees developed a number of computer-based programs to save labor and improve productivity.

ALLTEL prided itself on providing its customers with the latest in telecommunications technology, so when digital switching became possible, the company moved swiftly to install digital equipment in its telephone exchanges.

For example, before digital technology, field employees had to call their dispatchers for the next assignment and dictate descriptions of the job they had just performed. To recover the time spent dispatching and reporting, employees developed a voice-mail system for installation and repairs. That electronic innovation gained one man-hour per day for each installer and repair worker.

DISCUS (Distributive Information System-Customer Services), a revolutionary computer system developed in 1984, rid the company of costly paperwork in business offices and service centers. Business offices and customer centers all across a region could retrieve customer information with their computer terminals instead of combing through microfiche records.

In another cost- and time-saving effort, ALLTEL and Pacific Telecom, a provider of local and long-distance services in the Pacific Northwest, formed a partnership to create a flexible billing system that could handle billing and customer payments for long-distance carriers participating in the companies' equal-access programs. The system could also handle nonregulated sales, message processing, and centralized investigations of fraudulent long-distance calls.

In another endeavor, a computerized system provided detailed maps of the outside telephone plant for engineers. Engineers' work stations were linked to a host processor so that they could produce and access distribution and land-based maps as well as manhole, underground cable, and other detailed drawings.

Separately, a computer system enabled ALLTEL to monitor its switching facilities from one central location and correct any trouble by computer, saving the cost of dispatching repair crews.

Another program, called MIROR, computerized many of the functions of telephone service centers and switching facilities. Formerly, it would take one week to transfer three thousand customers from an electronic switch to a new digital call-processing system. MIROR reduced the task to one hour.

The labor-saving technologies, along with the rapid conversion to digital switching, produced sharp productivity gains throughout the decade. In 1984, ALLTEL employed one person for every 168 telephones, placing the company among the lead-ers in the industry, but five years later the ratio had improved to one worker for every 191 phones. These economies contributed significantly to ALLTEL's spectacular growth in earnings.

Equal Access

After the breakup of AT&T, the FCC required the Bell companies to offer "equal access" to their customers for competing long-distance companies—that is, their customers were free to designate any long-distance company as their carrier. As a result, more than 350 companies, most of them regional, sprang up to compete with AT&T. Originally the order applied only to the Bell companies, but early in 1985 the FCC extended the equal-access requirement to independent companies as well. The independents were not required to offer equal access in every instance but only from digital central offices where a long-distance company made a "reasonable request" for the service.

Before equal access, if a customer dialed "1," the area code, and a telephone number, a call outside the caller's local access and transport area (called LATA) was routed automatically over the AT&T network. With equal access, customers could designate the long-distance company they wanted to use. The local telephone company programmed its equipment to channel a call to the customer's preferred long-distance carrier when the customer dialed "1," the area code, and a seven-digit number. The choice was available to customers with either rotary or push-button phones.

Unlike many other independents, ALLTEL decided not to wait for a long-distance company to request equal access to its customers. In areas where ALLTEL had the necessary digital equipment and where the media had heavily publicized equal access, it tried to give its customers the same alternatives offered in the metropolitan areas. The company announced in August 1985 that it would convert about 135,000 customer lines in New York, Ohio, and Pennsylvania to equal access in 1986 and phase in other parts of the system in 1987 and 1988.

ALLTEL believed its customers should have a choice, and it believed customers shouldn't be penalized with inconvenience once that choice was made. While customers with push-button phones could already choose a long-distance company other than AT&T, it often was a nettlesome experience. They had to dial lengthy pass codes that totaled as many as twenty-three digits. People with rotary phones didn't even have that option. Speeding equal access to small towns and the countryside made ALLTEL the low-cost provider of cheap long distance, and it guaranteed maximum access to ALLTEL customers for any company that wanted to compete.

Ancillary Activities

While the core of the business remained the regulated telephone service and while the cellular and long-distance investments offered the prospect of super profits off in the future, the nonregulated activities of the company gave it immediate, dependable, and hearty growth year after year.

In 1984, the company formed a new subsidiary, ALLTEL Publishing, to coordinate advertising and sales for its 119 telephone directories. The new company would also handle printing and distribution of the directories. Though it was not intended to be a major profit center—only a step to control costs and standardize the quality of the directories—it would, in fact, become profitable. In October 1993, ALLTEL Publishing became a coast-to-coast operation when the company purchased the independent directory publishing business of GTE Corporation. Not only would ALLTEL now publish the directories of more than 125 independent telephone companies, it would also provide all the directory publishing services, including contract management, production, and marketing.

When Hugh Wilbourn at Allied and Weldon Case at Mid-Continent had detected the changes that were in store for the regulated telephone industry, they separately arrived at the wisdom that they should diversify. Almost simultaneously in the summer of 1970, they moved into the most rational auxiliary activity for a telephone company: telephone supply. Allied acquired Southern Telephone Supply Company, and Mid-Continent bought the Buckeye Telephone and Supply Company. Both had $5.3 million in sales in 1970. Revenues during the 1970s would grow at a rate of more than 25 percent a year. In 1983, the year the companies were consolidated into

Hudson, Ohio, remained an important market for ALLTEL as the newly merged company continued to diversify.

Despite its rapid growth, ALLTEL remained, in many ways, what it started out to be: a telephone company that basically served small towns and rural areas. The company considered it a special mission to provide telephone service that was as modern and reliable as that enjoyed in large cities.

ALLTEL Supply, their sales totaled $100 million. Once largely regional supply houses, they now marketed communications equipment and supplies to telephone companies and other utilities in all fifty states.

On November 23, 1987, ALLTEL entered into a definitive agreement with Contel Corporation to acquire a portion of its Texocom telephone equipment supply business. ALLTEL bought the part that served customers not affiliated with Contel. The purchase, set at $20 million, included the Texocom name, certain inventories, a customer base that generated $89 million in revenues in 1986, and other assets. Combining the customer bases of the companies produced economies of scale and made ALLTEL Supply one of the largest and strongest telecommunications equipment distributors in the United States.

It would become even larger and stronger in April 1989, when ALLTEL purchased all the shares of HWC Distribution, the largest master distributor of electrical and electronic wire and cable in the United States. The Houston-based company operated thirteen sales warehouses from Seattle to Tampa to Philadelphia and distributed specialty wire and cable products from more than three hundred manufacturers. Its products, distributed nationwide, were used in a wide variety of industries: telecommunications, computer networking, pulp and paper, petrochemicals, steel, mining, factory automation, and cogeneration. Its inventory included power and control cables for manufacturing and processing plants; shielded and unshielded power cables for burial in conduits, trays, and ducts; flame-resistant cables for use in airspace above office ceilings; and pre-

cision-engineered cables for use in data communications and broadcasting.

HWC continued to operate as an independent entity and sold exclusively through distribution, but its affiliation with ALLTEL let it expand more rapidly and let it serve distributors outside the United States. Ford said it was a strategic fit for ALLTEL's well-established distribution business. "It's a business we know and do well," he said.[3] HWC had enjoyed revenue growth of 26 percent a year in the previous five years, and its operating

Above: ALLTEL Supply sold a large array of telephone equipment and supplies in all fifty states.

Below left: In 1984, ALLTEL formed its own telephone directory publishing company, which proved both economical and profitable.

Below right: After the company acquired part of Texocom in 1987, ALLTEL became the nation's fifth-largest distributor of telecommunications equipment.

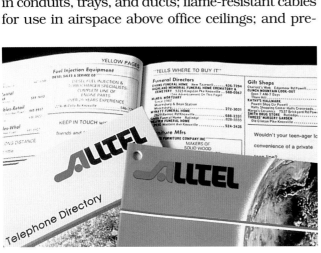

income had been rising 57 percent annually. The growth would be reflected at ALLTEL Supply with sales growing by $113 million and operating income by $13.4 million.

Overall, revenues and sales of all the company's distribution properties, including ALLTEL Systems and ALLTEL Communications, nearly doubled in one year, rising from $147.8 million in 1988 to $261.2 million in 1989.

ALLTEL Systems and ALLTEL Communications, both business communications subsidiaries, were outgrowths of the FCC opening the interconnect market in the late 1960s. Allied and Mid-Continent had established subsidiaries to market business communications products and services, and the business was strengthened in 1983 by Allied's acquisition of ComPath, an Oakland-based marketer of business telephone systems, a purchase that was completed as ALLTEL was formed. ComPath, with offices in fourteen California cities, was one of the largest marketers of business communications systems on the West Coast.

The company made another acquisition in 1988, Area Market Research Associates of Little Rock, a market research firm acquired from Cranford Johnson Robinson Associates of Little Rock, one of the leading advertising agencies in the Southwest. ALLTEL renamed the firm Sygnis and relocated it to ALLTEL Mobile's new headquarters at the Financial Center in west Little Rock. Sygnis employed twenty research professionals and more than two hundred part-time interviewers.

Natural Progression

In the late 1980s, leadership of the company began to pass from Weldon Case and his Mid-Continent team to the younger generation of management from Arkansas, all according to Case's plan.

Pierce Bray, the executive vice president and chief financial officer, retired in February 1985. Bray had been with Mid-Continent for fifteen years before the merger as executive vice president for finance and was a key figure in the development of the company and the formation of ALLTEL. Max E. Bobbitt, the young CPA who had risen

rapidly through the ranks at Allied, took on the duties of chief financial officer in addition to his role as executive vice president for nonregulated operations. Bobbitt had begun with Allied as director of accounting in 1970. His first job after college was with Arthur Andersen & Company, where his utility auditing work introduced him to Allied and Joe Ford.

In July 1986, two Mid-Continent telephone pioneers retired: Nelson H. Case, executive vice president for telephone operations, and Robert D. Bonnar, senior vice president and the controller for ALLTEL Service. Case's telephone career had spanned forty-two years, beginning at Western Reserve, the original Mid-Continent property. Bonnar had started his telephone career at the Ashtabula Telephone Company, another early Mid-Continent company.

Then, at the April 1987 board of directors meeting, Weldon Case announced that he was stepping down as CEO, and he recommended that the board transfer the title to Joe Ford. It was just such a transition that had impelled Case to explore the merger with Allied. The company, he said, would merge with a prosperous telephone company and acquire a fresh generation of vibrant management at the same time. Case's views were expressed in the company's internal newsletter shortly after his announcement:

There has always been a question of succession in our company. In fact, even before we considered the Allied merger, I made a list of three or four people who, if I were to be incapacitated, the board might look to as a replacement. One of the names on that list was Joe Ford. If you look back over the past few years, we have purposely had Joe Ford assume a great many areas of responsibility. For instance, Joe Ford has served on the

Chairman Weldon Case stepped down in 1987 as CEO of ALLTEL, turning over the reins to President Joe Ford.

board of the United States Telephone Association and the National Exchange Carriers Association. So you can see this is not a sudden decision, nor is it contrived. Rather it is something we have obviously been working toward for some time. It has all worked out exactly as planned.

Although no two people have the same personalities, I think Mr. Ford's objectives and mine have been more parallel than anybody I can think of— Joe and I have often spoken of that.[4]

For his part, Ford said little would change as a result of the new responsibilities.

Since the merger, Ford and Bobbitt had maintained executive offices in the riverfront office build-ing in Little Rock that Allied had finished shortly before the merger. Both had commuted frequently to Hudson, Ohio, the headquarters of Mid-Continent and then of ALLTEL. Gradually, the Little Rock complex would become the headquarters of the

---

Joe Ford, right, discusses telephone operations with top executives. From left, seated: Max E. Bobbitt, executive vice president and chief financial officer; Andre C. Belair, Northeast regional president; James F. Gadberry, Southwest regional president; and Frederick G. Griech, executive vice president for telephone operations; standing: Herbert H. McGaughey, Ohio regional president; and John T. Dunbar, Southern regional president.

nationwide operations, but Ford refused in an interview in 1987 to say that Little Rock was "the power center" of the company. If anything, a Stephens Inc. analyst said, "The company plane may be the power center."[5]

A Company of Winners

In 1990, Hugh Wilbourn, the founder of Allied and a director of ALLTEL, retired. Twenty years earlier, he had passed the torch to Joe Ford, his son-in-law. Though business analysts and the media credited Ford with being the entrepreneurial spirit behind the corporation's rapid acquisitions in the 1980s, Wilbourn and Ford shared similar philosophies. To both, employees and customer service were the keys to a successful business. "Our employees are our obvious strength," the new CEO said.[6]

Every year ALLTEL conducted employee training seminars, customer surveys, and motivational sessions, emphasizing that all of the company's success comes at the point where its employees interact with a customer. In a 1987 message to employees, the management cited a federal Small Business Administration study that concluded that only 14 percent of customers who leave a business do so because they are dissatisfied with the product and fewer still leave because of the price. Sixty-eight percent leave because the employees make them feel they aren't important. "Not at ALLTEL," Ford asserted.[7] As all aspects of the telephone business became more competitive, customer service grew more important than ever. "Our ability to sell in the competitive arena is not due just to our products, because other companies offer the same ones, but it is due primarily to our people and their ability to compete. Winners thrive on competition, and we want a company of winners," Ford told employees.[8]

ALLTEL was a favorite of security analysts and financial writers. Ford told the New York Security Analysts in December 1986 that the company had made the transition from a local telephone company to a high-tech growth company. It ranked 424th in net income among the *Forbes* 500 largest corporations, 492nd in sales per employee, 381st in assets per employee, and 278th in profits per employee.

The January 12, 1987, *Forbes* issue named ALLTEL the most improved company in the telecommunications industry. It noted that ALLTEL had experienced a 147.1 percent increase in its stock price over the previous five years—spectacular for that era. The magazine went on to emphasize ALLTEL's success:

> *Since the 1983 merger that formed ALLTEL, the company has bought into over 20 firms, including the acquisition of the 20,000-customer Heins Telephone of Sanford, N.C., and a $50 million partnership in three fiber-optic long-distance companies. And by spending $160 million annually on plant and equipment, Case has given his acquisitions a revenue boost that sent earnings per share for 1986 up by 8.7 percent, yielding 11.2 percent in net profits.*
>
> *The result? While ALLTEL is the smallest company of the top 20 on our list, its return on equity of 15.4 percent is among the best in the industry. During 1986 Wall Street responded accordingly, boosting ALLTEL's stock price by 50 percent during the year, to $41 recently.*[9]

ALLTEL's growth and earnings record in the seven years after it came into being were nothing less than phenomenal. In 1989, it posted a 10 percent dividend increase on common stock, ringing up its twenty-ninth consecutive increase that reached back to the formation of Mid-Continent in 1960. And stockholders received an additional dividend that year in the form of a three-for-two stock split—the second three-for-two stock split in two years. It would be tough to keep pace with such success, but during the next decade, ALLTEL would prove that it was, indeed, the best in the business.

In 1993, Systematics began serving customers from its new $20 million Technology Center—one of the nation's most advanced information processing facilities. *(Photo by Eric Myer.)*

CHAPTER TEN

THE INFORMATION SERVICES ARENA

1990–1999

Unlike some others in the telecommunications industry, ALLTEL, as an independent telecommunications company, is not prohibited from providing information services.

—Joe Ford[1]

TELEPHONES AND COMPUTERS followed a parallel history. Three decades before Bell cast his voice for the first time over a telephone, Charles Babbage and Augusta Ada King, the Countess of Lovelace and daughter of the English poet Lord Byron, designed a steam-powered "Analytical Engine," which, like a modern computer, could store a program, perform calculations, and print the results. But by the time German engineer Konrad Zuse built the first binary digital computer in 1938, the telephone was rapidly becoming universal.

World War II sped the development of computer technology just as it did telecommunications. And after the invention of the transistor in 1948 and then the integrated circuit ten years later, computers became progressively smaller, faster, more versatile, and more powerful. The development of programming language and the ability to store and change instructions for specific programs made them for the first time cost effective and productive for widespread use in business. A computer could print invoices and then seconds later calculate paychecks or design products. Both the purposes and the science of telephony and computing began then to converge.

The commercial potential of transmitting vast quantities of data over telephone wires was not lost on the industry. AT&T foresaw the possibilities, and Bell Laboratories was an early developer of computer technology. By the late 1960s, the Federal Communications Commission began looking at the relationship between telephony and computing and whether the government needed to regulate the competition that would surely ensue.

But it was not until 1990 that communications companies turned the long-talked-about convergence of voice and data into reality. ALLTEL was one of the first to leap into information services, and it was the most controversial move the company had made. The company would be both praised and doubted for its boldness in straying from the telephone business after it acquired a firm headquartered down the road from ALLTEL in Little Rock that had quietly become the nation's leading provider of data-processing services and software for the financial services industry.

To enhance its future earnings growth, ALLTEL entered a new core business area—information services—by adding fast-growing Systematics in 1990.

Systematics on Top

Systematics, Inc., was a classic entrepreneurial company. It was founded by employees who discerned a need in their industry that no one was serving and who had the gumption to try to fill it.

Walter V. Smiley, carrying degrees in industrial management and business administration from the University of Arkansas, landed a job as a systems engineer with IBM in the 1960s and soon left the company to become the data-processing manager for the First National Bank of Fayetteville in Arkansas. At that time, the data-processing industry was still rudimentary. Standardized software packages were rare. Only a few small service bureaus existed, so most banks found a way to process their own data. Smiley formed a friendship with the young data managers at two other banks, David Frantz and Hunter Gammill. After sharing frustrations, the three men started talking about a software development cooperative in which they would pool their knowledge, with one writing a loan system, another writing a deposit system, and so on. The banks, however, were resistant. Smiley was told he had a good idea but that he needed a venture capitalist.

Jon Jacoby, an executive vice president at Stephens Inc., the large Little Rock investment firm whose founder had sold the first telephone

company to Hugh Wilbourn and Charlie Miller, introduced Smiley to Jackson T. "Jack" Stephens, the Stephens president. They talked about the concept of a business that would offer data services to banks and other financial institutions, and Stephens agreed to provide $400,000 in capital. Thus in October 1968, Systematics, Inc., was born. Jacoby became a founding director and remained on the board into the 1990s. Stephens's only advice to the enterprise's founders was to "do what you say you'll do. If you make a mistake, fix it. And think long term."[2] It would not be Stephens's last role in the development of either Systematics or the telephone company with which it would eventually merge.

But it was hard to think long term in those days. Systematics started with eight employees and one customer, Union Life Insurance Company, owned, coincidentally, by Stephens. Systematics handled Union's data processing by remote from a small office at 411 Victory Street in downtown Little Rock.

"Our thoughts then were, 'There's a need, so let's go into business,'" recalled Smiley, the company's first CEO. "We weren't thinking about what we would become but about what to do the next morning. Our company was formed to fill the gap that existed, to satisfy the financial community's needs, and to try to solve many problems that had made them unhappy with their computer services."[3]

Systematics' idea was to combine many of the duplicated functions that were inherent in stand-alone data-processing services and to take advantage of the excess computer capacity that existed in most installations. Bankers, like other business executives, were excited about the potential of computer power, but the technology of the day was expensive and required leading-edge technologists and relentless software development to keep up with the expanding power of computers. Banks that could afford it bought big computer systems and hired programmers to develop custom software for them. Smiley's team understood banking and offered banks a chance

Walter Smiley founded Systematics in 1968 after realizing the need for a more advanced data-processing company.

to outsource their data processing (the term then was "facilities management") and thereby concentrate on banking and save money. Systematics advertised itself as "the will-do company with can-do people."

In 1969, Systematics started a centralized data center to process transactions for banks that didn't want to start such a data center in-house. Smiley's former employer, the First National Bank of Fayetteville, became its first banking client. There were the usual rough times for a start-up company. To cover one of its early payrolls, three employees had to drive to Mississippi to get a check from a customer, drive back to Little Rock, and deposit it. It would be nearly two years, June 1970, before Systematics had its first profitable quarter, but it never had another unprofitable one.

In 1972, the company stepped up its services. For larger institutions, generally those with deposits ranging from $250 million to $10 billion, it became a bank's data-processing department, furnishing innovative software, people, and equipment. It became a business partner with each bank, supplying custom services for that institution for five-year contracts. These facilities-management contracts would make up 90 percent of its business. For smaller financial institutions, it used remote processing contracts under which processing was done at remote locations that served several clients. Because its services were highly standardized, Systematics enjoyed economies of scale that individual banks didn't have, so it could usually provide services to the banks at a savings of 10 to 20 percent.

The company expanded at a rate the founders had never imagined. Banks outside the state, starting with the Bossier City Bank and Trust of Bossier City, Louisiana, hired Systematics as their facilities manager. By the end of 1977, both Systematics' revenue and the number of employees had nearly doubled from the previous year. The company became a national force that year, helped by the collapse of one of its largest competitors, and the pace would hardly slow.

ALLTEL Information Services keeps track of banking transactions around the world.

Shawne S. Leach, vice president of financial planning and performance analysis for ALLTEL, was a financial officer for Union National Bank in the 1970s, when Systematics presented its case for handling the bank's accounts. "My impression was that it focused strongly on problem solving and creating solutions," she said. "It was very customer-service oriented. They were very interested in understanding what the customer needed to achieve and finding a solution for that client objective. The company was filled with people who were thoughtful and who focused on creating new things, whether it was a new system or a new procedure or whatever it took to satisfy the client. Even now, I find that unit of ALLTEL to have the same sort of mindset."[4]

In 1980, Systematics diversified and began marketing software packages, commercial loans, deposits, financial management, and customer-information files, but it did so with some trepidation. "There was a great deal of concern at the time that if we sold customers software as stand-alone packages, they wouldn't need us," remembered Jerry Hart, a Systematics executive. "But the decision to sell software proved to be a wise one. Not only has it broadened the company's customer base, it has proven to be a very profitable segment of the business."[5]

On August 12, 1981, Systematics issued its first publicly traded common stock, eight hundred thousand shares on the over-the-counter market. Taking the company public raised its visibility, accelerated its growth, and gave employees a chance to own part of the company. Its revenues had grown from $13.3 million in the pivotal year of 1977 to $36.3 million.

At the same time, it announced the construction of a $35 million campus-style corporate headquarters on the western edge of Little Rock. By then, the company had a major presence across much of the South and beyond, and it had been looking at building its headquarters in a larger commercial center such as Memphis or Dallas. Systematics, however, decided to stay in Little Rock, which had a more stable economy and labor market, and began buying land owned by Charles M. Taylor near the crest of a bluff over the Arkansas River. Taylor's twelve-hundred-acre estate, which he called Pleasant Valley Farms,

raised Welsh ponies, Hampshire sheep, and cattle, and it was this picturesque farm and quail preserve that would become the growing Systematics campus. The architectural plans, which the company followed for the next twenty years, called for maintaining the rustic beauty of the terrain, developing an existing water course, and providing streets that avoided straight-line cuts through the trees so that employees and visitors could enjoy the outside beauty from every vantage point. The campus had a lodge for visiting executives and for employees who came to Little Rock for training. In 1984, it added a second building, in 1990 a third, and in 1993 a fourth, a seven-story technology center.

By the mid-1980s, a few of the nation's largest banks had contracted to outsource their data processing to Systematics. In the last six

months of 1987, the company announced nine new contracts with financial institutions, and in January 1988 it announced a cash dividend of $2 a share, compared with the usual quarterly 3 cents a share. A month later it announced eight more contracts with a combined value of more than $70 million over five years. It expanded overseas in 1987, contracting with CAP Financial Services of London and Bank Negara Indonesia of Jakarta. In another six years it would serve more than forty clients in thirty-four foreign countries and would open regional offices in London, Hong Kong, Singapore, and Bangkok.

John E. Steuri, assistant group executive of IBM's U.S. Marketing and Services Group at New Canaan, Connecticut, succeeded Smiley as CEO in October 1988. (Smiley stayed on as chairman for a time.) In the next quarter, the company reported a 20.8 percent increase in earnings, entered into eight new contracts with banks in the United States, and contracted to provide software to the Bank of the Philippine Islands in Manila, United Overseas Bank of Singapore, the Chase Manhattan Bank of Singapore, a branch of the United Overseas Bank in Hong Kong, and the Banco de Bogota in Colombia. In February 1989 Systematics signed a software leasing agreement with Manufacturers Hanover Trust Company, the nation's seventh largest bank, for which the advertising value was immense. Under the multimillion-dollar contract, the bank licensed Systematics' full line of integrated financial software for its retail-banking sector. Systematics was on quite a roll. It was regularly beating its toughest competitor, the Dallas-based Electronic Data Systems, the computer unit of General Motors, even in EDS's backyard. In February 1990, Systematics signed a ten-year deal with the $5 billion Team Bank of Fort Worth, which had forty-eight branch locations in Texas.

By the winter of 1989–90, Systematics was the top provider of data processing and software for financial institutions in the country, beating out EDS and IBM. Its sales were growing at a clip that sometimes hit 50 percent in a year, and it had contracted with megabanks like Manufacturers Hanover Trust, Republic National Bank, and California Federal Savings and Loan, each after extensive competitive analysis. Financial analysts were uniformly bullish about the company's stock. "We regard Systematics as the best-positioned banking software and data-processing-services provider in the country," wrote Alex, Brown & Sons. The committed long-term revenues of its data-processing services, the analysts observed, supported the more volatile, faster-growing, higher-profit-margin software-products industry.[6]

Systematics was making inroads into the top 490 banks and thrifts, where other software vendors had failed. Moreover, unlike its competitors, it

The courtyard of ALLTEL Information Services' campus in Little Rock offers a spectacular view of nature, which was carefully preserved during construction of the buildings.

had a large base of recurring revenues, most of it under contracts of five to ten years. Its service operations also gave it immediate feedback for its software-development group, raising the reliability of its software products. And the prospects for future growth were rosy, making Systematics a very appealing target for acquisition.

A New Hat for ALLTEL

Ford and the top ALLTEL brass had been talking about such an acquisition for several years and, indeed, there had been some discussion with Systematics' CEO and its largest shareholder in 1987. ALLTEL had a couple of advantages over other suitors. First, the regional Bell operating companies were prohibited by Judge Greene's Modified Final Judgment in the AT&T divestiture case from owning or offering information services, although that restriction was expected to be lifted sometime in the 1990s, perhaps as early as 1993. Investment analysts like Salomon Brothers expected the regional Bells to dive into the financial services market when they were permitted.[7] Independent telecommunications companies like ALLTEL, however, had no such limitations.

Moreover, Jack Stephens, whose control of 5.42 million shares accounted for 48 percent of the stock of Systematics, would sell to no one but ALLTEL. Stephens and his elder brother, Witt, had both a proprietary and a fatherly interest in the telephone company first organized by Hugh Wilbourn and Charlie Miller. Wilbourn and Miller had taken care of Witt's little hometown telephone company in the 1940s, stringing a line out to Witt and Jack's mother's house in rural Prattsville, and then had bought the company from Witt on credit. The brothers from time to time had arranged critical financing for Allied Telephone Company, and Stephens Inc. had acted as broker and investment adviser for ALLTEL, most recently in the purchase of CP National and the subsequent sale of natural gas and other properties that did not fit ALLTEL's long-term strategy.

The investment company, however, to avoid the appearance of a less-than-arms-length transaction, would play no such role in the ALLTEL-Systematics merger. The exchange of stock in the

transaction would leave Stephens as ALLTEL's largest shareholder, with about 8.7 percent of the outstanding shares.

Joe Ford and Systematics CEO John Steuri signed the definitive agreement on March, 2, 1990, subject to the approval of shareholders in April. ALLTEL would buy the data-processing company for about $530 million worth of new ALLTEL stock. Each share of Systematics stock would be exchanged tax free for 1.325 shares of ALLTEL stock. Systematics shares closed that day on the over-the-counter market at $30.25 a share and ALLTEL's at $33 a share in New York Stock Exchange composite trading. Systematics would be a wholly owned subsidiary but would continue to operate independently, with its own board of directors. Steuri and Ford issued this joint statement:

As we move further into the information age, technology and market forces are increasingly blurring the distinction between the telecommunications and the information services industries. The strategic merger of ALLTEL and Systematics is consistent with the convergence of these industries and gives the company proven capabilities and a strong customer base on which to build. In addition to the future opportunities this combination provides ... Systematics also brings a strong growth rate in earnings and cash flow to combine with ALLTEL's industry-leading financial performance.[8]

The combination produced a company with assets of more than $2.5 billion, annual revenues of $1.4 billion, net income of $175 million, and more than 11,200 employees.

Smiley, the Systematics founder, called the acquisition "a good synergy," and Ford termed it "a good fit." Smiley said ALLTEL's strong financial statement and its skills in acquisitions would help Systematics grow. On the other hand, Systematics' history of managing sophisticated computer centers should help ALLTEL manage its far-flung communications system.[9]

Executives of the companies had put together the deal quietly over about two weeks and announced it after the markets closed on Friday. Analysts professed surprise, and reactions were

ALLTEL Information Services has a proven track record of customized information technology solutions for its customers in the financial services and telecommunications marketplace.

mixed but decidedly favorable. Marianne Bye, an analyst with Shearson Lehman Hutton, called the merger "a major announcement."

It's a very big step into an area that's not exactly the same as ALLTEL has been involved in. But ALLTEL does have a successful record of diversifying and operating satellite businesses that enhance their overall core-business growth. Although it is certainly larger than some of their more recent non-core acquisitions, it does seem somewhat compatible with the way they have run their company in the past. Systematics has a superior reputation for quality.[10]

Jordan Cox, a data-processing and software industry analyst for the Johnston, Lemon & Company investment banking firm in Washington, D.C., predicted that the alliance would improve Systematics' ability to make acquisitions because it would be under the blanket protection of ALLTEL. On its own, an aggressive acquisition strategy would make people nervous because it could significantly damage operating earnings. He expected further acquisitions in industries outside banking that used data-processing expertise, and indeed ALLTEL would almost immediately expand into other industries.

Future Synergies

The lack of concrete examples of voice and data actually converging bothered other analysts, however. James Stork of the Duff & Phelps securities firm in Chicago said the merger presented opportunities "that aren't even imagined right now" but that the synergies were nebulous in the short term. He considered it more a financial transaction than a long-term strategy for harmonizing the two technologies.[11] Systematics' five-year average growth of 20 percent in revenues and 25 percent in income would elevate ALLTEL's solid but slower growth rates of 7.7 percent in revenues and 14.2 percent in income on its telephone, sales, and supply operations.

But the wisdom of the acquisition must be examined from the perspective of ALLTEL at that time, as Jim Hillis, a Systematics veteran who became vice president of ALLTEL's human resource development, pointed out. "While deregulation was clearly on the horizon, ALLTEL was a regulated telephone company with limited growth potential," he said. "If you looked at the information technology industry, you would have said, 'Here's someplace we can guess the amount of capital that we have available to us, and here's where we can get something that generates greater growth for the entire enterprise. That really was the underpinnings of the deal. On top of that was some perception of synergies between information technology and communication, but it was pretty much future oriented."[12]

The merger, Hillis observed, brought together different corporate cultures, one an operating culture (ALLTEL) and the other a sales culture. One company was accustomed to dealing with commercial bankers in large cities and institutions around the world, the other with residential and business customers in small towns and regional cities. But the cultures homogenized.

Although ALLTEL could only vaguely foresee the future ways in which the convergence of technologies might be fruitful, the consolidation promised one nearly immediate and compelling benefit. ALLTEL's own data-processing costs had risen 25 percent over a few years. Ford had concluded by 1987 that those costs had to come under control. ALLTEL also found it hard for a telephone company to attract and keep bright "techies," while a high-tech company like Systematics had no such trouble.

Though Jack Stephens and Walter Smiley had come to ALLTEL headquarters in 1987 to talk about a merger, it wasn't until 1990 that Systematics felt it had "its ship in order," according to Ford. In addition to streamlining ALLTEL's data-processing costs, Systematics also had a higher growth rate than ALLTEL, which was still largely regulated. "We knew the technology was changing and that there would be more opportunities for using computers in communications, but we didn't know exactly how," Ford said.[13]

The Virtuoso Jewel

Systematics became a part of the ALLTEL family on May 21, 1990. Six months later, the cele-

ALLTEL Information Services monitors customer transactions from around the world at its Little Rock, Arkansas, headquarters. *(Photo by Eric Myer.)*

brated synergy of the move came into sharper focus when ALLTEL signed a letter of intent to acquire the cellular telephone billing and information system of the Pennsylvania-based C-TEC Corporation. C-TEC was a diversified telecommunications and high-technology company that provided telephone, mobile, cable television, information, and communications services to a broad range of customers. It also had been an old client of ALLTEL Supply.

Systematics paid C-TEC $12 million for the rights to its Virtuoso software and some $3.6 million in royalties on new licensing fees. Significantly, C-TEC also entered into a long-term outsourcing arrangement for Systematics to provide nearly all data-processing services for C-TEC's telephone, cellular, and cable television operations. Systematics expected revenues from the management contract with C-TEC to range from $8 million to $12 million.

Gaining rights to C-TEC's Virtuoso software proved to be a coup for ALLTEL, which had been looking for a company to provide billing for ALLTEL Mobile Communications, its cellular telephone subsidiary. Virtuoso, which operated on both IBM's AS/400 and larger mainframes, was clearly the best system in operation in the country. Thus ALLTEL ended up with the best software for a cellular information system, plus the marketing and operating experience of the nation's most successful data-processing outsourcing company.

For twenty-two years, Systematics had provided data-processing services and had leased software to financial institutions. With the C-TEC acquisition, it was entering an entirely new field with vast opportunities for expansion, for now it could offer telecommunications companies the same benefits that it offered banks and thrifts. Its new Telecommunication Services Division could lease the Virtuoso software, or it could handle companies' data processing through an outsourcing agreement—both at considerable savings—and let the companies concentrate on what they did best. Virtuoso handled billing, credit and collections, equipment tracking, account processing, and the management of sales leads.

Virtuoso proved to be extraordinarily agile as well. By the end of the year, Systematics began a massive development project to enhance the Virtuoso billing and customer-information

management system for the needs of the United Kingdom and the world's first major personal communications network (PCN), assembled by Mercury One-2-One in London. After sixty thousand development hours—including consulting; problem management; and technical, operations, and business-process support—the enhanced Virtuoso system became operational in September 1993 and would expand to more than 60 percent of the United Kingdom by 1995.

Data Meets Voice

Despite the naysayers, it was the burgeoning telecommunications industry that offered a great opportunity for Systematics to expand. ALLTEL dramatically increased its market share in August 1993 when Systematics reached a ten-year agreement to process all the customer-service and billing records of GTE's cellular telephone operations. Terry Parker, GTE president of Telecommunications Products and Services, said Systematics had the most sophisticated software and outsourcing expertise in the country. A few months later Systematics added another major client when it signed a ten-year contract to provide complete outsourcing services for Citizens Utilities' 750,000-line telephone operations. It would run Citizens' billing, customer-service information, and engineering.

Personal communications services (PCS), an alternative form of wireless communications, offered another new and potentially dynamic market for which Systematics developed Virtuoso II, an advanced wireless customer-care and billing software. Virtuoso II eliminated many of the multi-step procedures that plagued other customer-record systems so that companies could develop competitively priced rate packages in a matter of hours rather than weeks. In 1997, ALLTEL implemented the Virtuoso II software in GTE's first PCS markets—Cincinnati, Seattle, and Spokane. The Virtuoso program was so uniquely beneficial that the International Engineering Consortium gave ALLTEL its 1997 InfoVision Award, which salutes products and services introduced over the previous year that have added new dimensions to the communications industry and to society. The software continued to be useful into the late 1990s. In 1999, under a $200 million contract, ALLTEL delivered its

As its financial service clients expanded into new markets to provide more convenient banking, ALLTEL expanded its software and service offerings to meet their needs. *(Photo by Eric Myer.)*

Virtuoso II system to Hughes Ispat Limited, a consortium that was building a wireless local loop system for Bombay, India.

Bigger Systematics

Backed by ALLTEL's strong financial statement, Systematics could follow a more aggressive acquisition strategy, and it wasted no time. In May 1990, at about the same time it closed the deal with ALLTEL, Systematics announced it would acquire Horizon Financial Software Corporation of Orlando, Florida, and consolidate it with its Mid-Range Systems Division, which had been established in 1989 to serve banks and thrifts with assets in the $100 million–$400 million range. Horizon was Systematics' chief competitor in the small-banking market. In October, Systematics bought Computer Dynamics of Little Rock, a mortgage-data processor that serviced two hundred thousand loans for banks and thrifts in six states. Then in February 1991 it bought Systems Limited of Hong Kong, a banking software firm that serviced clients involved in worldwide activities such as import-export documentation in France, India, Hong Kong, Singapore, Taiwan, Korea, and Indonesia.

Meanwhile, Systematics continued to add clients almost by the week. In December 1991 it announced the largest contract in its history with City National Bank of Beverly Hills, California, a ten-year deal that was worth between $350 million and $500 million. Systematics would service not only City National but about two hundred smaller banks that formerly had been serviced by City National. By winter's end, Systematics' backlog of committed revenues had surpassed $1 billion, up from $730.7 million a year earlier.

Lending Solutions

Despite its run of successes, Systematics seemed to be peaking by 1992, mainly because of the massive consolidation in the banking industry, which was the foundation of Systematics' business. Thus the company set out to diversify into rapidly growing sectors outside banking and telecommunications.

One such diverse sector was the mortgage industry. On February 28, 1992, Systematics became the nation's leading provider of software and processing services to companies that service single-family loans when ALLTEL purchased Computer Power Inc., a privately held company headquartered in Jacksonville, Florida. Founded in 1964, CPI was the nation's largest third-party processor of single-family mortgage loans. Its clients included about half of the top one hundred mortgage banks and top one hundred commercial banks, plus more than a third of the top one hundred savings and loans. Like Systematics, it also licensed its software products and provided consulting, training, portfolio conversion, and other services. Combined, Systematics and CPI processed nearly fifteen million mortgage loans. CPI became a division of Systematics Information Services, and eventually, as ALLTEL Residential Lending Solutions, it would become the most profitable part of ALLTEL's information services.

Jeffrey H. Fox, who at that time was with Stephens Inc. but who later would join ALLTEL to help run its information services, headed the due diligence panel for the ALLTEL/CPI deal. "The thing I most appreciated was how Jim Milligan and Bruce Andrews [of CPI] didn't answer the questions I asked, but they talked a lot. They thought they were answering my questions. I was young at the time, and they treated me like a kid with an assignment. But instead of being offended, I was tickled. It just told me more about them as people—that they were strong and independent-minded. It was a good business with good people, and that's what you want to buy."[14] Both Milligan and Andrews would join ALLTEL in senior management roles.

CPI's birth had been similar to Systematics'. When people mail their mortgage checks each month, the checks must be recorded and processed so that part of each one goes into escrow for insurance and real-estate tax payments and part to the holders of the mortgage. The escrow must be disbursed to the local government and the insurance carrier, and all of this data must be translated into usable information for the banks and mortgage companies.

Lowell Dent, founder and chairman of CPI, offered computer processing to local mortgage companies through a small service bureau and was frustrated that each client's job had to be done from scratch. He found a way to break each job into a series of standard steps. As a transaction moved through the system, it would trigger a separate software program to handle each task. Amazingly, he found it could offer these services to mortgage companies without making many changes in the process. With financial backing from David Hicks, who was then comptroller of Stockton, Whatley and Davin, one of the largest mortgage companies in the country, Computer Power Inc. was born.

In 1994, ALLTEL built a headquarters building for its mortgage operations in Jacksonville, Florida, which became home of ALLTEL Residential Lending Solutions. The building housed the twelve hundred mortgage-service employees and included state-of-the-art training, service, computer, and satellite facilities. Three years later, ALLTEL's mortgage-serving operations became the first service bureau in the country to integrate with Mortgage Electronic Registration Systems Inc. (MERS), the industry-owned utility designed to streamline the real-estate finance industry.

By century's end, the mortgage division would be the most profitable part of ALLTEL's information services operations. It owned more than half the national market (more than twenty million loans in 2000 were being processed on ALLTEL's mortgage-servicing package), and its clients included sixty of the top one hundred mortgage operations in the country.

In August 2000, ALLTEL announced it would offer a business-to-business mortgage-related billing and payment system called NewInvoice that would enable lenders to use the Internet to present, process, and pay default-related invoices.

That same month, the company signed an agreement to provide Internet technology to process mortgages for PricelineMortgage, the mortgage service available through Priceline.com. Consumers would be able to name their own mortgage terms, get guaranteed closing costs, and lock in their rate in as little as thirty minutes through the ALLTEL platform.

Also in August, ALLTEL announced a ten-year software agreement with Bank One Corporation, the nation's fourth-largest bank holding company, in which Bank One would utilize ALLTEL's Advanced Loan System for consumer lending, business banking, and community banking.

ALLTEL Residential Lending Solutions' phenomenal success sprang from two strategies. First, rather than develop a great technology and find problems to apply it to, the company's strategy was to identify a problem for the industry and then develop technology to solve it. Second, ALLTEL Residential Lending Solutions became a business partner with clients, working with them regularly to develop strategies and technologies to meet their goals. "Most companies in the technology business have attempted to provide solutions with pure technologists and then formed user groups or steering committees or something of that nature for analytical purposes," said Jim Milligan, president of ALLTEL Residential Lending Solutions. "We went beyond that. We not only worked with our clients, we actually hired their people."[15] Between two hundred and three hundred of Residential Lending Solutions' employees had been in the mortgage-banking industry.

In March 2000, ALLTEL Residential Lending Solutions formed a new company to provide mortgage administration and information technology solutions to the mortgage lending industry in the United Kingdom, with plans to expand into Europe. ALLTEL Mortgage Solutions, Ltd., was a joint venture with Bradford & Bingley Group of West Yorkshire, England, one of the leading mortgage lenders in the United Kingdom. ALLTEL owned 75 percent of the venture and provided the overall direction for the business.

Healthy Involvement

Another fetching target for ALLTEL in the midst of the heavy banking consolidation was healthcare, a sure-enough growth industry in 1992, when it was the national political preoccupation. In 1992 Systematics signed its first outsourcing agreement with a healthcare organization, Beverly Enterprises, the nation's largest nursing home chain. Then on October 1, 1993, ALLTEL acquired TDS Healthcare Systems Corporation, the world's largest privately held company that developed and marketed information systems software for the healthcare industry. TDS provided data processing for two hundred hospitals in the United States, Canada, and Europe.

Within three months of acquiring TDS, Systematics signed its first hospital-outsourcing contract at St. Joseph's Hospital in Parkersburg, West Virginia. In addition to billing and accounting services, Systematics developed the TDS 7000 Series software, which gave qualified physicians and other hospital workers instant access to a patient's lifetime medical history and records. There would be a growing need for the software as the healthcare industry evolved toward regional enterprises and as managing patient information became critical to controlling both the quality of care and its cost.

On November 1, 1994, ALLTEL acquired Medical Data Technology, a privately held company in Roseland, New Jersey, that provided data services to hospitals in the northeastern United States. Three years later, on January 24, 1997, ALLTEL joined Integrated Healthcare Solutions to create a new company that would provide healthcare information services worldwide. The new company, Eclipsys Corporation, united the employees and assets of ALLTEL Information Services-Healthcare and Integrated Healthcare Solutions. ALLTEL received $154 million in cash and took an equity position in the new company.

Solid Backing

Still, growth was sluggish by Joe Ford's standards, and the separate corporate cultures of the parent and the information subsidiary had not fully integrated. In 1994, Ford persuaded an old friend, William L. Cravens, to come out of retirement and be a troubleshooter for Systematics and ALLTEL's other information services. As an engineer, accountant, and sometime commercial banker, Cravens had worked with Allied Telephone

William Cravens brought a vast amount of experience to ALLTEL when he joined Systematics in 1994. He would later become the chairman of ALLTEL Information Services.

Company, Systematics, and ALLTEL and knew the operations and Joe Ford as intimately as anyone outside the company's immediate management could. He had done accounting work for the old Allied Telephone Company in the 1960s, had been the first auditor of Systematics, and as a commercial banker had bought a communication system from Allied and become an important client of Systematics. Cravens took the title of vice chairman and chief administrative officer at Systematics, and within three years it would be a much different business.

"Joe's view of the company was that he had about sixteen thousand employees, 35 to 40 percent of whom were in wireline business, a noncompetitive regulated industry," Cravens recalled. "Another 15 to 20 percent were in the cellular business, which was in a duopoly, and they really did not know what competition was. Then you had information services with 40 to 50 percent of the employees supporting primarily the banking industry. They thought they were competitive, but they really weren't. They were servicing smaller and mid-sized institutions that were rapidly being merged, and they had not really figured out how to attack and play in that marketplace."[16]

One reason Jack Stephens had been more than agreeable to the idea of merging Systematics and ALLTEL as far back as 1987, when Ford first broached it, was that he discerned the trend toward consolidation in the banking industry. There were even predictions that before the end of the century, all banking in the United States would be in the hands of no more than ten vast financial institutions. That prediction was amiss, but bank consolidation did accelerate in the 1990s, sped along by new federal banking legislation that had the effect of encouraging mergers and acquisitions.

Systematics traditionally had served the small and mid-sized institutions, but those institutions were consolidating with larger banks that performed their own data processing. As Stephens had calculated, the loss of this business slowed the company's growth by 1992. Somehow, Systematics needed to reach more of the large nationwide banks. Stephens had figured that ALLTEL's prestigious logo and capital base would give Systematics an entrée to the big banks, but though the ALLTEL brand had unquestionably opened doors, it hadn't come through to the extent that either he, Ford, or Steuri had hoped.

A key step to remedy this shortfall was to actually adopt the ALLTEL name, so in 1995 Systematics and the other divisions formed ALLTEL Information Services (AIS). The status and respect surrounding the ALLTEL name would help immensely in securing major clients as well as with acquisitions.

Cravens concluded early that the company needed youthful managers with keener competitive impulses. He talked to Ford about hiring Scott Ford, the CEO's son, away from Stephens Inc. "Absolutely not," Ford said; the family connection would be intolerable. Ford would later relent on his decision, but for now the younger Ford stayed with Stephens. Cravens also wanted to hire Jeffrey Fox from Stephens. Fox was a merger-and-acquisitions and corporate-finance specialist who had handled some of ALLTEL's acquisitions, including CPI, and Cravens was impressed by the way Fox quickly dissected a business. In February 1996, Fox joined ALLTEL Information Services as senior vice president for business development and special assistant to the chief operating officer. Six months later, he became the group president.

Fine-Tuning

Healthcare wasn't the only business that came under the magnifying glass. Fox evaluated each of AIS's businesses logically, weighing trends, leadership teams, and people. As Fox himself pointed out, he was recruited to run ALLTEL Information Services, to reevaluate its businesses, and to reorganize it, and that's what he did. Throughout the 1990s, ALLTEL repositioned itself, fine-tuning its

Jeffrey Fox, group president for ALLTEL Information Services, helped fine-tune and expand the business so that by the end of the decade, it had clients who did business in more than fifty countries.

services so that it was a more strategic, customer-focused business.

At the same time, the company continued offering top-of-the-line software and innovative conveniences to its customers. ALLTEL Information Services, in fact, was one of the first companies to introduce Internet banking capabilities to the banking industry. In 1995, when people were first realizing the value of the Internet as a technological tool, the company formed a strategic partnership with a small company in Atlanta called S1. "Given our interest in banking technology, we realized the power the Internet could provide for our customers and our customers' customers in the delivery of financial services," said David Slider, senior vice president and managing director for ALLTEL Financial Services' EMEA operations (Europe, Middle East, Africa). "We were able to bring together S1's software application with our operating capabilities and customers and introduce an Internet banking solution literally months and months before competitive offerings were able to take a product to their customers."[17]

A Consolidating Industry

The greatest challenge still was ALLTEL Information Services' inability to compete for the business of the megabanks as the small and mid-sized institutions vanished. In time, ALLTEL would learn to compete—it would learn to move fast and be flexible—but the rapid-fire consolidation in the banking industry made it tough for AIS to grow. As Fox pointed out, "We managed to grow our business despite consolidation. Bigger clients tend to buy differently from small or mid-sized clients. We have economies of scale to deliver in certain areas to anybody, big or small, so when a big client buys a small or mid-sized client, our whole value to the organization has to be transitioned, and sometimes that's hard to do."[18]

Despite the inherent transitional problems brought on by the consolidation shoot-out, Systematics did indeed grow. In 1992, the company added Chemical Banking Corporation, the country's second-largest financial institution, and NationsBank, the fourth-largest bank, to its client list, but they would be more than just two more clients. With NationsBank, the company developed the framework for the Model Banking Program, which reduced the number of redundant data-processing products, minimized the proliferation of systems, and implemented standard products and services quickly without interrupting service. The revolutionary program assisted in converting more than thirty-nine million customers to the NationsBank customer-information system and reshaped the sales and service environment for all the bank's locations.

NationsBank and BankAmerica merged in September 1998, and the resulting Bank of America became the third-largest financial organization in the world and the largest bank holding company in the United States with assets of $618 billion. The merger obviously would be a major blow to the software provider of one or the other of the companies, ALLTEL or M&I Data Services, but Bank of America ended up choosing ALLTEL—for a number of reasons.[19]

First, NationsBank had already standardized all of its data processing throughout the bank system and had integrated the banking centers and telephone banking. The old BankAmerica, on the other hand, ran its retail processing on three separate systems. M&I's software supported New Mexico, Oregon, Nevada, Texas, and Arizona; the software of Hogan Systems was applied in Oregon and Washington; and the bank ran a proprietary system in California. ALLTEL's Model Banking Program supplanted all three. ALLTEL, in fact, estimated that it would save Bank of America $1.3 billion over two years.[20]

In addition, Bank of America's goal was to become a single bank, not just in name but in the services delivered to customers throughout its twenty-two-state franchise, and ALLTEL's services could help it do that. The bank would use ALLTEL's Impacs direct-deposit account system, its Savings Time system for certificates of deposit and individual retirement accounts, and its Advanced Loan System for consumer lending. "We believe standardization results in a common customer experience, lower costs in operating its infrastructure, and

greater speed to market," said Drew Lockhart, senior vice president of consumer and commercial services with Bank of America.[21]

The significance of Bank of America choosing ALLTEL for the conversion was not lost on the industry.

ALLTEL emerged similarly as the winner in three major mergers involving Chase Manhattan Bank. Chase had selected Systematics' retail suite in 1987. Then through Chase's successive mergers with Manufacturers Hanover and Chemical Banking, ALLTEL's system survived evaluation and testing by the best technologists in banking. When Chemical and Chase Manhattan merged in 1996 to form the second-largest bank in the United States, the new bank needed to consolidate on one set of retail systems to maintain uniform and quality service to its customers in more than fifty countries. It chose ALLTEL's full suite of retail software to complete one of the most complex mergers in banking history.

Playing in the Big Leagues

First Union Corporation, which built the third-largest branch-banking network in the United States and the sixth-largest banking company through one of the most aggressive acquisition programs in banking, began employing ALLTEL's applications in 1993. The key to First Union's rise was its ability to move fast after an acquisition to cut its costs and enhance its revenues. The company would credit ALLTEL's software solutions with much of its success. When First Union acquired CoreStates Financial Corporation in 1998, the CoreStates accounts were converted to the First Union platform of services in eight months, saving First Union $10 million a month.

Then in June 1999, when Chase Manhattan Corporation, First Union, and Wells Fargo & Company founded Spectrum LLC, an electronic bill presentment and payment hub for banks, it was almost natural that Spectrum would ultimately choose ALLTEL to build the platform for the system. More than a dozen banks signed letters of intent to participate in the hub, a sort of automated teller-machine network to pass bills and payments between participating banks. At the outset, Spectrum chose an Open Financial Exchange

(OFX) model designed by Just In Time Solutions of San Francisco and Cambridge Technology Partners in Cambridge, Massachusetts. But before the system was in place, Spectrum switched to the more sophisticated Interactive Financial Exchange (IFX) technical model bid by ALLTEL and Intelidata Inc. It was a coup for the two companies, which were chosen from an original list of fifty companies, nineteen of which had submitted proposals. The billing switch engineered by ALLTEL and Intelidata validated transactions and then routed, settled, and logged them. Mike Steely, director of e-business solutions with ALLTEL, said its IFX system carried much greater auditing capability than the OFX system of the other companies.[22]

The international market gave AIS some of its most sustainable growth throughout the decade. The company sold its proprietary banking and cellular billing software and other services in a growing number of countries around the world. ALLTEL had established a presence in some of the countries through its international consulting business as far back as the 1970s, when it was still the Mid-Continent and Allied telephone companies. In April 1994, the company signed the then-largest international software and services agreement in the company's history with the Savings Bank of the Russian Federation in Moscow. In 1995, it signed its first

international outsourcing contract with a bank in the Republic of the Philippines. In February 1997 it signed one of the largest outsourcing agreements, a $276 million, seven-year contract with Colonial, an Australian-based financial services provider. By 1999, ALLTEL had financial and telecommunications clients in more than fifty countries and territories. Its banking system products were installed in more than thirty leading international banks, including twenty-three of the fifty largest institutions in the world. And thanks to the wizardry of the people at AIS, the company's financial services customers approached the year 2000 with unusual serenity. On March 5, 1996, nearly four years before the momentous date, ALLTEL was able to offer its Year 2000 Solutions for its institutional clients around the world.

By the end of the century, ALLTEL's lending software had assumed a dominant share of the American market and a growing part of the global market. More than one of every three dollars of consumer debt—$2 trillion of the $5.9 trillion outstanding—was processed on ALLTEL software and computing systems. That included the mortgages processed by Residential Lending Solutions as well as automobile loans and other forms of consumer debt. The company's Advanced Loan System was the retail lending software chosen by more of the top one hundred banks than any other vendor's application. It also was installed in fourteen major banks around the world.

Two of the three largest captive automobile finance companies used the ALLTEL software. In 1999, ALLTEL formed an alliance with Ford Credit Corporation, the world's largest automotive finance company, to develop, implement, and market auto-finance software. ALLTEL previously supplied the software for

ALLTEL Information Services employees work alongside clients to meet their information technology needs.

PRIMUS, a Ford Credit financial services subsidiary that served dealers and customers outside the Ford franchise system, and for Fairlane Credit, a specialty finance affiliate of Ford Credit. David Slider observed that the agreement with Ford Credit "was the final proof statement that ALLTEL was the leading provider of consumer lending software to the top-tier financial institutions in the world."[23] Moreover, it transformed the company into the dominant provider of core automotive lending technology.

In 1999, ALLTEL Information Services merged with Advanced Information Resources and developed an Advanced Commercial Banking System, the number one commercial lending solution to automate and streamline commercial loan and trading deals that stretched across countries and currencies. The multilingual application, which covered the complete cycle of a loan, from prospecting to deal closing, servicing, portfolio management, and loan trading, appealed particularly to organizations that managed globally diverse portfolios of commercial loans. Sixteen of the largest fifty global banks had chosen the system by the spring of 2000.

The benefit of the experience with all the system conversions and integrations gained through the banking consolidations of the 1990s would pay off handsomely when the company had to develop programs for the integration of major wireline and wireless systems that became part of the ALLTEL family in a series of mergers and acquisitions in the last half of the decade.

As the century ended, ALLTEL Information Services pursued an aggressive acquisition strategy. In rapid order, it formed an alliance with London Bridge Software Holdings of London to market collection and debt-management tools and bought Corporate Solutions International, the top consumer-loan-origination product; Southern Data System, a front-end system for the community-bank market; ACE Software Sciences, which produced the workflow-based mortgage-servicing software known as MaxMilion, which is designed to enhance the workflow capabilities of ALLTEL's Mortgage Servicing Package; the ACquire Report Management and Data Warehouse System, a client/server report-management and data-warehouse system for community banks that could be delivered via the Internet, intranet, or proprietary network; and Benchmark Consulting International, a privately held Atlanta-based consulting firm that specialized in measuring, designing, and improving operations processes for more than 150 financial service providers.

But as Jeff Fox pointed out, the company was able to grow not just through acquisition but internally, by reinvesting in its resources. The company made acquisitions to bring more value to its customers. This was the same reason it invested in new software and chose highly knowledgeable people with high integrity to run the organization. The net result of all this reinvesting was to become more of a partner with the customer rather than a vendor.

Fox had learned through his experiences at Stephens Inc. that, as he phrased it, "Commitment follows cash." If a company was not committed to investing in things of value for its customers, those customers would stop buying from the company. Following this simple philosophy, it was logical that AIS should reinvest in its software, its people skills, its acquisitions, and its alliances. "We have continuously made investments in things that we think our customers can benefit from," he said. "We're trying to get in a position where it's a good investment for our customers to come ask us for more help because we actually know how to listen to them and translate that into things that are helpful. And sometimes when they ask for help, we were already thinking about it before them and have the solution available. That's the virtuous cycle that forms a partnership versus a vendor-customer relationship. If we don't reinvest and offer our customers something good tomorrow, then we're just a vendor; we're not a partner."[24]

During the ALLTEL decade of the 1990s, the company experienced unprecedented growth and made decisive moves to extend its brand, even acquiring the naming rights to the stadium in Jacksonville, Florida. ALLTEL Stadium was chosen to host the 2005 Super Bowl.

CHAPTER ELEVEN

THE ALLTEL DECADE

1991–1996

Deregulation and the Telecommunications Act of 1996 have given us a lot of opportunities that we did not have before. I really think that competition has been good for us. We were willing to take some calculated risk and move into competitive areas. I'm sure some companies were afraid of competition, but we looked at it as another opportunity to expand our business.

—Joe Ford[1]

O N THE EVE OF ALLTEL'S ANN-ual stockholders meeting in Hudson, Ohio, in April 1991, a Little Rock business journal carried an article called "The ALLTEL Decade," the second in a series of articles about the company. Industry analysts, *Arkansas Business* reported, expected the 1990s to be a golden period for ALLTEL, which was already one of the best-performing companies in the industry.[2] Such hype is boilerplate for business publications, but the analysts had good historical premises for their optimism.

Perhaps more than any other telecommunications business, ALLTEL was a shareholder-driven company. From the year that Mid-Continent Telephone was formed in Hudson in 1960, ALL-TEL and its precursor had increased dividends every year for thirty consecutive years. And the smaller Allied Telephone Company had brought an even better shareholder-earnings and dividend record than had Mid-Continent. The analysts observed that Joe Ford, the Allied CEO who became president of ALLTEL, headed a younger and more aggressive management team that was taking command. Weldon Case, the genial and innovative founder of Mid-Continent, was retiring as ALLTEL's chairman effective with the stockholders meeting, and the widespread and correct assumption was that Ford would assume the joint roles of president and chairman.

The headline "The ALLTEL Decade" would indeed be prophetic. The company's growth would be phenomenal, and the string of consecutive annual dividend increases would run into the next century.

Preparing for Competition

ALLTEL had outperformed the industry because its leaders had been able to peer further into the future. Case in Ohio and Ford and Allied founder Hugh Wilbourn had discerned as early as 1970 that the telephone industry was rapidly maturing and that it could not sustain the tempos of growth to which their shareholders had become accustomed. Thus they had diversified into communications supplies and services and had jumped into the bidding for cellular franchises in the 1980s, even when that technology offered only speculative profits. In 1990, the wireline telephone business was still ALLTEL's staple and was still respectably profitable, but on the horizon Case and Ford glimpsed competition such as the industry had never seen.

With cellular operating income and customers nearly doubling each year, ALLTEL's cellular operations became an increasingly larger factor in the company's earnings growth.

Congress would not enact the Telecommunications Act that opened everything to competition until 1996, but Ford saw it coming in 1990. Technology, he told independent telephone company operators in West Virginia in December 1990, would force big changes in the way they did business. "Many of us with operating companies that serve more rural areas or isolated communities have a tendency to think advanced technologies will not have an effect on our operations," Ford said. In the past, telephone companies had no direct competition for service in their franchise territories, but new technological architecture "may open the door to competition to provide basic local service itself."[3]

Although rural markets would not be the most attractive to potential competitors at the outset, Ford's prophecy would be borne out in another six years. Long before that, competitive forces in the wider telecommunications field would affect telephone companies by driving rates and product prices downward. State utility commissions would hold hearings and order telephone companies to take steps to reduce their earnings.[4]

ALLTEL's strategy was to prepare for the competition well in advance by continuing to diversify outside the regulated wireline business, by concentrating on driving down costs and raising productivity, by staying ahead of the field in developing, testing, and implementing new technology, and, finally, by selling or trading properties outside the fast-growing Sun Belt and other areas the company was solidly entrenched, such as the Great Lakes. It would consolidate its position in those areas so that it would have a dominant market share. That way it would be in an impregnable position wherever and whenever the floodgates of competition opened.

Acquiring Systematics, the leading data processor and software supplier for the financial services industry, gave the company a third non-regulated business unit (in addition to the wireless and supply businesses) capable of making a major contribution to earnings growth. ALLTEL would further diversify the data-processing unit by acquiring and developing software for the wireless telephone, healthcare, and home mortgage industries. And when consolidations swept the banking and thrift industries, leaving it with dwindling

customers, ALLTEL successfully shifted its strategy to bring large national and international institutions into the fold.

While it was diversifying, ALLTEL also had to sharpen its focus. Across the system, it shed its less productive enterprises, activities that were foreign to the telephone business and financial services. In December 1988, ALLTEL had purchased CP National, a California-based utility. As part of the deal that brought ALLTEL 65,467 telephone customer lines, the company inherited a natural gas utility that served 67,900 customers in California, Oregon, and Nevada; small cable television systems that served parts of Southern California and the Navajo Indian Reservation; Denro, a subsidiary that had a large presence in the field of air-traffic-control communications equipment and naval-command systems and electronics; and Ocean Technology, another subsidiary that marketed maritime electronic gear. ALLTEL sold Denro to a subsidiary of the Firan Corporation and members of Denro's management in 1990, and it sold Ocean Technology to Whittaker Corporation, an aerospace company in Burbank, California, in 1992. Since it had a long experience in regulated utility service, although not in the natural gas distribution business, the company was serious about the West Coast gas business. But when it was unable to win an exemption under the federal Public Utility Holding Company Act, which prohibited holding companies from owning natural gas distribution companies, ALLTEL had no choice but to sell the gas property too.[5] Stephens Inc. brokered the sale. The Oregon and Northern California assets went to the Washington Water Power Company of Spokane, and the Southern California and Nevada assets went to the Southwest Gas Corporation of Las Vegas for $85 million altogether. In 1997, ALLTEL sold HWC Distribution, a supplier of specialty electrical wire and cable, which it had acquired eight years earlier, to Code, Hennessy & Simmons, a Chicago investment firm. The subsidiary's sluggish growth in the 1990s had been a drag on earnings.

Tech Testing

Beginning in 1968 with the Carterfone case, which allowed interconnections to phone systems, a series of judicial decisions and Federal Communications Commission rulings had thrown the telephone business open to competition. The rivalry to gain market share, in turn, seeded breathtaking technological innovation and entrepreneurial activity in the telecommunications business, and though not all of the breakthroughs were marketable innovations, many were. Either way, someone had to test whether there was sufficient demand for the products at a marketable cost.

Although ALLTEL was not a research and development company, its real-world know-how spurred its own share of development. In 1990, ALLTEL engineers developed the ALLTEL Message Monitor, a solid-state product that forwarded unanswered calls to a message service in the central office, allowing businesses to screen telephone calls and get to the urgent ones instantly. Jim Wagner of ALLTEL's Southwest region and ALLTEL Supply's marketers worked with a Canadian electronics firm to design and build the device, with ALLTEL Supply being the exclusive distributor in the United States. It went on the market in January 1991.

Each year the company increased its financial commitment to testing and putting new technologies into place by matching the technologies to certain markets. The industry was catapulted quickly from systems that transmitted voices over the wires to one that transmitted data and video as well—over the same wires. Early in the decade, ALLTEL began installing Signal System 7, the platform that permitted local exchange companies like ALLTEL to provide far more sophisticated voice and data services such as private virtual networks, wide-area Centrex, custom local area signaling service, and improved calling-card validation. By 1996, the advanced signaling software served nearly three-fourths of ALLTEL customers. ALLTEL also issued its own calling card in 1990; 355,000 were issued to subscribers the first year.

Much of the company's $300 million–plus capital budget each year was devoted to converting from analog to digital switches in the system's exchanges and to expanding the fiber-optic network. By 1994, a full 95 percent of the ALLTEL system was digital, and it had thirty-nine hundred sheath miles of fiber optics. Digital and fiber-optic technology raised the company's productivity every year to an industry-leading 283 phones per employee by 1994. But more importantly, fiber-optic and digital technology expanded the variety of services the company could offer and created potential new revenue sources. The prospect of rapidly and efficiently transmitting vast amounts of data over wires formerly used only for voice drove communications businesses to explore ways to get the technology into the marketplace quickly.

Using a small piece of equipment called a balun, ALLTEL in 1989 had begun to convert a customer's spare twisted pair—the standard copper telephone wire—into a transmission carrier that ran from a computer terminal to a company's main computer. Two baluns were needed for each terminal, one at the computer terminal and one at the central computer. Dick Hichens, ALLTEL Service Corporation's product manager for enhanced network services, visited each region to describe the new product and to demonstrate how installers familiar with voice technology could take the product into the data communications marketplace.

To achieve greater operating efficiencies and improve customer service, ALLTEL implemented the use of computer terminals that conduct several types of line tests, enabling installers to complete service orders more quickly.

In 1991, ALLTEL completed the first phase of an industry-leading New York trial, begun in 1987, of ISDN (Integrated Services Digital Network). ISDN provided users with an integrated voice, data, and video business solution that extended the benefits of digital technology all the way to the customer's telephone handset. The trials were conducted with Rochester Telephone Corporation, other telecommunications companies, and six large corporate customers, and they established ALLTEL as an important participant in the development of the technology. In 1992, the company began implementing ISDN and fiber-optic rings that connected customers to central office exchanges in selected markets in the Southeast.

Growing and Consolidating

While it was diversifying and implementing new technologies, ALLTEL continued its strategy of shrewd acquisitions and of repositioning itself in a national marketplace where new competitive pressures could exploit the slightest vulnerability. Skip Frantz, who served as executive vice president for external affairs as well as general counsel and secretary, explained ALLTEL's philosophy behind its acquisitions. "It's very common to do an acquisition that's dilutive on an earnings-per-share basis in the year that you complete it or possibly the year afterwards," he said. "But really the important question is, over a longer period of time, what does the acquisition provide in terms of the opportunity to increase your growth rate in earnings and overall enhance the wealth of the company in the marketplace? That's something that's sometimes difficult to gauge exactly, but it's kind of the test that we apply. Is this something that we believe will create long-term wealth for the stockholders of the company, and does it make sense in terms of supplementing or enhancing the businesses that we're in?"[6]

With these rationales in mind, in August 1990 ALLTEL bought 19.8 percent of Chillicothe Telephone Company in the mountains of south-central Ohio. It purchased the interest from the Cleveland Foundation for $5,275,000. Chillicothe, which had a record of solid growth, served twenty-seven thousand lines near ALLTEL's 236,000 Ohio customers.

Francis "Skip" Frantz, executive vice president of external affairs and general counsel and secretary, joined ALLTEL in 1990 and is responsible for the company's mergers, acquisitions, and business development.

The next year ALLTEL acquired Missouri Telephone Company, headquartered in Bolivar, Missouri, for $85 million. The acquisition added twenty thousand lines to the company's substantial holdings in southeastern Missouri. More importantly, the transaction gave ALLTEL interests (and customers) in several key cellular markets, including an additional 48 percent in the Springfield, Missouri, cellular system. The acquisition also gave ALLTEL 99 percent of the Springfield metropolitan market and a 29 percent interest in the St. Joseph, Missouri, metropolitan area, plus positions in seven more rural service areas in the region.

Another acquisition, in December 1992, gave ALLTEL coverage in twenty-five states—a peak number. In an exchange of stock, ALLTEL bought SLT Communications Inc. of Sugar Land, Texas, a booming western suburb of Houston. Access-line growth had been running from 8 to 9 percent a year, nearly triple the industry norm. SLT Communications added forty-two thousand lines to the ALLTEL system, raising the total number of wireline customers to 1.3 million. But it also gave the company an additional 328,000 potential wireless customers in Texas and Arkansas. The deal was valued at $157 million.

Over the next two years, the company would compress its traditional telephone properties from twenty-five to fourteen states while dramatically enlarging its customer base and the long-term profitability and productivity of its operations. In February 1993, ALLTEL and GTE Telephone Operations of Stamford, Connecticut, signed an agreement to exchange local telephone operations. ALLTEL gave up ninety-five thousand lines on the northern perimeter of its midwestern market—its operations in Illinois, Indiana, and Michigan—but gained 320,000 access lines in Georgia, mainly in rural areas and small towns that were formerly served by GTE. The largest towns were Canton, Winder, and Dalton. ALLTEL paid GTE $445 million. The exchange gave both companies compact territories.

The swap was welcomed in Georgia, where GTE had had numerous complaints and where it faced pressure from state regulators. ALLTEL said it would spend more than $343 million deploying system improvements. Harriet Van Norte of the Georgia Public Service Commission predicted that the transaction would improve telephone service in rural Georgia. "They [ALLTEL] are going to invest in equipment and service, and I think consumers will benefit," she said.[7] The company also hired more than one hundred customer-service representatives at a centralized service center in Dalton that would serve the entire state.

ALLTEL's territory shrank from twenty-five to twenty-two states as a result of the GTE swap, but its customers grew from 1.3 million to 1.6 million. The exchange was salubrious for ALLTEL since it surrendered three slow-growing markets in the Rust Belt for a larger and faster-growing market in the Sun Belt. The geographic advantages extended to other ALLTEL operations as well, especially to Information Services, which converted the 350,000 new lines to the telephone billing system.

Furthermore, the Georgia operations were near the center of ALLTEL's southern operations, which extended from the Carolinas to Florida, Tennessee, Alabama, and Mississippi. Combined with its existing forty-five thousand lines in Georgia, the transaction made Georgia ALLTEL's largest state operation. The company would widen its Georgia holdings in 1997 with the purchase of the Georgia Telephone Company, which had sixty-seven hundred rural customers near ALLTEL's wireless operations in the southwestern part of the state. That deal added two hundred miles of fiber-optic cable to the company's network.

In conjunction with the GTE deal, ALLTEL consolidated its five telephone regions to three and decentralized many of the functions to the regional level. "We had to change the structure of the company, and the managers had to feel good about it," said Mike Flynn, a group president for ALLTEL. "They had to help and contribute their leadership, but they could no longer have the fiefdoms they once had. They had to change the way they managed, but they also had to do it in a way that supported where we were all going." Joe Ford told Flynn that he was concerned that the company would become too centralized, but as Flynn saw it, ALLTEL needed "a tight/loose kind of thing where you have a tight strategic direction and a loose control over the operations so that they are accountable for what they do."[8]

The moves produced large operating economies, which further improved productivity and the company's strategic position in the face of the competition that was coming. The exchange and the economies would produce strong growth in revenues and operating income in 1994.

ALLTEL continued the repositioning in November 1994 when it signed definitive agreements to sell about 111,000 access lines in eight states—Arizona, California, Nevada, New Mexico, Oregon, Tennessee, Utah, and West Virginia—to Citizens Utilities of Stamford, Connecticut. It also sold its small cable television operations in California and in the Navajo Indian Reservation service area in four states. The transaction effectively reversed ALLTEL's 1988 purchase of CP National. (Over the previous two years, the auxiliary subsidiaries acquired from CP National

I N A LITTLE MORE THAN A DECADE, ALL-TEL had altered the skylines of its central markets: Little Rock, Jacksonville, Florida, Atlanta, and Charlotte. It also had emblazoned its name on major sports and entertainment arenas. In April 1997, the company acquired the naming rights to the former Jacksonville Municipal Stadium, home of the Jacksonville Jaguars of the National Football League. The Jacksonville facility became ALLTEL Stadium under a ten-year, $6.2 million contract with the city and the Jacksonville Jaguars. ALLTEL also

contributed $6 million to the construction of the ALLTEL Arena on the north bank of the Arkansas River in North Little Rock and $1 million as a Platinum Suite holder. The arena, built under a public-private partnership, became the ornament of a grand development along the riverfront in the twin cities and made the city the home of professional hockey and arena football teams.

Along with supporting public schools and colleges, the company took a proprietary and philanthropic interest in the sports of the com-

A POPULAR

PRESENCE

munities it served. In addition to the big arenas, it took sponsorships or naming rights during the decade to more than a dozen sports facilities around the country, including the Ice Den of the Phoenix Coyotes hockey team. It sponsored drivers Phil Parsons and Jimmie Johnson on the NASCAR circuit, as well as the ALLTEL 200, a NASCAR event at the North Carolina Speedway in Rockingham. In addition, ALLTEL would sponsor former USAC champion Ryan Newman's 2001 Penske racing effort to prepare him for a full NASCAR 2002 Winston Cup run.

Sponsorship of the sporting events and naming of the big arenas was an investment in raising the company's image and in customer and employee relations. Sponsoring three racing teams and two NASCAR events gave the company promotional and marketing opportunities. NASCAR fans were a loyal buying group, and sponsoring teams in a sport of growing popularity was a source of pride for employees.

Throughout the 1990s and into 2000, ALLTEL increased its brand presence through various sponsorships and affiliations with sports venues. The ALLTEL Arena in North Little Rock (opposite) is home of the Arkansas RiverBlades hockey team, and ALLTEL Stadium (opposite inset) in Jacksonville, Florida, hosts the Jacksonville Jaguars NFL team. The company also celebrated its partnership with the NASCAR circuit (this page).

had been sold.) Citizens Utilities paid ALLTEL about $292 million for the properties.

As a part of the same deal, ALLTEL paid Citizens $10 million for 3,600 lines in Pennsylvania that were contiguous to ALLTEL's service area. An auxiliary agreement with Citizens made it particularly advantageous. ALLTEL Information Services signed a ten-year, $400 million contract to process billing and information services for all of Citizens' 750,000 telephone lines. Citizens had acquired 500,000 lines from GTE in 1993 and was looking for a way to integrate its billing and management services.

The complicated arrangement was unusual for the industry and difficult to put together. "The whole purpose is to reposition, and that involves exiting some states where we have a small presence so that we can consolidate our efforts in the larger states," said Ron Payne, ALLTEL's vice president for corporate communications.[9] It shrank ALLTEL's territories from a high of twenty-five states before the exchange with GTE to fourteen states. While the loss of the properties would reduce revenues and operating income, the cash payment for the properties would be used to reduce the company's debt and interest expenses.

Market Penetration

While ALLTEL positioned itself better for long-term results, the short-term results were not bad. The total return to stockholders for a five-year term ending in 1994 outperformed Standard & Poor's 500 average, the Dow Jones industrials, and ALLTEL's traditional telephone peer group. (S&P added ALLTEL to its 500 Index in 1994 based on the company's size, market presence, and stock distribution.) But the traditional telephone operations, while showing consistent growth in absolute dollars, constituted a constantly shrinking part of the company's overall revenues and earnings. In ten years, the wireline operations' share of total revenues declined from 77 percent to 40 percent. Its share of operating income fell from 96 percent to 61 percent.

As the decade began, wireless was no longer a speculative operation. While it would not become profitable until 1992 because of the growing capital investment each year, it contributed

exponential growth in revenues and sales. And as it did in its traditional telephone operations, ALLTEL constantly searched for ways to acquire interests in its familiar Sun Belt territory through purchases or exchanges with other carriers.

The years at the end of the 1980s and the beginning of the 1990s were like the California gold rush. Companies scrambled to form consortia and obtain the remaining cellular licenses for smaller metropolitan and rural service areas and then to reposition their holdings in economically viable geographical regions. ALLTEL had done well, first obtaining minority interests in the midwestern industrial states and then trading them for or otherwise acquiring interests in its principal region, the Southeast, which also happened to cluster around its wireline properties. It succeeded in obtaining licenses for rural service areas (RSAs) clustered around its metropolitan statistical areas in the Southeast and in Arkansas, Missouri, and Texas. Many of its RSAs happened to sprawl along the interstate highway system, which had another advantage. Cellular users traveling along the heavily used interstates would pay roaming charges to ALLTEL for using its systems along the way.

The company strengthened its position in several key markets in 1991. It acquired the Missouri Telephone Company's cellular interests

Many of ALLTEL's rural service areas sprawled along the interstate highway system, which had another advantage. Cellular users traveling along the heavily used interstates would pay roaming charges to ALLTEL for using its systems along the way. *(Photo by Eric Myer.)*

the fastest-growing regions in the Southwest. It bought additional interests in three rural areas in Arkansas and Oklahoma and increased its position in one Missouri RSA and three Alabama RSAs. The acquisition of SLT Communications of Sugar Land, Texas, which had added wireline customers to the system, gave ALLTEL Mobile Communications another 328,000 potential customers. In the package came a 2.34 percent interest in the Houston, Galveston, and Beaumont metropolitan areas in Texas, an additional 1 percent in the Little Rock market, and small interests in four Texas rural areas. The package included Sugar Land Telephone; Peeples Telephone of Coolidge, Texas; Waterwood Communications of Huntsville, Texas; Tri-County Telephone of Garrison, Texas; Sweeny–Old Ocean Telephone of Brazoria County, Texas; and Perco Telephone Company of Perryville, Arkansas. Altogether, the transactions increased ALLTEL's potential wireless customers, or POPs, to 7.5 million. In the SLT deal, ALLTEL also picked up 6,300 cable television subscribers and a one-third interest in Metropolitan Houston Paging Services, one of the largest paging networks in Texas, serving 70,000 customers.

in Springfield, Missouri, raising its ownership from 51 percent to 99 percent. It also increased its interest in the Savannah, Georgia, market from 38 percent to 80 percent by acquiring the interests of Coastal Cellular, a unit of Coastal Utilities Inc. of Hinesville, Georgia. (It would acquire the last 20 percent of the partnership in 1997 from Pembroke Cellular Company.) Furthermore, ALLTEL activated thirty-two mobile systems in rural service areas during 1991, mainly around its metropolitan statistical areas in the Sun Belt, Missouri, and Arkansas, raising the number of operating rural systems to thirty-six. The clustering enabled the company to expand customers' service areas and reduce operating costs.

A year later, ALLTEL acquired an increased interest in both the Charlotte and the Springfield markets. And it bought operating control of the metropolitan territories of Fort Smith and Fayetteville, Arkansas—both in the booming northwest corner of the state, which was one of

By the end of 1993, ALLTEL had operating control or major interests in metropolitan and rural service areas in nineteen predominantly Sun Belt states, and it would continue to acquire additional interests in rural markets in North Carolina, Alabama, and Georgia. In 1995, an agreement with BellSouth Mobility established a managing interest for ALLTEL in a new limited partnership serving a number of markets, including Columbia and Florence, South Carolina. That same year, it acquired a Georgia rural market from United States Cellular in exchange for a West Virginia rural market, achieving complete coverage across southern Georgia. It also obtained a wireless license for Cleveland County, North Carolina, next door to Charlotte.

In 1995, ALLTEL's customers increased at the rate of 33 percent, and the wireless operations accounted for 70 percent of the growth in its operating income, less than ten years after turning on the first cellular customer. ALLTEL enjoyed excellent market penetration rates, and its sales costs were well below industry averages.

Upgrading

ALLTEL opened friendly retail outlets in addition to its traditional sales offices. On September 13, 1993, its first wireless store opened in Jonesboro, Arkansas, where customers could buy cellular phones and accessories and learn more about wireless technology. Laura Cook, ALLTEL's vice president and general manager for Central Arkansas, described the atmosphere of ALLTEL's early stores prior to the Jonesboro store's debut:

They were really more like a doctor's office or reception area where customers would walk up to a counter, and an administrative person would

find out what they needed and call a salesperson to the front to help. There were signs and posters in the front, but customers didn't actually see any phones. Once the salespeople found out what the customers needed, they would go to the back to find the phone and then get somebody to program it. They'd have to fax something over to the billing department and then take the customer to another person to pay for the phone and service. It took awhile before the customer's phone was actually going to be working.[10]

Above: ALLTEL's new wireless stores featured a complete line of wireless equipment and accessories. Many wireless customers purchased additional units for family members, for both convenience and safety. *(Photo by Eric Myer.)*

Left: As vice president and general manager for Central Arkansas operations, Laura Cook helps ensure that ALLTEL's retail stores are completely focused on the customer's needs.

As prices for cell phones dropped and rate plans became less expensive, ALLTEL recognized that it needed to pursue the next segment of customers—"which was your consumer," said Cook. "It was apparent that if we were going to enter the retail market, we had to jump into the business, and we couldn't operate the way we used to when cellular was much more business focused. It was a really big step for ALLTEL."[11]

In the Jonesboro store and in the retail stores ALLTEL opened thereafter, the phones were kept up front so customers could see them. "Retail customers want to come in, buy a phone, and get out, whereas before, the process of buying a cell phone was much longer, much more consultative." explained Cook. "We had to find a point of sale system, where the salesperson is the end all/be all for customers as far as the sale is concerned."[12]

By the beginning of 1996, ALLTEL Mobile Communications operated more than sixty retail stores and had significantly increased its penetration rates in the retail sector. It began offering its products and services at 120 Wal-Mart retail outlets and coordinating the Wal-Mart national cellular program in more than a thousand stores. Starting in the Charlotte market, it offered an array of new wireless services, including voice mail and wireless modem interface service, a critical component in clear wireless data transmission.

ALLTEL also announced plans to phase in an advanced digital technology for wireless systems. It chose Code Division Multiple Access (CDMA) as its long-term cellular technology and Motorola's advanced analog technology for deployment in all its markets. The technologies would still keep capital spending at the projected levels, but they would improve quality and also give the company a platform from which to provide new features that were coming on line. Further enhancing its service, ALLTEL (and fourteen other leading cellular companies) launched a new standardized dialing service called MobiLink, which made it easier to place and receive calls.

It wasn't until November 24, 1997, that ALLTEL offered digital wireless phone service in its first market, Central Arkansas. The digital phones gave customers greater range than any system in the market, and they carried the additional advantages of a longer battery life, more privacy, and greater clarity than the analog models.

To provide the high-quality network services throughout its territory, ALLTEL continued to invest in fiber-optic cable. On December 3, 1997, it announced plans to create a fiber-optic network throughout the southeastern United States and the Great Lakes region. It owned 6,077 miles of fiber-optic cable, and it would spend $40 million to build and acquire another 1,400 miles. By 1998, the company had one of the largest fiber networks in the Southeast.

Personal Communications Service

Part of the nature of technological revolutions is that they often carry the seeds of competition that can pose a peril for those who develop them. When ALLTEL began to investigate the potential of personal communications networks in 1990, it recognized the threat. Customers could be connected to the nation's telephone network with low-power wireless technology that would enable them to have a single telephone and number and communicate by their mobile phone wherever they went. A personal communications service (PCS)—as well as cellular technology—could transform how people thought about telephones. PCS would provide an alternative to traditional internal wiring because people could always carry their phones with them. For a company like ALLTEL, with a large wireline network, the PCS technology constituted a competitive threat of unknown quantity as well as another business opportunity.

Nevertheless, in 1993, ALLTEL Mobile Communications joined MCI Communications Corporation in a joint consumer trial of the PCS technology. The trial involved nine hundred ALLTEL customers in the Charlotte, North Carolina, area. Some of the customers had their home telephone systems disconnected and used nothing but their wireless phones. The others had the PCS instruments in addition to their regular home and business phones. The trial was a way for MCI and ALLTEL to test an array of new wireless services that could someday replace local telephone service.

In place of the incoming phone lines, homes and businesses testing the replacement wireless service were equipped with a fixed wireless interface, which was tied directly to each home's internal telecommunication wiring. The interface switched telephones, a computer modem, a fax machine, or other standard telephone equipment to available wireless service. Commercial users switched their PBXs and key systems at the office to the wireless service. The participants got a single telephone number so that incoming calls not answered in the home were automatically transferred to the portable phone. If the portable phone was busy or not answered, the calls were transferred to voice mailboxes. People could make unlimited local calls from home for a flat monthly fee that was comparable to their local telephone service.

The trial gave the companies some insight into the market potential of the PCS technology. The system clearly offered some big advantages to business people—if its reliability could be assured. Busy executives would have more time for leisure activities. They could wait for client calls on the golf course as well as at the office. People could always be in touch with family members or the office regardless of where they were.

In 1995, ALLTEL chose to participate in the PCS wireless market by investing $30 million in GO Communications, which would be a bidder in the FCC's "C" band PCS auction early in 1996. ALLTEL said the alliance provided the best opportunity to participate in the developing industry. Moreover, ALLTEL Information Services was to develop and manage GO Communications' information systems under a ten-year outsourcing agreement.

But in 1996, ALLTEL decided it needed to compete directly in the rapidly changing marketplace. The FCC opened bids on January 14, 1997, for "D" and "E" band PCS licenses. ALLTEL bid for and won licenses for seventy-three markets in twelve states, paying $146.5 million for the licenses. Later in the year, it withdrew its investment in GO Communications and realized a pretax loss of $1.8 million. The PCS licenses increased the company's long-term potential wireless customer base from nine million to thirty-four million. In addition to increasing ALLTEL's

ALLTEL used advanced digital technology for wireless systems, choosing Code Division Multiple Access (CDMA) as its cellular technology and Motorola's advanced analog technology for use in all its markets.

potential customers by nearly 400 percent, the PCS markets broadened the overlap of its wireline and wireless systems in the Sun Belt to 97 percent. By further expanding the company's ability to deliver a wide range of services across its markets, the licenses strengthened the company's competitive position in the markets and enhanced the long-term capital value of its communications assets.

The Telecom Act

If the winds of competition seemed brisk after the landmark regulatory decisions in the two decades after the Carterfone ruling, they would reach gale force in the final years of the century. On February 8, 1996, President Clinton signed the Telecommunications Act of 1996, the first major overhaul of telecommunications laws in more than sixty-two years. Its goal was to let any communications business in the United States compete in any market against any other. It was supposed to promote competition and reduce government regulation so that consumers could get higher-quality services and low prices and so new technologies could be deployed.

The law immediately and dramatically changed the ground rules for virtually every sector of the communications industry: local and long-distance companies, cable television, broadcasting, and equipment manufacturers. Now companies could merge and buy each other out. The FCC's and state regulatory agencies' job was to see that the competition actually took place and that it occurred on a level field. This was a tall order in a marketplace that had become tediously complex, much of it within territorial boundaries tightly controlled by government for a century.

Competition in the long-distance business had stimulated the growth of entrepreneurial companies like Sprint Communications Company and MCI Communications Corporation, which then had played a role in building the Internet in the 1980s. There was hope that the deregulation of local phone markets could drive down the cost of connecting with the Internet at high bandwidths. Internet access indeed would become one of the most competitive parts of the communications business as the century ended.

New Opportunities

In its 1996 annual report, ALLTEL told shareholders that while it could not predict how the new federal law and competition would affect its telephone operations, it was determined to take advantage of the opportunities that competition would provide.

It did not tarry. The company had already begun to move into the long-distance business in 1994 when it acquired an 8 percent interest in LDDS Communications (later WorldCom), the nation's fourth-largest long-distance provider. In the fall of 1995 ALLTEL introduced ALLTEL Long Distance,

a complementary service to its traditional telephone service, in several Pennsylvania markets. Customers liked having their local and long-distance service provided by one company and receiving one bill.

On April 11, 1996, two months after the president signed the Telecommunications Act, ALLTEL rolled out its long-distance service to customers throughout the company's fourteen-state wireline territories. Initially, it offered the service only to its local telephone customers. In Arkansas, the state Public Service Commission granted the license so quickly that it caught the company by surprise. It was May 15 before customers in the fifty or so Arkansas exchanges could be given long-distance service. The service was profitable in its first full year of operation, ending 1997 with 282,000 customers.

In June 1996, ALLTEL began offering local Internet access in ten markets: its service areas in North and South Carolina, Ohio, New York, Pennsylvania, and Georgia. The company acquired its first four hundred customers in Dalton, Georgia, where it had run its first Internet trial. The service was offered to Little Rock in January 1997. ALLTEL paid $12.5 million for a 5 percent interest in Apex Global Information Services of Michigan so that it could link customers directly with the Internet backbone rather than through providers. Scott Ford, who was then executive vice president of ALLTEL, said that it would be "thirty times faster than anything else in town."[13]

Like Father, Like Son

Hugh Wilbourn and Weldon Case, the patriarchs who founded the Allied and Mid-Continent telephone companies, would retire at the beginning of the decade, Wilbourn from the board and Case from active management of the company. Case would die suddenly at his home in Florida in the fall of 1999.

As the decade closed, the leadership of the company vaulted to another generation. In 1997, Scott T. Ford, Wilbourn's grandson and the son of CEO Joe Ford, became the president and chief operating officer. He came to the company partly owing to the upheaval in the industry brought on by deregulation and competition, and almost immediately he would take ALLTEL in dramatically fresh directions.

The younger Ford had earned a reputation as a whiz kid in the corporate finance division of Stephens Inc., the big Little Rock investment firm, putting together billion-dollar deals for Jackson T. Stephens, the president and cofounder. Ford had gone to Stephens as an assistant from a stint with Merrill Lynch after graduating from the University of Arkansas in Fayetteville in 1984 with a degree in finance.

The one career that had always been off limits for Scott Ford was communications, at ALLTEL in particular. Ford would recall a conversation with his father at the age of twelve, about the career he would pursue after school. "Well, whatever you end up wanting to do," his father said, "I'll help you in any way that I can, but we're not going to work together." The elder recounted his own experience working for the company headed by his father-in-law, Hugh Wilbourn. The pressure on the younger person because of the family association is too great, he said.

"We ended up shaking hands," Scott Ford said. "We made a deal that we wouldn't work together."[14]

But Bill Cravens, the confidant whom Joe Ford summoned to Systematics to reorganize the company early in the decade, told Joe Ford that he needed energetic and bold young leaders like Scott to take ALLTEL through the shoals of deregulation and competition. The two men agreed that no one in the telephone or data-processing business really knew how to compete, but still Ford was insistent that his son stay clear of ALLTEL. His rationale: "Too much family."[15]

Scott would learn much later that his boss, Jack Stephens, the largest stockholder in ALLTEL, also was urging Ford to bring his son aboard and put him in charge, out of reach of corporate politics. The elder Ford resisted.

But in November 1995 Joe visited his son at home almost nightly, and after the grandchildren went to bed, he would talk about the upheavals in

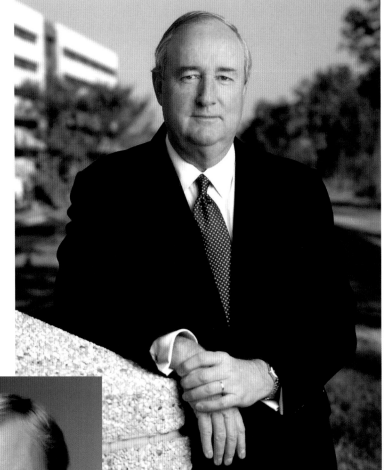

ALLTEL's future looked bright indeed in the capable hands of Joe Ford (above), who had led the company since shortly after the Allied/Mid-Continent merger in 1983, and his son, Scott Ford, who became ALLTEL's president in 1997.

the industry, the onset of fierce competition once the pending Telecommunications Act became law, and the management problems at the company.

"Well, aren't you in charge?" Scott asked his father one night.

"Yeah."

"Well, then either fix it or quit worrying about it."

"That's probably good advice," his father replied.[16]

The next January they caught a plane to play golf in a father-son tournament. Before boarding,

Ford told his son he needed to talk to him about something when they were in the air. On the plane Scott noticed that his father was staring at the newspaper but obviously not reading it.

"What's wrong? Are you all right?" Scott asked.

Joe put the paper down and said, "Everything in our industry is going to change with the 1996 act. A lot of companies that dominate the industry today will be gone. A lot of companies we've never heard of are going to be major players. The whole thing is up for grabs. We've got a chance with the asset base in place to make a real significant move forward, and we have a chance to lose it all, depending upon how well we play this. I want you to come to ALLTEL in a senior role and help me work through what we should do to make sure that we come out of this in the right way."

"What are you talking about?" Scott asked. "Doing what?"

"I don't know yet" was the reply. "You think about it over the weekend, and we'll talk on the way home."

The younger Ford triple-bogeyed almost every hole over the weekend. On the plane back, he wondered, "How many times does a father actually ask his son to come work with him on something that's meaningful to him where he actually thinks you can help?"

"Look," he told his father, "I'm inclined to say yes just because you've asked although, you know, I haven't been reading the annual reports. I don't even know what you do."

"Well, you know a lot about a lot of different businesses, and this is going to look like a different business than the one we grew up with," the father said.[17]

Scott Ford joined ALLTEL in January 1996 as executive vice president with responsibility for the company's communications businesses as well as the corporate staff functions. The younger Ford would become president in 1997, succeeding his father, who became chairman and CEO, and he assumed the additional duties of chief operating officer in 1998.

It didn't take long for Scott Ford to prove himself as a valuable addition to the company. "Joe Ford is a hard act to follow," said Josie Natori, a board member since 1994. "Yet Scott has fallen into his new role so smoothly. I'm really quite amazed at how he handles himself. He's taken up the baton so effortlessly, which is fantastic. It's been a great thing for the company."[18]

Though Scott Ford said he was pleased that ALLTEL had most of its assets in place—the wireless and wireline businesses, information services, and good employees who knew how to put technology together and take care of customers—he saw room for improvement on the cultural side. "It was the politics of a big company," Ford said, "people not talking to people, not sharing information. So we set about trying to find people who had the stomach for the kind of change that would get us out of that."[19]

Scott Ford said he used to spend much of his time just getting the people in wireless, wireline, and information services to talk to each other. "And I really encouraged Joe to do what he used to do," Ford continued. "I knew growing up that he walked hallways, shook hands, but as the organization had gotten to a size where there was a business leader over each of the businesses, he had correctly tried to give them room to run the business because he didn't want his presence to overshadow them. I told him to get back in the halls, talk to people, go see people again. The first two years after I started we spent just trying to wash that out."[20]

Convergence: One-Stop Shopping

Aside from improving the company's infrastructure, Scott Ford and his team also did much to move the company toward convergence of its wireless, wireline, and information services. Earlier in its history, diversification had been a central strategy for ALLTEL—a way to promote high growth once its old franchise business, the regulated telephone market, had matured. But in the late 1990s, ALLTEL's leaders began to see the company's strength in a sort of reversal of that policy. They called it convergence. "Convergence happens when different technologies become one technology, enabling different industries to meet the majority of their needs with a common technology platform," noted the 1997 annual report. The technology and expertise in one sector of the company would be applied to solving the problems of customers in another sector.

One of ALLTEL's first moves after Congress passed the Telecommunications Act in 1996 was to bundle all of its telecommunication services into one convenient package. In June of that year, Joe and Scott Ford (shown in insets) gathered together members of the media as well as thirty-two hundred ALLTEL employees to announce what this one-stop shopping would mean to ALLTEL's customers and to the company itself.

Convergence manifested itself in many ways. The seminal step was in applying the billing and customer-care specialties of the Information Services division to the vast telephone network of the company and then to competitors in the telephone industry. But the company would leverage its expertise and great experience in many other ways, offering clients more than cutting-edge software and outsourcing technology. ALLTEL could solve a range of communications and data-handling problems for businesses. Shaw Industries, the world's largest carpet manufacturer, used technologies provided by ALLTEL to link its Dalton, Georgia, plants in a network that enabled the company to monitor production at dozens of sites from a single location. For large national and international banks, the company provided not only data-processing software but expertise in managing mergers and acquisitions, designing banking infrastructure, and integrating and managing networks. When banking systems merged, ALLTEL could integrate the great variety of information systems that the bank inherited. For the Republic National Bank of New York, ALLTEL devised and implemented an infrastructure that routed and accessed information across hundreds of platforms worldwide and allowed the bank to achieve economies of scale. The company's mortgage-servicing division created Microsoft network's property finance forum, which allowed people to obtain information on-line about financing a new home. The screen, which looked like a small town, walked potential homebuyers through each step toward purchasing a home.

Technology, competition, and even the law had begun to erase the division between data services and voice services of telephones, between wireless and traditional telephone communication, and between other forms of transmitting data, voice, and video. Joe Ford described the convergence in a training video for employees.

Until recently, there was not much overlap between our telephone, cellular, and information services customers. They were distinct markets with different needs. However, as the technology driving the communications and information services industries has continued to converge, market distinctions are blurring. A banking client that *once looked to us to provide software or manage their information processing operations might now also have a need for someone to manage their data network or telephone call center. These are services that ALLTEL—with its vast experience managing technology and networks—can also provide.[21]*

The Telecommunications Act was the last portal to a truly competitive world where the company could employ its unusual strengths. It had an expansive and modern telephone network, a large wireless network, licenses for personal communication service (PCS) over a large territory—and, not coincidentally, all happened to overlap. ALLTEL had 2.7 million customers in fourteen Sun Belt and Great Lakes states. Its information subsidiaries were more cosmopolitan; they operated in every state and most of the countries of the world, but they had a dominant presence in the regions served by the telephone and wireless operations.

So ALLTEL was uniquely positioned. In 1997, it became the first in the industry to combine local wirelines and wireless businesses into a single organization that could provide truly integrated communications solutions for businesses and for residential customers. It had added traditional telephone products to its wireless retail stores and offered products across all of its sales channels—real one-stop shopping for all of a customer's communications needs.

On June 25, Ford gathered thirty-two hundred ALLTEL employees and the media on the lawn of the company's west Little Rock campus, home of ALLTEL Information Services, to announce that the company would package the full range of its telecommunication and information services for central Arkansas businesses. For the first time, a business could go to one provider for all those services—Internet access, wireless data transfer, network management, and local, long-distance, and cellular telephone services, plus a variety of other information services. The bundled services would be available for businesses quickly, and after another year or so they would be ready for residential customers as well. Customers could get any or all of the services, and on a single bill. Little Rock was the first market for the bundled services. Later they would be extended to ALLTEL's overlapping telecommunications markets in the other thirteen states.

Ford's announcement meant that the company was effectively starting a thirty-mile fiber-optic ring around the metropolitan area and linking downtown Little Rock and West Little Rock, where the Information Services campus is located. Although ALLTEL provided cellular service to the metropolitan area, Southwestern Bell had provided the only local dial service. ALLTEL would be competing with Bell for the telephone business of Central Arkansas firms. Later, it would offer dial service for residential customers as well.

Joe Ford summed up what offering bundled services would mean to businesses and to ALLTEL:

From the perspective of the business community, this represents the first time that a full set of communications solutions will be available from a single provider in Little Rock. As an increasing number of new products and services become available throughout the communications industry, we believe business customers will look to one company that can provide integrated communications solutions and help manage their increasingly complex networks more effectively. Whether it is managing a data network, providing local, long-distance, or Internet access services, or designing

a communications backbone network, we intend to be a full-service provider to Little Rock.... While we will continue to provide telephone, cellular, and information services in our respective market areas, we can no longer consider ourselves to be just in the telephone, cellular, or information services business. Today, we are in the business of applying our vast range of technological expertise and capabilities for the competitive advantage of and convenience of our customers.[22]

The company formed ALLTEL Communications Inc. and the Enterprise Network Services division to produce the integrated communications and data network services. Scott Chesbro, who had been president of ALLTEL's telephone operations in Georgia, headed the communications unit, and Cynthia Comparin, former vice president and general manager of network services with Nortel, directed Enterprise Network Services. Comparin said the new division was merging the management of computing services and its telecommunications programs into packages that any business could use.

Ford exhorted the thirty-two hundred employees he had gathered to spread the word: Businesses and individuals need think only of ALLTEL—no other company—for whatever communications service or product they needed.

In 1998, ALLTEL merged with 360° Communications, which turned ALLTEL into one of the largest wireless companies in the nation.

CHAPTER TWELVE

LEAVING A NATIONAL FOOTPRINT

1997–2000

I think we've hit a stride. I think it's just a matter of "keep expanding,
keep growing." I get up every day looking forward to it.

—Joe Ford[1]

I N THE SPRING OF 1997, ALLTEL took a very important step to improve its competitive position in the fast-changing telecommunications environment brought on by the Telecommunications Act of 1996. The company announced that it was combining three of its business units, ALLTEL Telephone Services Corporation, ALLTEL Mobile Communications, and ALLTEL Communications, Inc., into one new business: ALLTEL Communications. In essence, the company had consolidated its wireless and traditional wireline telephone operations into a seamless unit and had refocused all its diversified operations on the goal of being a one-stop provider of all the myriad communications services a business or a homeowner might want. That diversity—offering local dial service, long distance, all the wireless technologies, Internet access, paging, network management, and an unparalleled expertise in data management—was its leverage against far bigger competitors, including GTE and the spinoffs of the AT&T divestiture. Those companies could only talk about doing, someday, what ALLTEL was doing.

The step was part of ALLTEL's long-term strategy of moving the company from a product focus to a customer focus and from an internal management environment to a teamwork environment. "The goal," said Scott Ford in a statement, "is to be the best in the world in the acquisition and care of customers. This organization focuses the operating units on achieving that goal. We will gain efficiency by eliminating redundant efforts and, more importantly, we are empowering our people to focus resources on our customers and potential customers and deliver products, services, and solutions that they demand."[2]

The new ALLTEL Communications was organized into six market-focused areas. "We were creating layers in the organization," said Mike Flynn, who became president of communications operations after the restructuring. "Some of the people had telephone experience, some had wireless experience, and we were layering the management changes in order to mix the talent."[3]

Internally, the three new operating presidents were called "field generals" because, rather than working from an office, they were out in their assigned market areas, close to the customer. "We were developing people into a new class of manager in the business," Flynn explained. "We were

---

In 2000, ALLTEL launched its first nationwide calling plans in a campaign called Total Freedom.

training our people to have accountability, not here [at corporate headquarters], but at the customer level."[4]

In January 1998 ALLTEL waded further into the competition when it went head-to-head with Southwestern Bell for local dial customers in Little Rock. This was its first venture as a competitive local exchange carrier (CLEC), the term given to companies that competed against the traditional franchise local telephone company. That month, it sent out its first fully converged bill for an array of communication services.

In June 1998, ALLTEL launched its advanced digital version of wireless for the first time in Jacksonville, Florida. ALLTEL would have 36 percent of its wireless network converted to digital by the next year and was shooting for 100 percent by 2002. Digital wireless allowed the company to maintain revenue levels because it carried much more capacity than the widely used analog. The company profited by converting everything to digital, negotiating good prices with vendors through the growing volume of its commitments, limiting the variety of handset models, and then passing the savings on to customers.

The year 1997 was the best in ALLTEL's history. Revenues from current businesses rose 10 percent to $3.2 billion, and earnings per share had increased for the 37th consecutive year, this time by 13 percent. *Forbes* magazine ranked it high again in its profitability report, and its visibility, particularly in its franchise Sun Belt markets, had risen sharply. The company got consistently good press. The Federal Communications Commission reported that ALLTEL had the best record in the entire industry on "slamming," the illegal practice by long-distance companies of switching customers to their service without the customers' permission. The FCC said the complaints about ALLTEL numbered less than a tenth of one complaint per $1 million of revenues whereas other companies had as high as 28.26 complaints per $1 million.

But in the larger industry scheme, ALLTEL was not one of the giants. One of the results of the Telecommunications Act of 1996 was that the giants quickly became gargantuan. Although the major purpose of the act was to promote competition, the first impulse of the major communications play-

ers had been to make love, not war. In the first months after the act, major communications companies announced marriages: U.S. West and U.S. Continental Cablevision, SBC Communications (formerly Southwestern Bell) and Pacific Telesis (formerly Pacific Bell), NYNEX and Bell Atlantic, MFS Communications and WorldCom, and MCI Communications and British Telecommunications. The consolidations would continue. Despite all the advantages of ALLTEL's medium size—a close affinity with its markets, a streamlined and mobile management, and the ability to deploy technology and ideas quickly—heavily capitalized companies with a national footprint enjoyed other advantages that ALLTEL was intent on pursuing.

A 360° Boost

In the winter of 1997–1998, the consolidations, particularly as they affected the burgeoning wireless industry, were watched with keen interest in the management suites of ALLTEL in Little Rock and of 360° Communications in Chicago. Primarily a wireless provider, 360° had in its brief but spectacular history become the country's second largest publicly traded wireless company. It served customers in fifteen states from the Virginia suburbs of Washington, D.C., to West Texas.

When it began talks with ALLTEL that winter about a merger, 360° Communications was barely a dozen years old although its revenues for 1997 had hit $1.35 billion. And although the managements would find the cultures, business strategies, and personalities to be strikingly in sync, their histories were markedly different. While ALLTEL had developed from family-run businesses that started in the days of hand-cranked telephones, 360° sprang full blown from the head of Centel Corporation, one of the nation's largest independent telephone companies. It began in 1985 as Centel Cellular, a subsidiary of Centel Corporation. In 1988, the cellular company acquired United TeleSpectrum from Sprint, doubling Centel Cellular's revenues. Centel and Sprint merged five years later, and the cellular company became Sprint Cellular. Sprint spun off the cellular subsidiary in March 1996, and 360° became an independent, publicly traded company. Its core business was the cellular operation, but after it was spun off from

Sprint, it began reselling residential long-distance and paging services. It acquired Independent Cellular Network later that year, picking up markets in Ohio, Pennsylvania, Kentucky, and West Virginia with a combined population of 3.2 million. Like ALLTEL, it had begun bundling its services in 1997, giving customers a single bill for cellular, long-distance, and paging services.

Dennis E. Foster, a former Navy flier who had begun his communications career at AT&T, first at Ohio Bell and then Pacific Northwest Bell, was president and CEO at 360°. He had been offered a choice of staying with the parent company at the spinoff or going with the nervy, freewheeling cellular independent—an easy choice, he would say. But by 1998 the company needed to get bigger to be a player. Moreover, the agreement with Sprint limited 360°'s ability to issue stock to help fund acquisitions. Foster told 360°'s investment banker, Lazard Frères & Company, to put out the word that the company was available. "We had a good wireless network—a large company, growing well," Foster said. "But the only product that we owned that was facility based was cellular wireless. We resold long distance. We resold paging. I felt that given what was happening with the national footprint, it was only a matter of time. If you found the right partner and the right value, you should do it earlier rather than later."[5]

There were other suitors, larger companies, but 360° and ALLTEL had become familiar with each other through joint market trials of new technology in the Southeast. Their cellular markets in the Southeast and Sun Belt often abutted. Scott Ford, the new ALLTEL president, and Foster got together in the first of a number of meetings in Illinois. Foster joked that 360° was interested in buying all of ALLTEL's wireless properties. Ford said that maybe they should just get the two companies together. Foster and Ford, twenty years his junior, discovered immediately that they shared a vision of the industry's future and what a communications company should be.

"It may sound corny," Foster would say later, "but I trusted Scott. I always trusted Joe [Ford] just by reputation. I've never met anybody who did not trust Joe, and I have a high respect for his integrity."[6] Foster and Scott Ford bonded quickly,

Dennis Foster, former president and CEO of 360° Communications, brought nearly thirty years of valuable telecommunications experience to his new post as ALLTEL's vice chairman.

and the negotiations turned to decisions about the best people for jobs, how to maintain the entrepreneurial spirit at 360°, and how it should be integrated with ALLTEL's myriad operations. Foster described the meetings that followed:

From then on, we had our discussions on the back side of a racetrack, at a greasy-spoon hamburger place—biscuits and gravy at 7:30 in the morning. Clearly, it was the opposite of what people think about: smoke-filled rooms, hard-nosed negotiations, who's going to do what to whom. This was all team building, a little laughter, a couple of rounds of golf. I have two English mastiffs. One weighs 265 pounds, the other 200. As we got down to the next stages, there was Skip Frantz, Tom Orsini, who was a key player, Scott, me, Kevin Beebe, my counsel from Chicago, all sitting around our dining table with my two

English mastiffs under our feet, the cat on the lap of somebody. And we liked each other. We trusted each other. Very atypical.

This was a teamwork effort. We'd make a decision and move on. There wasn't going to be a turf war. Joe doesn't believe in that stuff. Scott does not believe in it. The people I brought down didn't believe in it. That made a significant difference in how quickly we could integrate the companies. That message was sent to everybody, internally as well as for the external market forces.[7]

The spirit carried over after the deal was struck. Kevin Beebe, who was executive vice president for 360°, described how they channeled their energies into making the merged company one. "No longer than thirty days afterward, the leadership team agreed that if anybody said, 'We used to do this at ALLTEL' or 'We used to do this at 360°,' they would be fined a buck. It wasn't the money; it was about the symbolism of not 'we' and 'they.' We were determined to be one company."[8]

On March 16, 1998, ALLTEL and 360° announced that they would merge in a transaction valued at more than $6 billion. The deal would make ALLTEL one of the largest wireless carriers in the nation with markets spread across much of the South and Midwest. The consolidated company would have $12 billion in market capitalization, $4.5 billion in annual revenues, $8.6 billion in assets, more than 5.6 million communications customers in twenty-two states, more than eleven hundred information services clients in forty-seven countries, and more than twenty thousand employees worldwide, four thousand of whom were integrated from the 360° operations.

The transaction was accounted for as a pooling of interests. Each share of 360° stock would be exchanged for .74 ALLTEL shares. ALLTEL assumed 360°'s $1.8 billion of debt, which troubled several analysts, who wondered if it might be a drag on earnings. Little Rock would be the headquarters of the company, and products would be sold under the ALLTEL brand. Ford said in a statement that

Both pages: Those who experienced the ALLTEL/360° merger said it was one of the smoothest transitions they'd seen. Whether at the closing table (below) or the public announcement (opposite), the relations between the two companies' executives remained affable, honest, and respectful.

the merger "creates a new, formidable competitor ideally positioned as one of the leading growth companies in the communications industry. The companies share a unique vision of the communications industry and what it will take to succeed in the future. The names of both companies are synonymous with quality, convenience, innovation, and value. Our combination of people, products, networks, technology, and geographic footprint provides the perfect foundation for the communications company of the future."

They shared other similarities despite their disparate histories. Both served primarily mid-sized cities and smaller communities. The combined companies had more than three thousand points of distribution, including 250 retail stores, 450 kiosks, and 2,500 sales employees in the cities and small towns. Both had adopted a strategy of bundling services in tightly focused geographic markets. Their territories often lay side by side. The merger would save the combined companies $100 million in the next two years by leveraging economies of scale in purchasing, administration, network operations, and technology. ALLTEL was building a 6,800-mile fiber-optic network connecting its service areas. That network provided an eco-nomical backbone for delivering additional communications services, as well as voice and data traffic. It would require only an additional eighteen hundred miles to tie 360°'s contiguous markets into the network. When the network was completed, transportation costs would be sharply reduced and traffic volume could increase substantially with little additional investment.

The merger involved no disputes over overlapping markets, only the advantages of contiguous territories. For example, 360° served much of North Carolina outside Charlotte, and ALLTEL was licensed for the Charlotte metropolitan area, which gave the company a more attractive offering across all of North Carolina.

More than two years after the deal, Eric Strumingher, a telecommunications analyst at Paine Webber, called it a "seminal event for the company.... While others are talking about bundling of services and being a company that provides one-stop shopping, ALLTEL is, of all the large companies, the only one executing that strategy well. There's no other company I know of at its size or larger that has completely torn down the structural barriers that exist between wireless and hard-line business."[9]

Under the merger agreement, Foster became vice chairman of ALLTEL, Beebe became a group president responsible for ALLTEL's field operations, and Jeff Gardner, senior vice president of finance at 360°, became senior vice president of finance at ALLTEL and later became chief financial officer. The ALLTEL board was expanded from eleven to fifteen to include four members of the 360° board.

By all accounts, the integration of 360° Communications and ALLTEL could hardly have

gone more smoothly. "An integration only works if it really is a merger as opposed to a takeover," said Jeff Gardner, who headed up the corporate integration effort from the 360° group. "ALLTEL had, in advance, crafted a plan that put many of us [from 360°] in very key roles early on, and I think that was the biggest key to the merger going so well. They gave us great opportunities and great leeway to run the business. So as a result, it has been one of the smoothest transitions I've ever been in."[10]

More Wireless Tendrils

As Joe Ford had predicted when he invited Scott to join the company two years earlier, ALLTEL was already a much different company from the one he had known for thirty-five years. Though the wireless operations had been the fastest-growing part of the business for nearly a decade, in 1997 the wireline sales and revenues still doubled those of the wireless operations. At the end of 1998, after the 360° merger, the situation had reversed. Wireless revenues and sales totaled nearly $2.1 billion, and all wireline revenues totaled $1.3 billion. Enlarging its wireless footprint would be the focus of its merger and acquisition activities for the next two years, but, unlike its larger competitors, ALLTEL sought

Jeff Gardner, formerly senior vice president of finance at 360° Communications, became ALLTEL's treasurer and senior vice president of finance after the merger.

another advantage. Its expanding wireless market gave it more opportunities for cross-selling its wireline products.

In the summer of 1998, the company struck a deal with Qwest Communications International to acquire fourteen hundred miles of fiber lines in Tennessee, Alabama, Georgia, Florida, North Carolina, and South Carolina and one thousand miles in Virginia, Maryland, Delaware, Pennsylvania, and Ohio. The dark fiber lines, which are best for transmitting voice, data, and video, put the company a step closer to interconnecting its wireline and wireless properties. The acquisition enabled the company to originate and terminate a full menu of voice and data traffic for its customers and to transport long-distance traffic to most major cities in the Southeast, along the eastern seaboard, and to the Great Lakes region.

In July 1999, ALLTEL signed two agreements that elevated the reliability of the twelve-state fiber network and made expansion of its capacity easier. It contracted with Fujitsu Network Communications, Inc., to supply synchronous optical network (SONET) fiber-optic transmission equipment for most of the network and entered into a deal with CIENA Corporation to provide dense wavelength division multiplexing equipment. The SONET technology was designed for extremely reliable, high-speed transmission over fiber-optic cable. The technology sent voice and data signals with a "protection path" in the opposite direction over separate fibers. It allowed the company to add tremendous capacity to the network wherever and whenever it was needed, easily and inexpensively.

ALLTEL's wireline franchise covered more territory and more customers in Georgia than any other state, and in August 1998 it expanded its reach again with the purchase of Standard Group, Inc., a small but key provider of local service in northeast Georgia. The privately held company had sixty-eight thousand local phone lines, paging clients, and a growing Internet access business. It served another twenty-eight thousand cable television subscribers and resold BellSouth's wireless phone service.

Simultaneously, the company announced that it would construct a $71 million campus on a sixty-eight-acre site in Deerfield Park, near the city of

Alpharetta in northern Fulton County, Georgia. The building would house nearly two thousand employees—about twelve hundred from its half-dozen offices in metropolitan Atlanta and another eight hundred who would be hired in its growing information services business in the state. The *Atlanta Journal-Constitution* said the announcement added luster to the Atlanta area's reputation as a high-tech haven. The building would be close to the headquarters of GTE Wireless, which used ALLTEL's Virtuoso II program for its customer billing. The Atlanta area also was headquarters for the company's telecommunication equipment supply operations.

ALLTEL was changing the skyline of Little Rock too. The company announced a $20 million expansion in its office park on the Arkansas River, the main corporate headquarters. The fifth building on the campus was completed in the summer of 2000. The original headquarters for Allied Telephone Company had been completed in 1982, the year before the merger with Mid-

Continent. Then in 1992, ALLTEL added a seven-story tower and a two-story addition at the center of the complex. A six-story building was completed in 1995.

Joining with Aliant

While the merger with 360° Communications was the largest and most consequential consolidation the company would make after ALLTEL's formation, it was only the first of several major acquisitions that would, in the space of two years, make ALLTEL one of the dominant wireless companies in the country. Although it had pulled back from its sparse western presence in the deal with

---

ALLTEL's headquarters in Little Rock expanded from its 1982 beginnings, when it consisted of a single building to house Allied Telephone. By 2000, the headquarters consisted of a sprawling campus along the Arkansas River.

Citizens Utilities, as the century ended it expanded its footprint westward.

On December 18, 1998, ALLTEL announced that it had agreed to buy Aliant Communications, a highly regarded telephone company that covered most of Nebraska, for $1.8 billion in stock and assumed debt.

Aliant had been an old family telephone company, much like the ones founded by Weldon Case in Ohio and Hugh Wilbourn and Charles Miller in Arkansas. It had been run by generations of the Woods family since its founding in 1904, although family members and a family company owned only about 9 percent of the stock in 1998. Mutual funds and financial institutions owned 60 percent of the stock. Thomas C. Woods III, grandson of the founder, was chairman of the company.

Aliant was founded as the Lincoln Telephone and Telegraph Company in the state capital of Lincoln by Frank H. Woods. Woods, who ran the company for nearly half a century, was one of the founders of the United States Independent Telephone Association and in 1912 headed the committee that struck the agreement preventing AT&T from buying and competing with independent companies. He negotiated the unified national toll system that put the industry on a sound financial basis and saved many early telephone companies from bankruptcy. Later his company became Lincoln Telecommunications Company and then changed its name to Aliant Communications in 1996.

Aliant was the franchise carrier of local telephone service for Lincoln and twenty-two surrounding counties but not the state's major city, Omaha, on the eastern border. It had 285,000 wireline customers at the end of 1998. Earlier in the year, the company had moved into the Omaha and Grand Island markets selling local service to businesses and apartment complexes in competition with U.S. West, one of the regional Bell operating companies.

But, like ALLTEL, it had enjoyed spectacular growth from its wireless operations. It had entered the cellular market in 1987, offering service in Lincoln. It became the managing partner of the Omaha cellular operation in 1991 and in 1995 acquired Nebraska Cellular, which gave it a seamless statewide cellular network that had access to 1.8 million potential customers. It had about 290,000 wireless customers in December 1998. Aliant had 10,000 paging customers and had moved aggressively into Internet service with 25,000 subscribers. Overall, the company had more than 1,600 employees.

Aliant had been a favorite of many Wall Street analysts for a decade. It was well managed and dominated its region like few independents in the country. Its earnings performance stacked up well against peer companies in the industry. The company had been mentioned as a target for a hostile takeover in 1989 and 1993, which prompted the board of directors to adopt measures to make it extremely hard to take over the company without the board's approval.

Joe Ford said the merger with Aliant would expand ALLTEL's geographic footprint "in a dynamic manner," and analysts generally saw the acquisition as a wise bargain for both sides. "This is one of my favorite telephone franchises in the country," said Salvatore Muoio of S. Muoio & Company

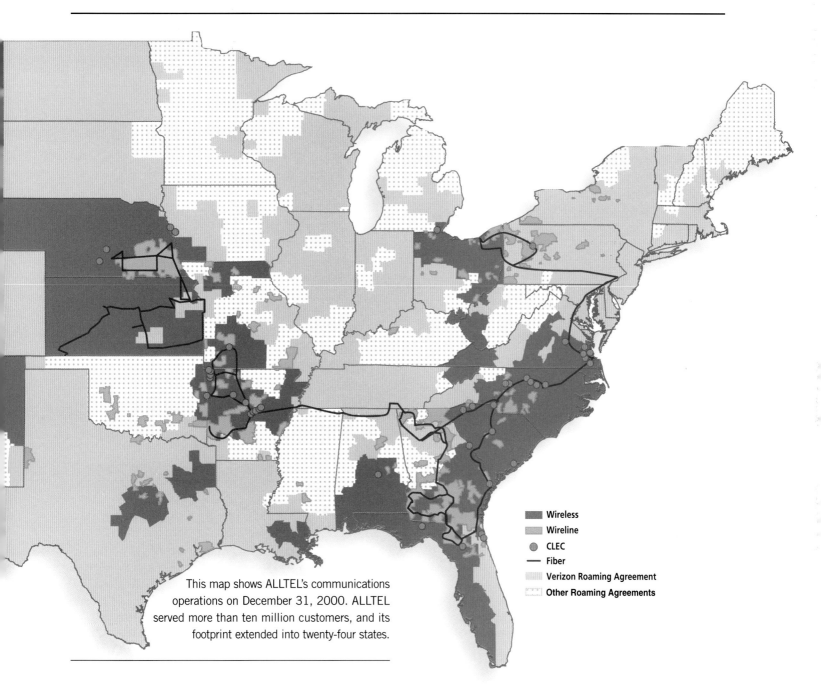

This map shows ALLTEL's communications operations on December 31, 2000. ALLTEL served more than ten million customers, and its footprint extended into twenty-four states.

Legend:
- Wireless
- Wireline
- CLEC
- Fiber
- Verizon Roaming Agreement
- Other Roaming Agreements

in New York. "They really dominate the whole state and are somewhat impervious to competition. It's a nice deal for ALLTEL."[11]

"This is the kind of plain-vanilla combination that has proven to work in the past," said Bette Massick Colombo, an analyst with Bear, Stearns. ALLTEL, she said, would see considerable cost savings, but it could improve its earnings even without savings. There was some overlapping of service, but the Nebraska system lay contiguous to ALLTEL's Missouri operations.[12]

"Both companies have been aggressive about rolling out Internet and long-distance service," Colombo said. "This is the kind of second-tier mentality because competition is not going to come to Nebraska first."[13] Indeed, the acquisition followed the company's strategy of moving into rural areas and small and mid-sized cities, which had milder regulatory and competitive environments, while other companies fought over metropolitan markets with far more customers. The powerful ALLTEL brand name and management would enhance the value of the franchises in the small-town and rural markets.

Robert J. Venable, vice president of equity research for Robert W. Baird & Company in Milwaukee, said ALLTEL's strategy of buying in less-populated markets was a wise one because there were solid growth rates, less competition, a stable base of customers, and a favorable regulatory environment. He observed that the company picked its acquisition targets wisely, choosing well-managed companies that moved ALLTEL closer to becoming a one-stop market where businesses and individuals can buy local telephone service, long distance, cellular, paging, Internet service, and personal communications services.[14]

Manifest Destiny

In a separate transaction announced the same day, ALLTEL acquired all the assets of Durango Cellular Telephone Company in southwestern Colorado. The Durango service area was adjacent to ALLTEL's cellular coverage in northern New Mexico.

Six months later, in June 1999, with the Aliant merger still pending before regulatory agencies, the company filled in the gap in its midwestern wireless operations by acquiring Liberty Cellular of Salina, Kansas, a privately held company operating under the name Kansas Cellular, and its affiliate, KINI LC. Liberty's market embraced all of Kansas. ALLTEL picked up 150,000 customers in fifteen rural service areas covering all or part of 100 of Kansas's 105 counties. Liberty enjoyed 35 percent more coverage than all its competitors in Kansas combined.

The network was adjacent to ALLTEL's Missouri operations and the Aliant network, the purchase of which was soon to be consummated. Liberty also offered paging, long-distance, and Internet services, and it operated a state-of-the-art digital network with more than 1,350 miles of fiber-optic cable. The transaction, which was accounted for as a pooling of interests, was valued at $600 million, including about $90 million in debt.

In April, ALLTEL had picked up another fifteen thousand customers with the purchase of BellSouth Mobility's wireless operations in Dothan,

Alabama, which gave the company continuous coverage across southern Alabama and into adjoining Georgia and Florida.

Every month, ALLTEL moved its bundled services and billing into more of its territory. It was a strategy most of its large competitors, still under regulatory restraints imposed by the AT&T divestiture and the Telecommunications Act of 1996, could not match. ALLTEL pressed its advantage in advertising campaigns throughout its markets and in the national media. An article titled "Sell a Phone, Get a Bike," which appeared in the February 22, 1999, issue of *Forbes,* had a lot to say about the "once sleepy" company:

> AT&T, MCI Worldcom and Bell Atlantic all talk about one-stop shopping for long-distance, local, wireless and other telecom services. But talk is cheap. Local provider ALLTEL Corp. is one of the few phone companies doing a lot with the idea of bundling....
>
> Unlike its much bigger competitors, ALLTEL's strategy is to acquire regional cellular properties and pitch those customers products like local service, high-speed data lines, paging and Internet access. ALLTEL's bosses, the father-and-son team of Joe T. and Scott T. Ford, are doing this at a time when national operators like AT&T and Sprint are seizing most of the growth in the wireless industry. The Fords think they can get more mileage out of their marketing dollars by cross-selling from wireless to wired services....
>
> It seems to be working. In Little Rock the Fords claim to have snagged, from SBC Communications, phone customers representing one-quarter of all the business lines in the city. This is after less than one year of offering local service....
>
> In its costly acquisition of AirTouch Communications, Vodafone is buying subscribers at $4,300 apiece. Scott Ford, ALLTEL's president, has a cheaper way to get business. He introduced a referral plan for ALLTEL employees: Bring in a new wireless customer and get 40 points; a new local customer and get 30. Accumulate 500 points and you can get a bicycle for your kid. This particular marketing gimmick should cost about $14 per subscriber.[15]

Still, ALLTEL labored under one major handicap. Its footprint was smaller than those of nationwide providers like AT&T and Sprint, which could offer one-rate plans to people calling and traveling across the country. That would change in February 2000, when ALLTEL seized the opportunity created by the ambitions and legal problems of three of the world's largest wireless companies.

Bell Atlantic, the nation's second-largest local telephone company and one of the largest wireless companies, agreed to merge with GTE Corporation and then to fold their combined wireless unit into a joint venture with Vodafone Airtouch P.L.C. of Britain, the world's biggest wireless carrier, to form a new company called Verizon Wireless. This plan would form the biggest wireless operation in the country. But to comply with federal regulations, Bell Atlantic and GTE had to first divest themselves of major overlapping parts of their wireless networks—areas embracing a fifth of the nation's population, about 45 million people. ALLTEL obligingly offered to help.

In a deal announced on February 1, ALLTEL agreed to exchange its wireless properties in Nevada and eastern and midwestern states for overlapping Bell Atlantic and GTE properties in other parts of the country, mostly in Florida and the Southwest. ALLTEL surrendered nearly 1 million customers to the new combined company but gained more than 1.5 million. It paid $600 million, but the properties it received appeared to be worth at least $4 billion based on valuations in other wireless deals. The deal took care of about 14 million of Bell Atlantic's and GTE's 45 million overlap. It also made ALLTEL the fifth-largest wireless carrier in the United States.[16]

For ALLTEL, it seemed like a deal made in heaven. The company would dump properties trapped in the middle of Bell Atlantic's territory but gain valuable real estate in the Sun Belt, where it could leverage its new wireless service for new long-distance, local dial, Internet, and paging services. It would jettison its majority and minority interests in forty-two relatively small markets in Illinois, Indiana, Iowa, Nevada, New York, and Pennsylvania and gain twenty-seven markets in Arizona, Alabama, Florida, Ohio, New Mexico, South Carolina, and Texas. Bell Atlantic's properties in the Southwest served about 700,000 customers in the Phoenix, Tucson, Flagstaff, El Paso, and Albuquerque areas under the brand name of Cellular One.

In a statement, Joe Ford said, "This transaction is an innovative approach to finding solutions to remain ahead of the competitive curve in the fast-changing communications industry. It enhances ALLTEL's geographic market clusters and increases our customer base."

Charles Pluckhahn of Stephens Inc. agreed that the deal greatly enhanced ALLTEL's competitive position. "This lets them transition from a balkanized, locally biased patch-quilt of systems toward the national footprint that is the paradigm of the future," Pluckhahn said. "I think this is a very, very smart deal for them."[17]

Much of the new ALLTEL territory was in Florida, from Tampa to Pensacola, and in the metropolitan Cleveland, Akron, and Canton areas, around Mid-Continent Telephone Corporation's old grounds. ALLTEL already served much of the Florida panhandle. The deal would give it access to a cluster of major growing markets, including Tampa, Sarasota, Bradenton, Fort Myers, and Lakeland, running through the Panhandle and down Florida's booming Gulf Coast. ALLTEL's new markets gave it 5.8 million subscribers, but its potential customer base, or POPS, rose 15 percent to 46 million.

A key part of the deal for ALLTEL was a roaming agreement with Bell Atlantic and GTE that allowed each of the companies to roam onto the others' networks at significantly reduced rates. Shortly after the transaction, ALLTEL rolled out its Total Freedom plan, which allowed customers to use digital wireless phones to call from anywhere in the United States to anywhere else in the country, at any time and for one flat rate—no roaming or long-distance charges. The company also debuted a more limited Regional Freedom plan in select markets. Joe Ford said that the new rate offerings allowed ALLTEL to compete for local customers with competitive national pricing.

To help launch the Total Freedom plan, ALLTEL signed country music superstar Faith Hill. Beginning June 12, 2000, Hill began appearing in television, print, and radio ads in ALLTEL's markets. The company chose Hill as an ALLTEL spokesperson because she had broad consumer appeal, especially in the twenty-five-year-old to

Total Freedom
Anywhere. Anytime.

fifty-five-year-old bracket, which was ALLTEL's target market. She also, according to Kevin Beebe, is "a person who shares the same down-home values as our company. As a working parent who is extremely focused on both her family and her career, Faith knows the importance that communications play in staying connected, especially when she is out on the road or traveling."[18]

"I am very pleased to be working with ALLTEL," Hill said. "They pride themselves on simplifying the lives of customers—a concept with which I can certainly relate. If ALLTEL's service is good enough for my mom, it's good enough for me."[19]

Though the mechanics of ALLTEL's swap with Verizon may have been somewhat difficult for investors to understand, CFO Jeff Gardner said it was a very easy deal to complete from a financing perspective since ALLTEL generated so much free cash flow. "The exchange of properties allowed us to really strengthen our competitive position in the Midwest, in the West,

Kevin Beebe (shown above at microphone and in inset) became group president of ALLTEL's communications services after serving as executive vice president of operations at 360° Communications. In 2000, Beebe had the pleasure to announce that the company had signed country music phenomenon Faith Hill as a spokesperson to launch the company's Total Freedom plan. Hill appears in print, television, and radio ads and is even featured on ALLTEL's prepaid calling cards.

and in the Southeast," he said. "And at the end of the day, we added some 700,000 customers and picked up the opportunity to sell not only wireless, but wireline, through our CLEC business and long distance in those new markets. We paid a very fair price for those markets, and the fact that we were able to get a national roaming agreement was really the thing that may have created the most value with the deal."[20]

In October 2000, ALLTEL was able to extend its wireless footprint all along the Gulf Coast, from New Orleans to Southern Florida, when it purchased wireless properties in New Orleans and Baton Rouge from SBC Communications. ALLTEL gained about 160,000 wireless customers and 300,000 paging customers, upping its wireless customer base to more than six million. The new market areas also included about two million potential customers.

Internet Expansion

Meanwhile, ALLTEL continued to expand its Internet services into new areas. Joe Ford told the *New York Times* that the Internet was "the thing that's out there. I'm convinced people are going to be more on the go in the future than they have been in the past. They want access to information and we want to give it to them."[21]

In August 2000, the company launched a new wireless Internet service called Web-Unwired in ten markets, which covered forty-six cities in Arizona, Arkansas, Florida, New Mexico, North Carolina, Ohio, and Texas. Using the service, customers could access Web services and content over their mobile phones, whether they were sending and receiving e-mail, viewing Web sites, or accessing a daily planner. Though ALLTEL was not the first company to offer wireless Internet service, it was the first wireless Web provider to give its customers starting-point options, or, as Kevin Beebe described it, "the power to prioritize the information and tools they find most important."[22]

ALLTEL retail store representatives would help customers customize their service so that it was immediately ready for use, letting them choose one of four different menu versions to appear on their home page. Other providers of wireless Web services offered only predetermined links. As Scott Ford observed, "ALLTEL is going to make it simple and convenient for our customers to communicate, transact business, and stay in touch via the Internet when they are on the go."[23]

Elsewhere in the company, ALLTEL Information Services had for some time been offering a number of e-commerce and Internet applications to banks, mortgage companies, and telephone companies, and it was not about to let new opportunities slip by. The Internet, said Jeff Fox, "is very radically changing the economics of our customers' business. Our business is a function of their business. We don't have a business if they don't have a business. So the ability for us to understand how our customers' business is being changed by the Internet and translate that into things that we can help our customers improve or change is what we do. It's fundamental."[24]

John Haley, an ALLTEL senior vice president and the chief technology officer, envisioned a

dynamic future for Internet technology. He and his team were working on a Web portal that would be super-localized for specific calling areas. "A lot of the Web is focused on a set of applications that are nationwide in scope," he said. "If you want to buy a television on the Internet, you can comparison shop, and it will be a very satisfactory experience. But that's not something you do every day. On the other hand, you may want to check the weather every day. You may have to get in your car every day and run around doing errands, and if you're a typical American, you have fifteen things to do but only have time to do ten. We want to make those tasks easier by providing Web service at the local level. We're committed to making people's lives simpler every day."[25]

Good Communications

Through the whirlwind of new deals, products, and services, ALLTEL didn't lose sight of its own communications systems—how it related to the media and its customers and how it communicated internally among its employees. George Smith, vice president for ALLTEL's media services, said that when he joined the company in 1996, ALLTEL was "the best kept business secret in America." One of Smith's jobs was to give the public a consistent message. At that time, the company had six different Internet sites under different names, so he and his team merged the six sites into ALLTEL.com. At the same time, they started an intranet to ensure that ALLTEL employees were always well informed about the company's activities as well as the competition and the industry in general. "I don't think anybody has taken it quite to this level, giving employees information about things going on that don't have to do with their immediate jobs and how things outside of the company affect them," said Smith.[26] Moreover, employees could e-mail Media

By the end of 2000, ALLTEL had 24-hour call centers in Little Rock, Macedonia, Phoenix, and Toledo, Ohio, as well as a Bundled Service Center in Raleigh, North Carolina. The 1,300 customer service representatives in these locations handle approximately 820,000 customer calls per month.

Services with any questions they might have about the operation of the company. Smith said they received as many as seventy to eighty questions a week.

The media services team also performed research on industry events and posted a daily analysis in a forum called "ALLTEL Today" on its intranet site. Other communications vehicles included a monthly newspaper called *ALLTEL Times,* which updated employees on company and industry news, and *@ALLTEL.Us,* a quarterly magazine that explored the interests and hobbies of ALLTEL employees and which became an electronic magazine in late 2000.

Customer Focus

ALLTEL was certainly starting the century off on the right foot. The deals it had made with 360°, Aliant, and Verizon had positioned it as the country's sixth-largest wireline phone company and the fifth-largest wireless provider with ten million communications customers in twenty-three states. At least part of the company's success in finagling great deals was due to what ALLTEL's senior vice president of strategic planning Keith Kostuch dubbed "a world-class deal team" led by Joe Ford and Scott Ford. "Frankly," Kostuch said, "ALLTEL doesn't have a lot to learn about making deals. It's a world-class acquirer and integrator of properties."[27]

When asked about his acquisition philosophy, Joe Ford replied that when he got into the business, he knew he could "either grow or go.... I'm a firm believer that you have to take advantage of opportunities as they present themselves, and they don't always present themselves when you'd like to have them. We just try to be aware of anybody that might be interested in selling and be prepared to take advantage of that, if we can."[28]

As a telecommunications company, ALLTEL never lost sight of the importance of communicating with its employees. The company uses several methods to keep employees up to date, including *ALLTEL Times,* a newsletter, and *@ALLTEL.Us,* an electronic magazine.

Investors, analysts, and employees of ALLTEL are quick to attribute much of the company's success to chairman and CEO Joe Ford, whose vision, instincts, and amazing people skills helped transform a small rural phone company into a leader in the communications and information services industries.

ALLTEL also owed much of its success to its focus on the customer. "It's really all about sales and service in the communications business," said Mike Flynn. "You can have a strategy and manage that strategy, but if you don't execute to selling and acquiring new customers and if you don't execute to a service standard that's better than your competitors', you're not going to win. Joe Ford knows that, and he knows that as we become

bigger, the risk of losing sight of that objective is greater."[29]

As far as Kostuch could see, the biggest change that ALLTEL needed to prepare for was dealing with the actual size of the company. "We've grown extraordinarily rapidly," he said. "There are certain natural growth point limits. ALLTEL has already transcended several of those, from being a really small business to being a mid-size business and from being a mid-size business to being a *Fortune* 500 business. But there's another gap that happens somewhere, and we're in the midst of it now."[30]

As the company grew, ALLTEL began shifting the way it did business to ensure that its focus on the customer didn't get swallowed in the enormity of the company's infrastructure. "We knew we needed to change from being an operationally excellent company, one that has had a very sound record of acquiring companies and integrating them and driving synergies and being more efficient at the end of the day, to now being a customer-satisfaction-focused company," said Dan Powell, market-area president in ALLTEL's Mid-Atlantic region. "Now we spend just as much time and attention on delighting the customer with our service and experience and on delivering valued product in the eyes of the customer."[31]

One of ALLTEL's strategies for staying customer focused was to measure itself from the customer's perspective using what it called a Customer Service Index, in which ALLTEL asked customers how it was performing. The company knew that a customer's perception of service may be completely different from internal measurements.

The company also began offering its "Always Up2Date Guarantee" in October 2000, which allowed Total Freedom and Regional Freedom customers to easily update their rate plans and equipment on a regular basis. Every six months, ALLTEL would analyze customers' phone usage and notify them if there was a better rate plan available, even if the new plan would cost less than the current plan. Customers would also receive a $100 credit toward a new phone every two years.

In addition, ALLTEL updated its retail stores to make them more customer focused. "With the original retail store setup, we had glassed-in cases that contained the phones that formed a sort of barrier between the sales representative and the customer—which worked perfectly because back then, sales people were really there to do one thing: sell," explained Laura Cook. "Today customers can go in and have anything taken care of, whether they need help with their bill, want to make a payment, or want to buy something. And we no longer have that glass counter as a barrier. Now we have several stations where the sales and service rep and the customer can sit closer in a more personable setting."[32]

And, of course, ALLTEL would continue to conduct its business with honesty and integrity, treating its employees, its shareholders, and its customers with a profound sense of responsibility and respect.

Joe Ford's individual efforts were even recognized by the United States Telecom Association (USTA). In October 2000, the USTA awarded Ford its highest honor, the Distinguished Service Medallion, in recognition of his outstanding contributions to advance the telephone industry and USTA.

Throughout the corporation, executives praised Joe Ford for his values and strove to emulate his model of doing business. "Joe has very high ethical standards," said Dennis Foster. "It's very obvious he has a very high level of compassion. He cares about people. I've seen a zillion CEOs that do okay in the boardroom or on Wall Street, but they're like a fish out of water if they're down in an installation center or a retail store. But Joe isn't that way. He knows people. He remembers people."[33]

"Joe is very consistent about his values, and that's communicated constantly," added Mike Flynn.[34] Jeff Fox described him as "a world-class CEO.... He's willing to take risk, and he allows people to grow beyond their résumés."[35] And Jerry Fetzer, vice president of shared services, said, "As long as I've been with ALLTEL, I've been able to do what I think is the right thing. Joe Ford has created a culture that says we're going to work hard, we're going to be aggressive. But we're going to do it with ethics and integrity."[36]

But perhaps it was Joe Ford himself who best summed up the business philosophy that had helped ALLTEL grow into a $7 billion company with more than 26,000 employees: "I look at business as a people-to-people thing—honesty, integrity, respect—and I do business on that basis."[37]

A SHORT HISTORY OF GOVERNMENT POLICY ON TELECOMMUNICATIONS

1880s and 1890s A few states begin regulating telephone service and rates.

1910 Congress enacts a law giving the Interstate Commerce Commission authority over some aspects of the interstate telephone industry. As the Bell system acquires 495,000 independent telephone companies in three years, federal and state regulators and legislative bodies express concern about an emerging monopoly.

1912 Presidential candidate Woodrow Wilson advocates strict enforcement of monopoly laws and begins investigating AT&T's plans to buy independent telephone companies. AT&T eventually is charged with violating antitrust laws. The postmaster general prepares a bill for introduction in Congress that would nationalize the telephone industry.

N. C. Kingsbury, vice president of AT&T, works out a compromise with the Justice Department under which AT&T disposes of its Western Union stock, discontinues acquisitions of phone companies except in special circumstances, and arranges for long-distance toll connections with independent phone companies. The Kingsbury Commitment formed the basis of the industry's growth for the century. The formal letter containing the agreement is sent in 1913.

1913 The Interstate Commerce Commission issues an order providing for a uniform system of accounts to be used in regulating telephone companies.

1917 The Kingsbury Commitment is modified to allow AT&T to acquire some independent companies if there is an equal exchange of property.

1918 President Wilson issues a proclamation placing the telephone industry under control of the U.S. Post Office Department during World War I, but day-to-day management remains with the companies.

1919 The Post Office Department returns ownership of the telephone companies to private hands.

1921 The Willis-Graham Act allows mergers of telephone companies without antitrust fears, which supplants key provisions of the Kingsbury Commitment. AT&T is buying up independents rapidly.

1922 AT&T promises the United States Independent Telephone Association (USITA) that it will not buy or duplicate independents except in special cases, in spite of authority in the Willis-Graham Act.

1934 President Franklin D. Roosevelt signs the Communications Act, creating the Federal Communications Commission to regulate the interstate telephone business. Formerly, the Interstate Commerce Commission had jurisdiction.

1947 The Rural Electrification Administration (REA) and the Bell system announce development of forms for telephone companies and REA cooperatives for power line carrier telephone service and joint use of pole lines.

1949 Congress authorizes the Rural Electrification Administration to make loans to telephone companies at 2 percent.

The Justice Department files a civil antitrust suit against AT&T and Western Electric alleging that they are trying to monopolize the telephone equipment market.

1952 REA and telephone equipment manu-facturers sign the first research contracts to develop a multiparty subscriber carrier and low-cost point-to-point microwave radio.

1956 A consent decree is signed in the antitrust case against AT&T restricting AT&T to the provision of regulated telephone service and Western Electric to equipment. But the court does not order AT&T to divest itself of ownership of Western Electric.

1957 The FCC directs the Bell system to permit customers to use the Hush-A-Phone and similar devices that connect to the telephone unless Bell can prove the devices will harm equipment or service.

1958 The FCC directs AT&T to cut its rates for privately leased telephone circuits by 15 percent.

1960 AT&T Long Lines Department applies to the FCC for approval of space communications experiments using active satellites.

1950s and 1960s Federal courts reject efforts by manu-facturers to make equipment for use with the telephone. (A Bell agreement in 1899 prevented the inter-connection of non-Bell equipment to the network.)

1961 AT&T and National Aeronautics and Space Administration sign an agreement to launch Telstar satellites in 1962.

1962 The world's first international commu-nications satellite, Telstar, is placed in orbit.

President Kennedy signs legislation creating a private corporation, Communications Satellite Corporation, to develop an international communications system using satellites such as Telstar.

1968 The FCC reaffirms the appellate court's findings in the Carterfone case. (Carterfone was a coupler that allowed for direct conversation between two-way radios and telephones with no electrical connection between the two.) The FCC says that AT&T must prove that a device will harm the network for it to be prohibited. Thus is the interconnect industry born. The FCC gives MCI, which had developed a microwave network, authority to compete against AT&T for long-distance customers.

1969 The FCC licenses Microwave Communications Inc. (MCI) to construct and operate an interstate radio link and to lease private-line service to business users in competition with AT&T Long Lines.

1960s thru 1990s The FCC opens a series of computer inquiries to settle regulatory jurisdiction over phone service and tariffs.

1971 The FCC announces a comprehensive investigation of AT&T, including its rate of return, costs, ownership of Western Electric, and service pricing.

The FCC expands the MCI decision and orders the Bells to provide local connections to independent long-distance and data transmission carriers and their customers.

1972 The FCC rules that telephone holding companies may not control community antenna television (CATV) systems in areas served by their telephone companies and orders divestiture by June 30, 1974.

1973 The REA telephone loan program is converted to insured loans, made from a fund that was established by payments from borrowers on prior loans. Most loans will be available at 5 percent.

1974 MCI files an antitrust suit against AT&T and the Bell companies in U.S. District Court in Chicago alleging that AT&T violated the Sherman Antitrust Act by attempting to monopolize the business and date the communications market.

The FCC begins hearings on economic impact of competition in the telephone business. The Justice Department files another antitrust suit against AT&T charging that it uses its monopoly power to suppress competition.

1976 FCC regulations permit the unlimited resale and shared use of private line facilities.

1977 The FCC, in the Execunet decision, allows customers to dial alternative carriers from any residential or business telephone.

1981 In its Resale and Shared Use decision, the FCC allows unlimited resale and sharing of interstate telephone service, including switched services, which means anyone can buy long distance and retail it to end users.

1982 A settlement is announced, and eight months later, U.S. District Judge Harold Greene enters a Modified Final Judgment. AT&T is to spin off its twenty-two telephone companies, which are to focus on local exchange service. AT&T keeps Western Electric, its long lines, and assets to provide interexchange long-distance service. AT&T retains Bell Laboratories. Seven regional telephone holding companies, the "Baby Bells," are allowed to enter nontelecommunication businesses subject to the court's approval.

1984 The FCC requires equal access, first with Baby Bells and then all telephone companies. Companies begin the task of modifying switching equipment so that long-distance providers can have equal access to their local exchange networks. Equal access allows customers to dial 1, an area code, and seven digits anywhere in the United States.

Traditional long-distance subsidies of local calls end. The FCC develops a system of access charges to replace the old system of settlements between AT&T and local carriers. The FCC later establishes the National Exchange Carrier Association to administer the new system.

1986 The FCC authorizes shared tenant services, requiring telephone companies to allow competitors—mostly small private companies serving resorts and residential developments—to operate within the telephone companies' service areas.

Developers are allowed to use their own exchanges (PBXs) to provide telephone service to their communities, bypassing the telephone companies.

Cellular services are authorized. Wireless telephones can offer dial tone and local exchange service in direct competition to local telephone companies so that cell phones often become a substitute for traditional wireline telephone service.

1987 Judge Greene, on a motion of the Justice Department, removes the blanket restrictions on regional telephone companies for everything but long distance. However, they still cannot enter manufacturing.

1988 Telephone billing and collection services,

formerly the exclusive domain of telephone companies, are opened to competition. Credit-card companies, among others, may now bill telephone customers and accept payment for telephone services.

1990 The FCC ends the traditional rate-of-return regulation of local exchange carriers by which it regulated a company's earnings. It adopts instead a system of incentive-based caps on the prices local carriers can charge each year.

1991 The FCC grants licenses for experimental personal communications networks (PCNs) designed specifically to substitute for and compete directly with local wireline telephone services.

1992 Nearly everything telephone companies offer is opened to competition except the "link and port." Traditionally, the link and port were considered a single unit but now must be unbundled into two services. (The port is the connection to the switch; the link to the port can be provided by anyone.)

1996 Congress passes the Telecommunications Act of 1996, a sweeping law that changes the whole environment. It opens local telephone markets to competition. (It opens the door for ALLTEL to enter the long-distance business as well and allows it to enter competition with Bell outside ALLTEL's traditional rural systems.) Megamergers in the industry follow.

NOTES TO SOURCES

Chapter One

1. Joshua Graham Baldner, *The Telephone: Impact and Expansion,* http://www.beloit.edu/~amerdem/students/baldner.html, September 2000.
2. Herbert N. Casson, *The History of the Telephone,* copyright 1999, Rector and Visitors of the University of Virginia, http://etext.lib.virginia.edu/modeng/modengC.browse.html, September 2000.
3. Tom Farley, *Private Line Telephone History,* part 1, http://www.privateline.com, September 2000.
4. Casson, *History of the Telephone.*
5. Ibid.
6. Ibid.
7. "History of Rural Telecommunications," NTCA Web site, http://www.ntca.org, September 2000.
8. Baldner, *Telephone: Impact and Expansion.*
9. Quoted in "History of Rural Telecommunications," the NTCA Web site at http://www.ntca.org, September 2000.

Chapter Two

1. "ALLTEL Architect Attracts Admirers," *Log Cabin Democrat* (Conway, Arkansas), 24 September 1990, 14.
2. Hugh R. Wilbourn Jr., interview by Ernest Dumas, tape recording, 6 January 2000, Write Stuff Enterprises.
3. Wilbourn family genealogy, Gene Wilbourn, 1994, 1.
4. Edward G. Hopkins, Brig. Gen. (Ret.), interview by Ernest Dumas, tape recording, 26 January 2000, Write Stuff Enterprises.

5. Hugh R. Wilbourn Jr., interview.

6. Ibid.

7. Ibid.

8. Ibid.

9. Ibid.

10. Ibid.

11. Ibid.

12. "ALLTEL Architect Attracts Admirers," 14.

Chapter Two Sidebar

1. Ernest Dumas, "Government 'Partner' of Brothers," *Arkansas Gazette,* 28 June 1977, 1.

2. Ibid., 5A.

3. Ernest Dumas, "Brothers Envy of Wall Street," *Arkansas Gazette,* 26 June 1977, 1.

Chapter Three

1. Weldon W. Case, commencement address at Ashland University, Ashland, Ohio, 11 May 1991.

2. Dr. Raymond M. Hyser, associate professor of history at James Madison University, Harrisburg, Virginia, interview by Ernest Dumas, tape recording, 8 February 2000, Write Stuff Enterprises.

3. Ibid.

4. Raymond M. Hyser, "A Study in Cooperative Management: The Business Career of James W. Ellsworth (1849–1925)," (Ph.D. diss., Florida State University, 1983), 436.

5. Hyser, interview.

6. Thomas H. Case, interview by Ernest Dumas, tape recording, 1 February 2000, Write Stuff Enterprises.

7. Weldon W. Case, address to the Newcomen Society of the United States, Cleveland, Ohio, 16 May 1985.

8. Ibid.

9. Thomas Case, interview.

10. Ibid.

11. Ibid.

12. Ibid.

13. Ibid.

14. Weldon W. Case, commencement address at Ashland University, 11 May 1991.

15. Ibid.

16. Thomas Case, interview.

17. Ibid.

Chapter Four

1. Hugh R. Wilbourn Jr., interview by Ernest Dumas, tape recording, 6 January 2000, Write Stuff Enterprises.

2. Samuel E. Morrison and Henry Steele Commager, *The Growth of the American Republic, 1865-1950,* (n.p., n.d), 777.

3. *Encyclopedia Britannica Book of the Year, 1948,* s.v. "Information Department, American Telephone and Telegraph Co."

4. *Encyclopedia Britannica Book of the Year, 1949,* s.v. "Information

Department, American Telephone and Telegraph Co."

5. Hugh R. Wilbourn Jr., interview.

6. Robert Partridge, interview by Ernest Dumas, tape recording, Washington, D.C., 1 March 2000.

7. Emon Mahony, interview by David Patten, tape recording, 19 July 2000, Write Stuff Enterprises.

8. Hugh R. Wilbourn Jr., interview.

9. Ibid.

10. Sarah Rhodes Benton, interview by Ernest Dumas, tape recording, 2 March 2000.

11. Hugh R. Wilbourn Jr., interview.

12. Harry Erwin, interview by David Patten, tape recording, 20 July 2000, Write Stuff Enterprises.

13. Charles Hinkle, interview by Jeffrey L. Rodengen, tape recording, 7 March 2000, Write Stuff Enterprises.

14. Bruce Kinzel, "In the Race at a Slower Pace," *Arkansas Democrat*, 16 November 1986.

15. Ray H. Thornton Jr., interview by Ernest Dumas, tape recording, 20 January 2000, Write Stuff Enterprises.

16. W. Rupp, equipment and building engineer, AT&T, New York, letter to H. R. Wilbourn Jr., 9 July 1962, from ALLTEL archives.

17. "A Sorry Sight, an Editorial," *Sheridan Headlight*, 11 July 1963, 1.

18. Letter from Warren E. Bray, vice president and general manager of Southwestern Bell of Arkansas, to Thomas D. Wynne Jr., mayor of Fordyce, Arkansas, cited in *Arkansas Gazette*, 8 July 1965, 5A.

19. "Telfast Used, Bell Thwarts It 48 Hours Later," *Arkansas Gazette*, 12 June 1965, 1.

20. Thornton, interview.

21. "Allied Seeks Injunction in Federal Court," *Fordyce (Arkansas) News-Advocate*, 17 June 1965, 1.

22. "A Tiny Rival Sues AT&T on Dialing," *New York Times*, 19 June 1965.

23. "Goodby Hand-Crank, Hello Touch-Tone," *Financial Trend*, 18–24 November 1974, 12–13.

24. Ibid., 13.

25. David Reynolds, interview by David Patten, tape recording, 7 March 2000, Write Stuff Enterprises.

26. Elsie Johnson, interview by David Patten, tape recording, 7 March 2000, Write Stuff Enterprises.

27. "Goodby Hand-Crank, Hello Touch-Tone," 15.

Chapter Four Sidebar

1. "Explosion, Fire Destroy Phone Facility," *Harrison Daily Times,* 16 January 1979, 2.
2. "Blast Levels Phone Building at Harrison; Loss $5 Million," *Arkansas Gazette,* 17 January 1979, 1A, 4A.

Chapter Five

1. Weldon W. Case, "People: The New Philosophy of Acquisition," preprint of article accepted for publication by *Harvard Business Review,* date of authorship uncertain.
2. George McConnaughey, interview by David Patten, tape recording, 29 August 2000, Write Stuff Enterprises.
3. Thomas H. Case, interview by Ernest Dumas, tape recording, 1 February 2000, Write Stuff Enterprises.
4. Philip F. Searle, president of the Northeastern Ohio National Bank, remarks at the retirement of Weldon W. Case, 1991.
5. Robert D. Bonnar, interview by David Patten, tape recording, 22 August 2000, Write Stuff Enterprises.
6. Weldon W. Case, commencement address at Ashland University, Ashland, Ohio, 11 May 1991.
7. *The Mid-Continent Story* (Elyria, Ohio: Mid-Continent Telephone Corp., 1965), 6.
8. Weldon W. Case, "People: The New Philosophy of Acquisition."
9. Ibid.
10. Ibid.
11. Anne O'Herron, interview by David Patten, tape recording, 18 August 2000, Write Stuff Enterprises.
12. Thomas H. Case, interview.
13. Anne O'Herron, interview.
14. Thomas H. Case, interview.
15. Mid-Continent Telephone Corporation Annual Report 1968, 6.
16. Weldon W. Case, "Mid-Continent Progress Report," address to Cleveland Society of Security Analysts, Cleveland, Ohio, 29 October 1969.
17. Andy Coulter, interview by David Patten, tape recording, 7 March 2000, Write Stuff Enterprises.
18. "Mid-Continent Moves into Fully Electronic COs," *Telephone Engineer & Management,* 1 March 1971, 26.
19. Weldon W. Case, "'42 Heads a Firm of Telecommunications Specialists," *Case Alumnus,* winter/spring 1983, 9.

Chapter Six

1. John Steele Gordon, "The Death of a Monopoly," *American Heritage*, April 1997, 16.
2. Ibid., 18.
3. *Intercom*, published by Mid-Continent Telephone Corp., December 1973.
4. "An interview with Weldon Case," *Telephony*, 22 October 1973, 43.
5. Jim Flowers, "Fight under Way in Telephone Field," *Arkansas Democrat Gazette*, 28 July 1974, 1D.
6. "Hugh Wilbourn Analyzes the Industry's Problems," *Telephony*, 7 October 1974, 37.
7. "Rates Will Rise on Home Phones, Speaker Predicts," *Birmingham News*, 11 November 1974.
8. "Hugh Wilbourn Analyzes the Industry's Problems."
9. "USITA Elects Hugh Wilbourn New President," *Telephone Engineer & Management*, November 1974.
10. Joe T. Ford, interview by Ernest Dumas, tape recording, 21 February 2000, Write Stuff Enterprises.
11. "Hugh Wilbourn Analyzes the Industry's Problems," 37.
12. Ibid.

Chapter Seven

1. Letter to Shareholders, ALLTEL 1983 Annual Report.
2. Will G. Staggs, interview by Jeffrey L. Rodengen, tape recording, 8 March 2000, Write Stuff Enterprises.
3. "Hugh Wilbourn Analyzes the Industry's Problems," *Telephony*, 7 October 1974, 62.
4. Americo Cornacchione, interview by David Patten, tape recording, 8 March 2000, Write Stuff Enterprises.
5. Allied Telephone Company 1982 Annual Report, 4–5.
6. Mid-Continent Telephone Corporation 1982 Annual Report, 2.
7. Allied Telephone Company 1981 Annual Report, 2.
8. Ibid.
9. Allied Telephone Company 1982 Annual Report, 5
10. Philip F. Searle, text of speech given at Weldon Case retirement dinner, 1991.
11. Ibid.
12. Joe T. Ford, interview by Ernest Dumas, tape recording, 21 February 2000, Write Stuff Enterprises.
13. William Zimmer, interview by David Patten, tape recording, 18 August 2000, Write Stuff Enterprises.
14. "Mid-Continent, Allied Telephone Agree to Merge," *Wall Street Journal*, 1 July 1983.

15. *Intercom*, published by Mid-Continent Telephone Corporation, July 1983, 1.

16. "Mid-Continent, Allied Agree to Merge," *Plain Dealer* (Cleveland), 25 October 1983, 1D.

17. "Alltel Corp. Formed by Mid-Continent Merger," *Akron (Ohio) Beacon Journal*, 25 October 1983, C5.

18. "Message to Employees," *Intercom*, September 1983, 1.

19. "ALLTEL Chosen as New Company Name," *Intercom*, September 1983, 1.

20. "ALLTEL Poised to Diversify, Expand," *Crane's Cleveland Business*, 23 October 1983, 2.

21. Carl Tiedemann, interview by Melody Maysonet, tape recording, 29 August 2000, Write Stuff Enterprises.

22. "ALLTEL Merger Creates Vast New Opportunities," *Intercom*, November 1983, 3.

Chapter Eight

1. Joe T. Ford, interview by Jeffrey L. Rodengen, tape recording, 7 March 2000, Write Stuff Enterprises.

2. "Ford Gives Glimpse of Year Ahead," *Intercom*, December 1984, 2.

3. Ibid.

4. Frederick J. W. Heft, interview by David Patten, tape recording, 9 August 2000, Write Stuff Enterprises.

5. John Dunbar, interview by Melody Maysonet, tape recording, 13 November 2000, Write Stuff Enterprises.

6. Ibid.

7. "Joint Agreement Reached to Provide Cellular Radio Service to Top 29 Markets," *Intercom*, July 1982.

8. Dunbar, interview.

9. Ibid.

10. Ibid.

11. "Cellular Pioneers Look Back on the First Decade," *Intercom*, April 1994, 2.

12. Ibid.

13. Ibid., 3.

14. Randy Wilbourn, interview by David Patten, tape recording, 8 March 2000, Write Stuff Enterprises.

15. "Cellular Pioneers Look Back on the First Decade," 3.

16. Jim Kimzey, interview by Jeffrey L. Rodengen, tape recording, 7 March 2000, Write Stuff Enterprises.

17. James Gadberry, interview by David Patten, tape recording, 7 March 2000, Write Stuff Enterprises.

18. Randy Wilbourn, interview.

Chapter Nine

1. "Ford: Our People Are Our Obvious Strength," *Intercom*, April 1987, 1.

2. Jerry Fetzer, interview by David Patten, tape recording, 7 March 2000, Write Stuff Enterprises.

3. "ALLTEL to Purchase HWC Distribution," *Intercom*, March 1989, 2.

4. "Weldon Case to Remain Chairman," *Intercom*, April 1987, 1.

5. "ALLTEL's LR Base Powerful," *Arkansas Gazette*, 15 January 1989, C1.

6. "Ford: Our People Are Our Obvious Strength," *Intercom*, April 1987, 2.

7. Ibid., 1.

8. Ibid.

9. *Forbes*, 12 January 1987.

Chapter Ten

1. "ALLTEL and Systematics to Merge," PR Newswire, Little Rock, Arkansas, 2 March 1990.

2. "Systematics: The First Twenty-Five Years," 1993, 2.

3. Ibid.

4. Shawne Leach, interview by Jeffrey L. Rodengen, tape recording, 8 March 2000, Write Stuff Enterprises.

5. "Systematics Celebrates 25 Years," *Intercom*, October 1993, 2.

6. Alex, Brown & Sons, Inc., Research, Computer Services Group, 7 April 1989, 3.

7. "Transaction Processing—Pathway to Profitability," United States Equity Research, Salomon Brothers, October 1992, 24.

8. "$500 Million Joins ALLTEL, Systematics," *Arkansas Democrat*, 3 March 1990, 1.

9. C. S. Heinbockel, "ALLTEL Deal Excites Market," *Arkansas Gazette*, 6 March 1990, 1D.

10. David Smith, "ALLTEL Proxy: Chair Given $1.5 Million," *Arkansas Democrat*, 13 March 1990, 1C.

11. C. S. Heinbockel, "ALLTEL Pins Hopes on Synergy," *Arkansas Gazette*, 11 March 1990, 1D.

12. Jim Hillis, interview by Jeffrey L. Rodengen, tape recording, 8 March 2000, Write Stuff Enterprises.

13. Joe T. Ford, interview by Ernest Dumas, tape recording, 21 February 2000, Write Stuff Enterprises.

14. Jeffrey H. Fox, interview by David Patten, tape recording, 25 August 2000, Write Stuff Enterprises.

15. Lauralee Wilson Shapiro, "The 'Big Fish,'" *ALLTEL Times*, July 2000, 6.

16. William L. Cravens, interview by David Patten, tape recording, 7 March 2000, Write Stuff Enterprises.

17. David Slider, interview by David Patten, tape recording, 5 September 2000, Write Stuff Enterprises.

18. Fox, interview.
19. "BofA's Mass Conversion of Old Accounts Begins," *Future Banker,* March 1999.
20. Carol Power, "BankAmerica Merger Tilts Retail Software Playing Field," *American Banker,* 11 February 1999.
21. Ibid.
22. "ALLTEL Intelidata to Create Spectrum's Switch," *Bank Technology News,* May 2000.
23. Slider, interview.
24. Fox, interview.

Chapter Eleven

1. Joe T. Ford, interview by Jeffrey L. Rodengen, tape recording, 7 March 2000, Write Stuff Enterprises.
2. Rex Nelson, "The Alltel Decade," *Arkansas Business,* 15 April 1991.
3. "ALLTEL President Delivers Message of the Future," *Intercom,* December 1990, 1.
4. Ibid.
5. Jerry Fetzer, interview by David Patten, tape recording, 7 March 2000, Write Stuff Enterprises.
6. Skip Frantz, interview by Jeffrey L. Rodengen, tape recording, 7 March 2000, Write Stuff Enterprises.
7. Shelley Emling, "ALLTEL to Take Over GTE's Phone Service in Georgia," *Atlanta Constitution,* 13 October 1993, 8F.
8. Mike Flynn, interview by David Patten, tape recording, 7 March 2000, Write Stuff Enterprises.
9. Andrea Harter, "ALLTEL Sells Phone Lines to Citizens," *Arkansas Democrat-Gazette,* 30 November 1994, 1D.
10. Laura Cook, interview by Melody Maysonet, tape recording, 10 November 2000, Write Stuff Enterprises.
11. Ibid.
12. Ibid.
13. Andrew Moreau, "ALLTEL to Hook Up LR to Internet," *Arkansas Democrat-Gazette,* 28 October 1996, 1D.
14. Scott T. Ford, interview by David Patten, tape recording, 8 March 2000, Write Stuff Enterprises.
15. William Cravens, interview by David Patten, tape recording, 7 March 2000, Write Stuff Enterprises.
16. Scott T. Ford, interview.
17. Ibid.
18. Josie Natori, interview by David Patten, tape recording, 18 September 2000, Write Stuff Enterprises.
19. Scott T. Ford, interview.
20. Ibid.
21. Introductory remarks for *Allsourcing* video, transcript, 19 April 1996.

22. Remarks by Joe T. Ford, 25 June 1996, Little Rock, Arkansas.

Chapter Twelve

1. Steve Barnes, "A Not-So-Little Phone Company from Little Rock," *New York Times,* 10 September 2000.
2. "ALLTEL to Combine Wireline, Wireless Operations," 26 March 1997, Little Rock, Arkansas.
3. Mike Flynn, interview by David Patten, tape recording, 7 March 2000, Write Stuff Enterprises.
4. Ibid.
5. Dennis E. Foster, interview by David Patten, tape recording, 9 March 2000, Write Stuff Enterprises.
6. Ibid.
7. Ibid.
8. Kevin Beebe, interview by Jeffrey L. Rodengen, tape recording, 7

March 2000, Write Stuff Enterprises.
9. Barnes, "Not-So-Little Phone Company."
10. Jeff Gardner, interview by David Patten, tape recording, 19 July 2000, Write Stuff Enterprises.
11. Lawrence M. Fisher, "ALLTEL Buying Top Phone Company in Nebraska for $1.5 Billion," *New York Times,* 19 December 1999, 1C.
12. Ibid.
13. Ibid.
14. Melinda Norris, "ALLTEL Taking Wal-Mart Approach," *Omaha World-Herald,* 27 December 1998, 1M.
15. Christopher Palmeri, "Sell a Phone, Get a Bike," *Forbes,* 22 February 1999, 92.
16. Seth Schiesel, "Bell Atlantic and GTE Swap Wireless Systems with ALLTEL," *New York Times,* 2 February 2000, 16C.

17. Michael E. Kanell, "ALLTEL Wireless Unit Passes BellSouth's," *Atlanta Journal and Constitution,* 2 February 2000, 1D.
18. "ALLTEL Signs Agreement with Superstar Faith Hill," PR Newswire, Little Rock, Arkansas, 24 May 2000.
19. Ibid.
20. Gardner, interview.
21. Barnes, "Not-So-Little Phone Company."
22. "ALLTEL Offers First Ready-to-Use Wireless Internet Service," PR Newswire, Little Rock, Arkansas, 23 August 2000.
23. Ibid.
24. Jeffrey Fox, interview by David Patten, tape recording, 25 August 2000, Write Stuff Enterprises.
25. John Haley, interview by David Patten, tape recording, 20 July 2000, Write Stuff Enterprises.

26. George Smith, interview by David Patten, tape recording, 8 March 2000, Write Stuff Enterprises.
27. Keith Kostuch, interview by David Patten, tape recording, 19 July 2000, Write Stuff Enterprises.
28. Joe T. Ford, interview by Jeffrey L. Rodengen, tape recording, 7 March 2000, Write Stuff Enterprises.
29. Flynn, interview.
30. Kostuch, interview.
31. Daniel Powell, interview by David Patten, tape recording, 25 August 2000, Write Stuff Enterprises.
32. Laura Cook, interview by Melody Maysonet, tape recording, 10 November 2000, Write Stuff Enterprises.
33. Foster, interview.
34. Flynn, interview.
35. Fox, interview.
36. Jerry Fetzer, interview by David Patten, tape recording, 7 March 2000, Write Stuff Enterprises.
37. Joe T. Ford, interview.

INDEX